Where the Tigers Were

కకక

Where The Tigers Were
Travels through Literary Landscapes

DON MEREDITH

UNIVERSITY OF SOUTH CAROLINA PRESS

UNIVERSITY OF SOUTH CAROLINA *BICENTENNIAL*

© 2001 Don Meredith

Published in Columbia, South Carolina, by the
University of South Carolina Press

Manufactured in the United States of America

05 04 03 02 01   5 4 3 2 1

Library of Congress Cataloging-in-Publication Data

Meredith, Don, 1938–
    Where the tigers were : travels through literary landscapes / Don Meredith.
        p.   cm.
    Includes bibliographical references and index.
    ISBN 1-57003-380-3 (cloth : alk. paper)
    1. Literary landmarks.   2. Authors—Homes and haunts.   3. Setting
(Literature)   I. Title.
    PN164 .M455   2001
    809—dc21   00-011816

Again for Josie—the gypsy who first dreamed these journeys ...

Very well then—he would travel. Not all that
far, not quite to where the tigers were. A night
in a wagon-lit and a siesta of three or four
weeks at some popular holiday resort in the
charming south . . .

Thomas Mann, *Death in Venice*

It is curious how the most dismal place after
twenty-four hours begins to seem like home.
. . . You get accustomed in a few weeks to the
idea of living or dying in the most bizarre surroundings.

Graham Greene, *The Lawless Roads*

Contents

Contents

Acknowledgments

My first thanks are to my editor, Barry Blose, for his dedication and perseverance in seeing this book through to publication. I owe gratitude to Daryln Brewer, the former editor of *Poets & Writers,* for suggesting I put the collection together and seek publication. My thanks, too, go to Therese Eiben of *Poets & Writers,* and her supportive staff. For their help and encouragement over many years, I thank Gorman Beauchamp, George Garrett, Philip Parotti, and especially Paul Ruffin of *The Texas Review;* and Ali Zaidi, Tom Maliti, and Parselelo Kantai of *Executive Magazine,* Nairobi.

I can never adequately thank everyone who has helped me on my travels, but would like to mention the people of Korčula, Croatia—especially Darko and Lučka Lozica and their extended family, and Frano Grbin, Pero and Eli Granić, Stanka Krailavić, and Igor and Melena Jeričević. I would like to express my appreciation to everyone who provided encouragement and hospitality along the way: in Greece, Sabek Kororo, Will and Mavis Manus, Sheila and Stergos Markiou, and Giovanni Zaneto; in Italy, Pippo and Licia Greggi, Rita Marignano, Rosamond and Guido Ottaviani, Andrew Porter, Joan and Geoff Rutkowski, Jeffrey Smart and Hermes Desane, Floriano Vecchi, William Weaver, and especially Jean Cootes and the late Merritt N. Cootes; in East Africa, Judy Aldrick, Bunny and Jeri Allen, Lucas Auma, Dot and Barry Clark, Peter Kandie, Safari Charo Kazungu, Wilson Keemani, Carol and Lars Korschen, Sammy Lewa, Steven Maina, Francis Makokha, Roland Minor, Zahid Rajan, Cynthia Salvadori, Mary Stone, Dan Suther, Asha Thamu, Errol and Sbish Trzebinski, Jony Waite, Michel van Steene, Ali and Irene Zaidi, and Rose Mbwambo of the Tourist Information Center, Dar es Salaam; in Wales, the Vicar Jones and the people of Laugharne and Swansea; in Vietnam, Doan, Trinh, Trung, Vu T Phuong Trang, and special thanks to Phan Ngoc Thanh for his editorial help; in the Middle East, Signora Cressaty and the staff at the Pension Roma in Cairo, Madam Christina, Rabia Mohammed Ahmed, Abdullah Hassan Abud, Basan, Mahmoud Bedeir, Talal Naif Abd Mahfouze, Abu Saleh, Moustafa Mohammed El Sayde, Aleya Serour of the American University in Cairo Press, Elizabeth Todd, Yusef and his Plymouth Magnum, and particular thanks to the staff of the Syrian Embassy, Cairo.

For keeping me in touch with the "real" world, my thanks go to the late Lynn Arden, to the late Mary Anne Ashley, to Herb Beckman and Sue Wilkens, Ruth Belmeur, Patricia Brent, Michael Bry, Charles Chapin, Jim and Trudie Collins, the late Ruth Costello, Neil Davis, Jim and Lynn Deis, Barbara Fuller, Victor, Marjorie and Amy Garlin, George Gutekunst, Jim and Jana Hamilton, Marvin Lichtner, Clyde Meredith, Joe and Brenda Michals, Joe and Maidee Moore, Jeannie Raiser and Roy Brown; and particular thanks to Joan Kloehn and the late Robert Peterson. My deep gratitude goes to Jean Crotty Guthrie for her friendship, sound advice, and help above and beyond the call.

I extend my thanks to the young Syrian who took me off the train in Deraa, then paid my bus fare to Damascus, and to the cab drivers, waiters, bartenders, hotel clerks, fellow nomads, and all those who have made my travels possible and full.

Finally all appreciation goes to my wife, Josie, whose counsel and editorial help have been crucial and whose courage and imagination set us on the road.

Where the Tigers Were

Prologue

HIGH ON A HILL above windswept Swansea Bay stood an ordinary white house with tall windows trimmed in blue. A plaque distinguished its front: DYLAN THOMAS WAS BORN IN THIS HOUSE OCTOBER 27, 1914. The tall windows, the gleaming brass plaque, drew me across the road and onto the steps. I rapped at the door. And an adventure began, an extraordinary passage into the literary landscape of this Welsh genius with the booming voice and remarkable poetic gift.

It was spring, 1963. In January I'd sailed from New York aboard the *Lista,* a rust-bucket Norwegian tramp making her last transatlantic crossing—and my first. After landing at Le Havre I began a two-year journey across Europe, from Ireland to Yugoslavia. I was passionate about all things "European," my imagination kindled by the works of Beckett and Camus, Hemingway, Fitzgerald, Joyce, Eliot, and Pound. In Paris I lingered in the cafés of Montmartre and Saint-Germain-des-Prés: the Brasserie Lipp, Le Dôme, Le Lapin Agile. Like others before and since, I sought the landmarks where the legendary comrades of the Lost Generation had talked through the dazzling Parisian nights. Perhaps, even now, I might catch a glimpse of Jean-Paul Sartre and Simone de Beauvoir lunching at Les Deux Magots.

I returned to Europe in 1968 and lived there for the next dozen years, first on Korčula, a Dalmatian island, then on a farm in Italy's Tuscan hills. Later, like a nomad needing to move on, I roamed the Middle East, India, and Southeast Asia, eventually landing in East Africa, where I now live on a small island off the Kenya coast. But that first European trip is what I remember best. First journeys, like first love affairs, are so immediate, so poignant, that their essence, their subtlest shifts in mood and perception, their smallest details, stay forever.

No portion of that European trip is more vivid than the weeks I spent in Dylan Thomas' Wales. So intense was the experience that when I felt compelled to write about it twenty-five years later, my thoughts came in a rush as if, quite literally, it had happened yesterday. Swansea. Mumbles. Carmarthen. Laugharne. I realized just how closely linked Thomas was to his Welsh landscape. "This is Thomas country to its roots," I wrote. " . . . land and sea, it rings in every line."

As my travels continued, I sought out poets and novelists who, like Thomas, had captured the essence of a city, a region, a land, and used their works as guides, much as another traveler might look into *Fodor's* or a *Guide Bleu*. The essays in this collection describe the books and writers I've found, and the literary landscapes they've opened to me.

———

Traveling rough, what I call "going against the grain," means bargain hotels in out-of-the-way streets, cheap restaurants, public transportation—donkeys and camels where possible, buses, boats, trains, the occasional taxi when all else fails. Despite minor discomforts, there are definite advantages. Among them the spirit of serendipity, the traveler's boon companion, is set free to work its magic. The unexpected loan of a seventeenth-century sea-captain's house on the island of Rhodes led to the rereading of Lawrence Durrell's island books and to the discovery of the author's beloved Greece among the groves and villages of Mount Attaviros, and to writing "The Pagan Soul: Lawrence Durrell and the Marine Venus." As a girl Madame Christina, the Greek restaurateur who appears in "The House on Rue Lepsius," had often seen Constantine Cavafy pass in the street. This noble old lady, with her stories of the Alexandrian poet, I encountered by pure chance. The unbidden Rabia Mohammed Ahmed, the polyglot street hustler, turned up like a jinni from *The Arabian Nights* to pilot me through the puzzle of Naguib Mahfouz' Cairo, while Abdullah Hassan Abud, the Syrian schoolteacher from *A Dangerous Man,* so curious about Mister Alfred Prufrock and Colonel Lawrence, was a product of serendipity if ever there was one. Repeatedly, fortune provided the source of significant discoveries.

You may argue that my methods are less structured than might be, less academically stringent. Using fortune as accomplice has meant giving up the niceties of reservations, timetables, appointments with writers, scholars, literary journalists. At the risk of anticlimax, I've written things as they've happened, forgoing the invention of epiphanies and climaxes where none exist. Attempting to keep myself in the background, I've tried to give space to my surroundings and sources of inspiration.

Sometimes I have set out to unearth characters and settings and failed. During my 1995 trip to Egypt, I was very disappointed not to meet Naguib Mahfouz—sadly, an assassin's attempt on his life had incapacitated the Nobel laureate. In "The Only *Mzungu* Afoot," an account of Maria Thomas' novel of transition in postcolonial Tanzania *Antonia Saw the Oryx First,* I speak of my inability to discover the real-life models for Thomas' African healer, Esther Moro, and the white doctor, Antonia Redman. Still, my stay in Dar es Salaam was rich in both literary and personal rewards. "These two extraordinary women," I wrote, "must remain fictional as probably they should, creations of deep insight, sympathy and spirit, wise and complex portraits [of the] imagination." You don't always find what you seek, but in the seeking sometimes find more.

———

Walking, book in hand, along a foreign back street where in some fictional netherworld two imaginary characters once met, has given meaning to experiences that might otherwise appear classically absurd. What is the purpose of witnessing some Middle Eastern backwater or down-at-the-heels African port, then passing on? Only context gives meaning, even if that context is a snapshot of yourself squatting before a third-rate monument or the exhilaration of placing it in literary circumstances, of illuminating a corner of an author's world.

What I chose to write of are works of literature suited to unraveling cultures, peoples, countries. This is one traveler's way of unearthing something personal and abiding about a place as he plunges in—uncommon guidebooks to literary landscapes.

Hijani House
Lamu Island, Kenya

The Fox

A Memoir of Dylan Thomas' Wales

BREAKFAST, AS USUAL, was something grotesque. Sausages paddling in their own blubber. Tinned spaghetti on toast. It was years before Elizabeth David would introduce "cuisine" from the cloudless Mediterranean, and Britain was awash in bad cooking. Surfacing through cookhouse smoke, Francesco bore platters of scorched eggs, charred stacks of cold toast. Beyond steamed windows an iron Welsh rain slashed across Swansea Bay. Francesco was Neapolitan, and his Welsh wife was in Italy visiting his mother, savoring the sun and *calamari fritti*. Before leaving she'd taught Francesco "British cooking." With thumb and forefinger fiddling a tenor's mustache, he grinned and watched me eat.

With breakfast finished, the dishes done, Francesco buttoned himself into a scarlet mackintosh. "I'll give you a lift," he said. A lift? The rain had let up and a puny March sun slanted across the back garden. Francesco swung a sea-green muffler around his dark throat. "You'll want a ride up Cwmdonkin Drive to see the house."

It was barely a decade since Dylan Thomas' death. Like many students in the 1950s, I'd read his poems and could recite stanzas from "Fern Hill" and "Do not go gentle into that good night." I'd listened to him on Caedmon recordings, read John Malcolm Brinnin's controversial account of the poet's New World odysseys in *Dylan Thomas in America,* and, as an undergraduate, attended a reading but missed the faculty party afterwards where Thomas did his famous "barking dog" act and nipped the ankle of a notable Spenserian.

Now, I stood above Swansea and its rain-spattered bay, waving Francesco on to his errands. Number 5 was a high white house with tall, attenuated windows. The differences between it and other houses on the breezy upsweep of Cwmdonkin Drive were the sky-blue trim and the plaque at the front:

Dylan Thomas
was born in this house
October 27, 1914

No sign it was open to the public—it wasn't a museum—and I didn't plan to barge in. I'd hitched to Swansea on my way to Fishguard to catch the ferry to Ireland. A quick look at the poet's birthplace seemed apropos. But the tall windows, the commemorative plaque, drew me across the road and onto the steps. I rapped at the door.

Mr. Williams was a small, weathered man with smoky hair and eyes the blue of the window trim. He shooed me into the parlor, apologizing: "Wife's shopping . . . know she'll want to meet . . . made cookies . . . water on for tea." He vanished into the back of the cookie-fragrant house. The parlor was crowded with lamps. I studied the nearest. Hand-lettered on its vellum shade were the lines of "In my craft or sullen art":

Not for the proud man apart
From the raging moon I write
On these spindrift pages . . .

Other shades, other poems, each drawn with the delicacy you'd expect from a Sung scroll. "From Love's First Fever." "After the funeral." "The force that through the green fuse drives the flower."

"You've discovered my passions." Williams carried a tray of tea things, a heaping plate of oatmeal cookies. "Dylan's poems and calligraphy."

I helped myself, sweetening the bitter tea with spoonfuls of sugar, wondering what I'd done to deserve this welcome.

Williams had been a friend of David John Thomas, Dylan's father, who had bought 5 Cwmdonkin Drive in 1914, a few months before the poet's birth. When "D. J." sold the house in 1936, Williams had the notion that someday he'd like to live here. The chance came shortly after D. J. Thomas' death in December 1952.

Muffled in a crumpled cardigan, he led me upstairs to Dylan's bedroom. Here, in a small, wallpapered space, with bed and chair for furniture, puffing Woodbines and sipping bottled beer, Thomas had produced the poetry of his first two books: *18 Poems* (*Sunday Referee*, 1934) and *25 Poems* (J. M. Dent, 1936). Of the latter Dame Edith Sitwell wrote in the *Sunday Times* (November 15, 1936): "The work of this very young man (he is 22 years of age) is on a huge scale . . . I could not name one poet of this, the younger generation, who shows so great a promise, and even so great an achievement."

I took in this perfectly ordinary room in which an odd, round-faced young Welshman had created "so great an achievement." Clearly, I thought, genius can triumph in the most commonplace surroundings. Maybe there was hope for us all. Then I was led back to the parlor to see Williams' manuscripts.

They were penned in black ink on pale vellum, the characters faultlessly drawn. Eventually he would pen all of Thomas' poems. He'd begun with "I see the boys of summer." Next was "Light breaks where no sun shines," then "Altarwise by Owl-light." When the poems were finished, he had the short stories to look forward to, then the radio scripts. He'd completed *A Child's Christmas in Wales* and, between poems, was lettering *Under Milk Wood*.

Over more tea the conversation turned to travel. Williams found my planned two-year trek around Europe daunting and confessed he'd never been abroad. "Wales is big enough for me." He spoke of Mumbles and the Worm's Head, St. David's, Carmarthen and Laugharne, his warm voice full. And I began to think I'd like to see something of this corner of Wales Dylan Thomas had spun into a universe.

————

The shambling double-decker bus creased the morning drizzle and squeaked to a stop. Mumbles. A few shops, the trio of pubs Thomas knew well: the Marine, the Antelope, the Mermaid. Weekend bungalows overlooked water the color of old coins. I walked west along a gravel track over high cliffs. A feeble sun shone on the Bristol Channel, which mauled wedges of beach below.

Bowed beneath a canvas rucksack, I hiked through morning and into afternoon, passing through Bishopston, where Dylan Thomas' parents lived after Cwmdonkin Drive, and where the poet, by then married to Caitlin Macnamara, often stayed. Although, in a letter to the poet Vernon Watkins, he claimed, "I'm not a countryman" and today we associate him with endless boozy nights in endless pubs, Thomas had a cosmic understanding of the natural world. His poetry brims with it. Of the time of their marriage in Cornwall, Caitlin has spoken of weeks spent walking the cliffs and wandering the hedgerows. This trudge out the Gower Peninsula was one of his beats.

From Bishopston to Oxwich over heathland, along dizzying drops above a frantic sea, the sun a tepid presence among scrappy clouds. On a hilltop, in the midst of wildflowers and golden gorse, stood the roan walls of a ruined castle. Wild ponies, streaming tatters of winter shag, galloped off like zebra on the Africa of the imagination.

At Port Eynon I sipped beer and played skittles in the only pub, ate Scotch eggs off a napkin spread on the bar. After a night at Ivy Jenkins' house on a hill above the sea, I set off along cliff tops in morning sunshine.

By noon I'd reached Rhossili: a deep, unprotected bay, a massive finger of stone pointing into the Atlantic—the Worm. I took a room in a high, sheep-white house, dumped my rucksack, then started for the headland. The tide was ebbing as I crossed the "reef" and mounted the great granite hump where I warmed and rested myself above the silvered sea through a long, gull-screaming afternoon.

Thomas often rode the bus here from Swansea, carrying a book and his lunch, walking onto the Worm's Head at low tide to spend the day reading. Once, he'd fallen asleep and been trapped by the incoming water. It was midnight before he could cross the "reef" and walk the eighteen miles home in the dark, seeing, according to Bill Read's *The Days of Dylan Thomas,* "diaphanous young ladies in white who vanished as he approached."

———

The morning bus back to Swansea was jammed with schoolchildren, their voices fluting as if English were a tongue of pure music. Their sounds were so joyful I laughed aloud, and they thought me daft. If the Welsh are famous as singers of language, and Dylan Thomas clearly was, the people of the Gower are Wales's Carusos, their simplest exclamations ravishing melodies.

The kids were still crooning as I swung down in Swansea's High

Street and hitched west aboard a gravel truck driven by a mild young man with a fag on his lip. We rode across green fields and greener hills, and I was left outside a gray pub in gray Carmarthen.

Inside, a half dozen weathered locals in tweed caps stubbly as sheep leaned across the bar, lamenting with the aproned publican, who swiped a dingy towel around the innards of a beer glass. Some deadbeat had died and left a sizable tab. Now it would never be paid. Six tweed caps nodded and there was a chorus of sympathetic *ayes*. One by one they told stories of this wretched freeloader who had mooched countless pints and shillings and packets of fags from them all. They paid no attention to me as the publican brought another pint. Soon it was clear that the madcap bamboozler who had charmed them out of their money was Dylan Thomas—now ten years dead. There was pride in their complaining. Not to have been sponged off of by Dylan seemed inadmissable, like sobriety or virginity.

———

Billy Pritchard, a pale boy in gum boots and oversized fedora, led me to the Great House and unlatched the door. An annex of Brown's Hotel, the Great House stood along Laugharne's King Street, a hundred yards from Brown's on the opposite side. My room was across a lightless parlor big as a meadow. Apparently I was the only guest. "Lights don't work," Billy warned. "Carry a torch, for when you come back from the pub."

I walked into the dusk along a street of seventeenth- and eighteenth-century slate-roofed houses, past Brown's, where Thomas drank, and the Cross Hands, his father's local, and down a slope to the ruined Norman castle and Castle House, where Richard Hughes, author of *A High Wind in Jamaica,* had lived. In the autumn of 1938, while Thomas was living up the street at Sea View ("a tall and dignified house at the posh end of this small town," as Thomas described it) Hughes lent him the gazebo in the castle garden to complete work on *Portrait of the Artist as a Young Dog,* unaware the poet was plundering his wine cellar deep within the castle walls.

Now the gazebo was lost in weedy tangle. I walked on, "sadly staring over the flat, sad, estuary sands, watching the herons walk like women poets" where the Eve-hipped cockle-women still worked the inner shore. Chilled and thirsty, I hurried back along the darkening street to the beery warmth of Brown's Hotel.

Ebbie and Ivy Williams, who ran Brown's in Thomas' day, were gone. Tony was behind the bar, thick, dark, and friendly, a talkative man who'd never known Thomas but who'd heard enough yarns about him to want to spin a few himself. I sipped a tepid pint of best bitter at a table near the window. A photo of Dylan and Caitlin taken here in 1938 hung behind me. Caitlin, with a half-smile, turns her strong, beautiful face to speak to someone nearby, while Dylan, just twenty-four, gazes dark-eyed into the camera as if he would take possession of it. Papers, cigarettes, a large bottle, a pint mug, a half-pint glass crowd the table then as they do now. The table was the same. I sat in Dylan's chair; Caitlin's was empty.

In George Tremlett's 1992 biography *Dylan Thomas: In the Mercy of His Means,* the author speaks of tens of thousands of visitors, many of them American, now in their sixties and seventies, who come to Laugharne each year to stand by Thomas' grave, drink at Brown's, visit the poet's house, now a museum. In the spring of 1963 there were no tourists save myself, and there can't have been many before me. The nodding tweed caps in the Carmarthen pub were not actors in a pageant. Mr. Williams, a little lonely, had taken my appearance as a chance for unexpected society. And if there were graduate students in Laugharne grinding out dissertations, they were thickly wrapped in Welsh wool and Welsh accents and were invisible, at least to me.

"Down in Wales," Tremlett writes, "Dylan Thomas is still regarded as 'a bit of a boyo' rather than a literary figure of world importance." He was a "boyo" to Tony, who poured himself a beer and joined me, pointing across the road toward the Pelican. This was the house Thomas leased for his parents when he and Caitlin moved permanently to Laugharne in 1949. Tony spoke of Thomas' funeral: because the casket was too wide to bring through the door of his mother's house, six Laugharne friends had lifted it through the window and into the waiting hearse, and deep in the viny churchyard the poet Louis MacNeice, in profound distress, had dropped a package of sandwiches into the grave.

There were stories of Thomas the drunkard, the charmer, the talker, the comedian, the mooch, the friend, the card player (chummy games of nap with Ebbie and Ivy Williams in the front window of Brown's), the flatterer of ladies—the stories that make up the legend—but little of Thomas the poet.

The evening wore on; business picked up. Tony got busy behind the bar. I ordered more beer, warm and thin, and pork pies as appetizing as K-rations. About ten a booming party in coarse suits and shaggy ties settled around a nearby table. Tony leaned over the bar. "Court of Aldermen," he said, sotto voce. "Chancellor, constables, and His Lordship the Mayor, would also be the Vicar Jones."

The vicar, young, small and blond, wore a clerical collar and a pious black suit. He saluted me with a tankard of ale. "Bring a chair," he said, waving me to his table. "We've this minute adjourned a corporation meeting and we've a prodigious thirst." Though my glass was full, he ordered more beer and introduced me around: there were Williamses and Lewises, Evanses and Davieses, and "Jenks the Chemist," a bright star in this small, affable firmament.

It wasn't Dylan Thomas "Jenks" spoke of but Laugharne itself, a place Thomas had called "timeless, beautiful, barmy (both spellings)." With a population of roughly four hundred adults, it's approximately the size and shape it was when the castle was built about 1300. An English-speaking town in the midst of Welsh-speaking Wales, it's kept its traditional government: a corporation headed by a portreeve—term for bailiff or mayor at the time of the Norman Conquest—a chancellor, a recorder, a court of aldermen, and four constables, each equipped with a wooden billy.

The corporation owned much of the surrounding land and twice each month met to discuss rents and leases. Every October the men of Laugharne attended the Portreeve's Breakfast, a thin excuse for an all-day drinking spree, a day when pubs never closed. But the Common Walk was the big event, a day observed every three years when the citizens, led by the portreeve and his council, walked the corporation's twenty-six-mile boundary. Every turn along the way had its own peculiar name, and if someone didn't know a name, he was turned upside down and whacked on the bottom with a constable's billy.

The Common Walk was coming up in a few weeks, and the mayor invited me along. "You'd be excused from the naming business, of course. Wouldn't want a guest having his bottoms smacked." But Constable Williams grinned beneath the bill of his shaggy cap, flourished his truncheon, and said he'd think long and hard before exempting an itinerant Yank.

In the noise and camaraderie of Brown's Hotel, lingering a few weeks in order to walk over the Welsh hills and fields with the eccentric and convivial citizens of this odd little town was tempting. I was still mulling it over when more beer arrived. I checked my watch. It was late: 11:10. Ten minutes past closing. Then the door burst open and two bobbies rushed in.

Choking down the evidence, I swallowed a full pint of best bitter while everyone laughed. Everyone but the bobbies who rounded on our table. "Would that be Constable Williams with a pint on the table before him?" asked a tall bobby made taller by his domed helmet. "And it's after hours. Aren't you ashamed of yourself, Dan?" Innocent as an angel, Dan Williams gazed into his beer as if it were morning tea.

The short bobby looked from face to face. Brass buttons strained across his bulging front. "Alderman Davies, Alderman Lewis, Constable Watkins, 'Jenks the Chemist!' I'm shocked, Jenks, deeply shocked, to find you, pillar of the community, here after hours, swilling the devil's brew." He leaned over the table and looked "Jenks the Chemist" in the eye. "We can run you in, Jenks, we surely can, and should. But what would poor Mrs. Jenkins think when she woke to discover you in jail?"

The tall one turned to the vicar. "Your lordship," he said, "it's distressing indeed to see you, mayor of Laugharne, vicar of St. Martin's, partaking of alcoholic beverage in a public establishment at this late hour. And leading an unsuspecting foreigner"—here he nodded at me—"into the paths of criminality. Maybe we'll hear a sermon on the subject come Sunday."

The bobbies bowed deeply, strode to the door, then wheeled on the assembled boozers. There was laughter and applause for their performance. They knew, of course, the story of the first two policemen ever sent to Laugharne, the two who disappeared without a trace. "We've taken names," the short one said. "We'll be back in ten minutes," the tall one went on, "and we expect to find you gone! Or it's jail for the lot of you!" Turning, they vanished into the drizzly Welsh night. The vicar ordered more beer.

I was pretty muzzy-headed. "I don't think I can drink another in just ten minutes."

"Ten minutes?" the Vicar asked. "What do ten minutes have to do with the drinking of beer?"

"Before the bobbies come back."

"Ah, it's the bobbies worry you. Well, don't fret about the bobbies.

The bobbies won't be back tonight. We'll be fortunate indeed if the bobbies should come back tomorrow."

———

Beer-filled, I stumbled home under a Welsh sky black as the vicar's waistcoat, bumped torchless among chairs grazing like steers across the black pasture of the Great House parlor, and slept into Thursday morning.

After breakfast, a waking cholesterol nightmare, I walked out Victoria Street to the Cliff—already called "Dylan's Walk" in 1963, the poet's only "official" recognition in Laugharne—and along the path to the Boat House. "My seashaken house / On a breakneck of rocks," as Thomas wrote of it in the prologue to *Collected Poems*.

The Thomases moved here in the first week of May, 1949, and it was home until Dylan's death in New York on November 9, 1953. A boxy, two-storied house perched on stilts over the Taf Estuary, it's inaccessible by car and difficult enough on foot, its roof almost level with the path. A steep walk led to the front door. No one was about, so I took a chance, went down and followed a catwalk around the house to a spindly balcony above the Estuary—the balcony where Dylan and Caitlin were photographed with the poet John Malcolm Brinnin while planning Thomas' second American tour.

No one answered my knock. Through mullioned windows I saw an ordinary room, a Welsh room with china dogs and doilies, books and chintz, a room whose owner I didn't know. The Thomases were gone from Laugharne: Caitlin in Italy with the children, Colm, Aeronwy, and Llewelyn; D. J. and "Granny" Thomas both dead.

If the room no longer echoed the poet's well-honed vowels, the view over the Estuary did.

> In the mustardseed sun,
> By full tilt river and switchback sea
>   Where the cormorants scud,
> In this house on stilts high among beaks
>   And palavers of birds
> This sandgrain day in the bent bay's grave
>   He celebrates and spurns
> His driftwood thirty-fifth wind turned age;
>   Herons spire and spear.

Across the "full tilt river and switchback sea," loud with shorebirds sailing the outgoing tide, cows fed in milky grass on the Llanstephan Peninsula, where the Williams clan, Thomas' mother's family, once lived. Visible across the Taf from the Boat House was Pentowin, where Aunt Ann and her husband, Jim Jones, farmed before moving to Fern Hill, just over the fields at Llangain. This is Thomas country to its roots—land and sea, it rings in every line. But he was no more a regional writer than were Joyce, Faulkner, or Dickinson. From the mud of the Taf and Towy, he'd molded the universe.

———

Walking back, I stopped to see Dylan's Shack on the Cliff a few hundred yards from the house. Built originally to house Laugharne's first automobile, Thomas wrote here during the last years of his life. In what he called his "workshed," there were a stove, bookcase, photos pinned to the wall—Auden, Edith Sitwell, Marianne Moore, Frank Harris—and his work table before a window overlooking the estuary of the Taf and Towy rivers to the sea. Now it stood deserted and locked, looking for all its poetic past like a garage once more.

———

I spent the afternoon on Pendine Sands, along a sunny curl of Carmarthen Bay, but was back in Laugharne by teatime. In the parlor at St. Martin's vicarage I sipped orange pekoe among the china dogs and chintz while the Vicar Jones, being most mayoral, opened a deep box of time-worn oak and displayed his emblem of office: the chain of solid gold cockle shells he wore on ceremonial occasions. Tea with Yanks apparently wasn't one of those occasions, but he lay the chain in my hands. A shell was added each time a new portreeve took office. This had gone on at least since Wales was incorporated with England in 1536. The chain was long and heavy. If I stayed for the Common Walk, the Vicar said, he would don it and, in his role as mayor, act as my guide. But I had to beg off. The Common Walk was weeks away, and I'd promised to be in Ireland for the anniversary of the Easter Rising.

———

After tea and scones and a view of the mayor's golden chain, I

13

climbed the ivied slope behind St. Martin's Church and stood beside a wooden cross:

IN

MEMORY

OF

DYLAN THOMAS

DIED

NOV 9

1953

R.I.P.

Someone had left spring blossoms. I snapped an early rose from the church's arbor and added it. For a while I sat in pale sunshine, then set off through late afternoon for Sir John's Hill.

It was dusk when I turned from the road and mounted a path through dense oaks. Beyond the trees the sea and estuary wore a platinum sheen that turned slowly coral, then salmon and gold. In the sunlit distance lay Llanstephan, Llanybri, and Fern Hill. To the north, under Milk Wood, Laugharne was in shadow, the castle, the clock tower, the slate-roofed houses along King and Gosport Streets, Sea View, the Pelican, Brown's, the simple crosses in St. Martin's Churchyard a tremulous blue, intangible as wood smoke.

On this shore of the Estuary a single point was touched by light: the Boat House, small, spindly, forgotten, the "seashaken house" from which the poet watched the mute ferryman taking his boat across the river to the family and farms of Dylan Thomas' childhood. To live and work in such a place was to see again

the woods the river and sea
Where a boy
In the listening
Summertime of the dead whispered the truth of his joy
To the trees and the stones and the fish in the tide.

The light held a moment, bright and golden, then the sun dipped behind the hill and the Boat House, too, went blue and impalpable.

I hurried down a tunnel between trees, darkness splashing over me like iced ale. It was cold, Laugharne far away. Suddenly, in the failing light,

I saw him: the fox. With bonfire fur, waiting and watching, vigilant, his businesslike muzzle honed. He was a big animal, unblemished, astonishingly alive. I stopped, and he waited, measuring me, familiar and inevitable. In that dimming silence, he cried once only.

> [T]he foxes on the hills barked clear and cold,
>   And the sabbath rang slowly
>   In the pebbles of the holy streams.

Then, with a flash of his flaming tail, he turned and was gone.

2

The House on Rue Lepsius

C. P. Cavafy in the City of Alexandria

MADAM CHRISTINA GAZES down from the tall cashier's desk and fluffs her blond hair. She's nearly eighty, a gaunt figure with good bones, ivory skin, and lively eyes. She would resemble Edith Piaf, had the great French chanteuse lived to this venerable age. For the past forty years Madam Christina has run Alexandria's Elite Café, a cheerful spot with deep booths, a superb collection of old art posters, and big sash windows opening onto Sharia Safia Zaghloul.

In the days of Constantine Cavafy, when Alexandria was more Greek than Egyptian, Sharia Safia Zaghloul was called Rue Missala, and on it, at the Café Al Salam and the Billiard Palace, the poet often picked up transient lovers. Had Madam Christina known Cavafy? She smiles down from the high desk. On the wall above her shoulder is a pastel drawing of the poet, hair slicked back, tired eyes fixed on a middle distance. Beneath it is a framed manuscript: "At the Café Door."

> Something they said beside me
> made me look toward the café door,
> and I saw that lovely body which seemed
> as though Eros in his mastery had fashioned it.

The strong handwriting in Greek builds toward architectural permanence.

"I used to see Cavafy," Madam Christina says, her rich voice strong and passionate. "But only from a distance. I was young, and he terrified me. He was a very important poet, always impeccable, a cape draped across his shoulders, a flower in his lapel. Very dandy. He dabbed his cheeks with rouge and splashed rose water around his eyes to brighten them.

"He was the last of nine children, you know, all boys, and Hariklia, his mother, desperately wanted a girl—her only daughter had died in infancy. So she dressed Constantine as a girl—long hair, dresses, ruffles and bows. It was this, I think, that turned him homosexual. He picked up boys along the street just here. There was a billiard parlor nearby, and a café where he found young men. At the time I saw him he was growing old, very thin, a white scarf at his throat. He was suffering from cancer of the larynx. He lived not far, on Rue Lepsius, in a flat above a bordello, just the other side of Saint Saba, the Greek Orthodox church. Around the corner was a hospital—where he died."

> The aging of my body and my beauty
> is a wound from a merciless knife.
> I'm not resigned to it at all.
> I turn to you, Art of Poetry,
> because you have a kind of knowledge about drugs:
> attempts to numb the pain, in Imagination and Language.
>
> Melancholy of Jason Kleander,
> Poet in Kommagini, A.D. 595

Outside, a calèche, a leather-hooded horse-drawn cab, pulls to the curb. The cook and a waiter hurry out to unload a huge silver fish. When they've wrestled it through the restaurant into the kitchen, Madam Christina excuses herself to see that the fish is fresh and carefully cleaned.

———

Though living in relative obscurity in Alexandria most of his life, Constantine Cavafy (1863–1933) is now regarded as perhaps the most important and original Greek poet of the twentieth century. He was introduced to English audiences by his friend E. M. Forster, championed by T. E. Lawrence and Arnold Toynbee, and published in T. S. Eliot's *Criterion*. But his concision, absence of rhetoric, and frank treatment of homosexual themes were unfashionable in modern Greek poetry, and he was not taken up by the Athenian literary establishment. He lived a quiet, some say circumscribed, life in Alexandria, never wishing to publish a volume of his poetry during his lifetime, though he gave friends privately printed pamphlets and broadsheets of his poems.

Cavafy's English connection is not surprising. His mother took him to England in 1872, where, over the next seven years—from the age of nine to sixteen—he became familiar with English poetry, especially the works of Shakespeare, Browning, and Wilde. He absorbed British ways and was so fluent in English that he was said to speak Greek with a British accent.

The family returned to Alexandria in 1879 but in 1882 again moved abroad, this time to Hariklia's family home at Yeniköy, a few miles up the Bosporus from Constantinople. They remained, living in genteel poverty, for the next three years, during which time Cavafy wrote his first poems. In 1885 the family returned to Alexandria where, except for an occasional journey to Athens, Cavafy lived for the rest of his life.

———

When Madam Christina remounts the great desk, there's a faraway look in her eye. "Cavafy's is a first-class tomb," she says, her voice suddenly soft and dreamlike, "you can be sure of that. A marble monument, not the cement you get in second class. He's buried with Hariklia and the sister that died as a baby. Ah, in those days things were done right. Alexandria was Paris. Thousands of Greeks, English, Italians. Very cosmopolitan. Very European. Concerts every day—all the great American and European artists performed. And parties and balls; the cafés full. Every month a different artist showed his paintings on these walls. My parents were Greek, but I was born here. There were almost a half million Greeks then; now there are only three hundred. My family's all gone—to Athens. My sons, every one. There's nothing for them here. No hope. But I have a nice flat and this business. I come every morning to see that the fish is fresh. I visit Athens now and then. But I'm home here. Like Cavafy, I have no place else to go."

> You will always end up in this city. Don't hope for things
>   elsewhere:
> there is no ship for you, there is no road.
> As you've wasted your life here, in this small corner,
> you've destroyed it everywhere else in the world.

———

After ten days of smog, traffic, and grit in crowded, horn-blaring Cairo, the clear, iodine-scented sea breeze of Alexandria is balm to my smoky soul. I've taken a corner room at the old Acropole Hotel on Midan Saad Zaghloul. Though the elevator isn't working and I've lugged my bags up five flights, it's a fine old Alexandrian building, and the view from my terrace—an ornate confection fit for a pasha—looks across Midan Saad Zaghloul to the Corniche and the blue sweep of the harbor.

On the seafront next door stands the Hotel Cecil, an Alexandrian institution whose guests over the years have included Churchill, Noël Coward, Somerset Maugham, and Lawrence Durrell. But the Cecil's recently been bought by an international chain, and modernization has dispelled its romantic ambience suggestive of age-old intrigue and corruption.

A bronze statue of the twenties nationalist leader Saad Zaghloul stands atop a granite plinth amidst the palms and hedges of the Midan. Beyond it spreads the Italian consulate, a graceful old Mediterranean villa, and over the tram lines, across from Ramleh Station, the Hotel Metropole. The upper floors of the Metropole once housed the Ministry of Public Works' Third Circle of Irrigation, where the twenty-nine-year-old Constantine Cavafy became a clerk, and where he worked for the next thirty years, retiring as an assistant director in 1922. Downstairs is the Trianon Patisserie, one of the poet's favorite cafés. It's easy to imagine him, after a day at what must have been a dry, irksome job, drinking at a table on the terrace overlooking the square or in the cool, paneled barroom.

> It's sad, I admit. But we who serve Art,
> sometimes with the mind's intensity,
> can create—but of course only for a short time—
> pleasure that seems almost physical.
> That's how in the bar the other day—
> mercifully helped by alcohol—
> I had half an hour that was totally erotic.

Like the Cecil, the Trianon has undergone a recent facelift and is now glitzy and expensive, though always packed with well-heeled Alexandrians.

———

Describing a visit to Alexandria in his book *Slow Boats to China,*
Gavin Young says that a Cavafy Museum is housed on the top floor of
the Greek consulate. Guidebooks agree. But I arrive on a Friday, the
Moslem holy day, and the consulate is closed. I spend an hour over coffee at the Trianon, then stroll along Sharia Safiya Zaghloul. After noon
prayers it's thronged with shoppers—the women in head scarves and
long skirts, a few of them veiled, while the men sport slacks and casual
shirts. The Acropole Hotel's mustachioed night clerk, Khalid al-Hakim,
has scrawled a crude map on which I've noted a few of Cavafy's haunts.
From Sharia Safiya Zaghloul I turn into another busy shop-lined street
and at number 39 Tarïq al-Hurriyyah, across from the Amir Cinema, find
a blue awning with white lettering: PASTROUDIS. A dim, high-ceilinged
place with dark paneling, beveled mirrors, and Deco chandeliers, Pastroudis was a Cavafy refuge and a landmark cited in Lawrence Durrell's
Alexandria Quartet: "We will walk the whole length of Rue Fuad thus
and take a lengthy public coffee on the pavement outside Pastroudi." I
order an iced Stella, the sour Egyptian beer, and am told politely by the
waiter "No alcohol" on Friday. I settle for "a lengthy public coffee," then
consider the connections between Cavafy and Durrell. The lietmotivs of
excess and loss, nostalgia, and futility found in Cavafy's poetry are echoed
in Durrell's *Quartet.* And though Cavafy died in 1933, some time before
Durrell's arrival in Alexandria, the English novelist translated several of
Cavafy's poems in the *Quartet* and used the Greek poet in crafting Balthazar. In *Justine* he describes this pivotal character: "To have written so
much and to have said nothing about Balthazar is indeed an omission. . . .
I see a tall man in a black hat with a narrow brim. . . . He is thin, stoops
slightly, and has a deep croaking voice of great beauty, particularly when
he quotes or recites. In speaking to you he never looks at you directly—
a trait which I have noticed in many homosexuals. . . . Often I have
entered his little room in the Rue Lepsius—the one with the creaking
cane chair—and found him asleep in bed with a sailor. He has neither
excused himself at such a time nor even alluded to his bedfellow. While
dressing he will sometimes turn and tenderly tuck the sheet round his
partner's sleeping form." Later, in *Justine,* he places the two characters
together—the fictional and the real: "The sulking bodies of the young
begin to hunt for a fellow nakedness, and in those little cafés where Balthazar went so often with the old poet of the city, the boys stir uneasily."
Durrell's footnote reveals Cavafy to have been "the old poet of the city."

It's as if Alexandria, with its decadent grandeur and crumbling edifices, the dank sea-smell of cramped spaces, the feeling that a great past has slipped quietly away and left a dissolving present, a future without promise, turned these two writers inward to mine veins of loss and decay.

> . . . Since nine o'clock when I lit the lamp
> the shade of my young body
> has come to haunt me, to remind me
> of shut scented rooms,
> of past sensual pleasure—what daring pleasure.
> And it's also brought back to me
> streets now unrecognizable,
> bustling night clubs now closed,
> theatres and cafés no longer there . . .
>
> Half past twelve. How the time has gone by.
> Half past twelve. How the years have gone by.

———

With Khalid's map in hand, I set out through the Alexandrian evening. The stores along Sharia Salah Salem are alight, the sidewalks crowded. A boy passes, selling cotton candy, the sticky pink stuff strung along a lengthy pole. A handsome young man with a movie-star smile sprawls legless on the pavement, begging in a modest way. When I give him a couple of Egyptian pounds, his smile broadens and he thanks me in impeccable English. Seated outside his shop, a barber in a white smock examines Khalid's map. It bears a street name in Arabic script. "Not here," he says, gesturing. "Three blocks further." Finally a round little waiter at the Bendrot Restaurant, wiping his hands on a soiled apron, leads me around a corner and shows the way.

The Rue Debbane [des Bains] is narrow and dim with a collection of tailor shops still open for business, their windows eerie with ghostly dress forms draped in fabric. There's a hole-in-the-wall teahouse, "The Engineers of Typewriters and Counting Machines," a dental lab, and, surprisingly, the Austrian consulate. Alexandria's Greek literati once gathered in the Rue Debbane at Grammata, a bookshop run by Cavafy's friend Stephen Pargas, known to acquaintances as Nikos Zelitas. There Cavafy joined Zelitas and a group of literary compatriots in the evenings.

But though I prowl the street from end to end, a second then a third time, there's no sign of Grammata. Shopkeepers eye me suspiciously and shake their heads: No, no one remembers a Greek bookshop. Must be the wrong street.

Midway along the Rue Debbane is the blank side of an old church, Greek letters inscribed above a gateway leading to a garden. More lettering on the church wall: *Boreja Sao Pedro*. An odd mix of Greek and Portuguese. A man, in muted *galabieh* and inky turban, stops, takes the map from my hand, then scrawls something in Arabic. "Sunday," he says. "Church open." He goes his way, leaving me alone in this dark street where Constantine Cavafy sometimes surfaced, seeking companionship.

———

Two soldiers, helmeted young men with automatic weapons and country grins, draw to attention before a wrought-iron gate. Behind them is an imposing three-story building of tan stone, the blue and white of the Greek flag snapping from a pole high on its roof. It's Saturday, the consulate closed, but after a long, hot walk over badly broken streets, I hope to stake a claim. The soldiers, seeing things differently, bring their weapons to port-arms and block my way. Then the taller of the two, a gangly youth whose skinny neck can barely support the weight of his steel helmet, relents and nudges the gate open with his boot. I follow him up broad steps and wait while he rings the bell. A factotum appears, an old man in white, peering around the half-opened door.

"Cavafy Museum?"

"Monday," the factotum says. "Open Monday—ten o'clock. Please to come then."

———

After onion soup and a crisp salad at the Elite, then coffee on the terrace of Pastroudis, I follow Tariq al-Hurriyyah to Sharia Nabi Daniel. It's a cool evening, the sea's salt smell drifting in from the Corniche. After wandering dim alleyways, I come upon the Greek Church of Saint Saba.

> Whenever I go there, into a church of the Greeks,
> with its aroma of incense,
> its liturgical chanting and harmony,
> the majestic presence of the priests,

22

dazzling in their ornate vestments,
the solemn rhythm of their gestures—
my thoughts turn to the great glories of our race,
to the splendor of our Byzantine heritage.

Saint Saba is a disappointment. The old monastery, torn down and rebuilt in 1970, is now a clumsy, overdecorated, top-heavy structure crowded with "Greek" columns and too many arches.

In a lighted shop across the street, a young man peers from behind a collection of leather handbags. Cavafy's old Rue Lepsius has been renamed Sharia Sharm el Sheikh. Neither name means anything to the clerk. But when I mention the Pension Amir, Cavafy's building, he brightens and steps outside to direct me down a side street. "Two blocks, then turn left."

This brings me to a neighborhood food shop on a narrow alleyway with no apparent name. No one's heard of Rue Lepsius or Sharia Sharm el Sheikh until a fat man in white nightshirt, the boss probably, heaves up from a capacious blue couch at the back of the shop, nods his massive skull, then points along the street and gestures first turn to the right.

Rue Lepsius is a short, dark street of potholes, rubble, and unlit buildings. Robert Liddell, in *Cavafy: A Critical Biography,* says the Rue Lepsius is "dingy and ill-famed," while in *Slow Boats to China* Colin Young writes: "Cavafy's street . . . is not smart or picturesque; on the contrary, it is almost a slum." To me, Rue Lepsius is no more squalid than countless other streets in Egypt—or anywhere else in the world.

At the end of the block a lighted sign advertises Happy Home, a small shop selling ball-point pens, curling irons, and cheap plastic dishes.

He idled his way down the main street
and the poor side-streets that led to his home.

Passing in front of a small shop
that sold cheap and flimsy things for workers
he saw a face inside there, saw a figure
that compelled him to go in, and he pretended
he wanted to look at some colored handkerchiefs . . .

Behind the counter a pretty young woman in a head scarf looks up from her Koran. She's uncertain about the Pension Amir. "Cavafy house?" I hold four fingers aloft. "Ah," she says in flawless English, "you wish number four." As she leads me outside and indicates a building down the block, two small boys materialize to become my guides. "Give *baksheesh! Baksheesh!*" they shriek hilariously, leading me to a dingy building. A half dozen tarnished plaques in Arabic script are mounted on a scarred wall beside locked doors. One among them, it's brass gleaming, is in Greek: K. Π. ΚΑΒΑΘΗΣ [C. P. Cavafy].

———

Ten o'clock Monday morning, the long three-day weekend finally over. The gangly young soldier snaps a salute, mounts the steps and stands aside as the great double doors of the Greek Consulate swing wide. The white-clad factotum is all smiles as he leads me into a downstairs office where a distinguished, silver-haired gentleman in a costly blue suit resides behind acres of desk.

"May I be of help?"

"The Cavafy Museum, please."

"Ah, the Cavafy Museum." While a tanned hand brushes back silver hair, a long pause chills my enthusiasm. "I'm afraid," he says at last, "the Cavafy Museum is no longer here. It's been moved back to Cavafy's flat on Rue Lepsius."

Enthusiasm returns. To give a sense of his life, Cavafy's flat is plainly more appropriate than the consulate for the poet's manuscripts and mementos.

A hand dips into a drawer and draws out a mimeographed flyer. "This may help you find your way."

On the flyer is a map, little better than that drawn by Khalid al-Hakim. Hand-lettered across it:

VISIT Cavafis Museum

Open Daily 9–2

Monday: <u>Closed</u>

———

Happy Home is open, though the young woman reading her Koran is gone, replaced by a stout man in caftan and *kofia*. I buy a notebook and a cheap pen, the kind that inevitably smears and splotches my clothes like those of a Dickensian scrivener. My baksheesh-seeking urchins fail to appear. They are, I trust, in school. So, Monday or no, I start along Rue Lepsius to number 4.

There is no sign of the Pension Amir, which in Cavafy's day was a brothel, though it may still exist behind closed shutters. The entrance to number 4 is open, the tall double doors pushed wide. The stairs mounting through the building's core echo hollowly as I climb to the third floor landing where a polished brass plaque on a solid door reads "ΜΟΥΣΘΙΟ ΚΑΒΑΘΗ."

The bell is answered immediately by a twenty-year-old in work clothes who holds a paintbrush in one hand, a bucket of whitewash in the other. I'm in luck. Not wishing to disappoint a visitor, even when the museum is officially closed, he smiles and steps back, then vanishes as quickly as he came, leaving the door open behind him.

First there's a foyer with a screen inlaid in mother-of-pearl, a lantern of colored glass, ornate tables and chairs. Opposite, a corner room with oriental carpets, red plush chairs, a rococo writing desk. The ceilings are tall, none of the rooms large. Tables are spread with Cavafy's books and manuscripts and mementos of his spare life. In the photographs and drawings he's mustached and dashing, a sophisticated bon vivant, forever young. Nowhere is he tired, disillusioned, old, though these are the rooms where he aged, lived alone, suffered cancer, wrote his haunting, evocative poems.

> This room, how familiar it is.
>
> Here, near the door, was the couch,
> a Turkish carpet in front of it.
> Close by, the shelf with two yellow vases.
> On the right—no, opposite—a wardrobe with a mirror.
> In the middle the table where he wrote,
> and the three big wicker chairs.
> Beside the window was the bed
> where we made love so many times.
>
> They must still be around somewhere, those old things.
>
> Beside the window was the bed;
> the afternoon sun fell across half of it.

25

> . . . One afternoon at four o'clock we separated
> for a week only . . . And then—
> that week became forever.

The workman suddenly reappears, handsome and trim in his paint-spattered clothes, and I'm sure Cavafy would like this young man knocking about his flat. In the kitchen, which a second workman is plastering, the first shows me Cavafy's ornate brass bed propped against a wall. Like the plaque at the door, it gleams with frequent polishing.

For an hour I wander these half dozen rooms. I have the place to myself—not a sound but the two young men at their work. At the back, across the hallway from the kitchen, is the bath—a white tile cubicle sterile as an operating room. At the front, next to the corner room where Cavafy wrote, is a room where the bed will go when the painting is done. French doors open onto a balcony overlooking the street—the Rue Lepsius. From here, beyond the tin roof of the Greek Garage, stand a cluster of palms and the tower of Saint Saba. Down the block, on the corner of Safia Sultan Hassein, is the derelict Alexandria Theatre, once the Greek Hospital. Looking over the poet's old quarter, I think of Madam Christina: "He lived not far, on Rue Lepsius, just the other side of Saint Saba, in a flat above a bordello."

"Where could I live better?" Cavafy once asked. "Below, the brothel caters for the flesh. And there is the church which forgives sin. And there is the hospital where we die."

He died there in 1933, after receiving last rites from a Greek Orthodox priest. As his final act, he drew a circle on a sheet of paper, then placed a period at the circle's center.

———

It rains at dawn. The morning is cloudy and cool. One thing left I want to do. After breakfast I ride a crowded tram out Sharia Iskandar el-Akbar, past the Greek consulate, and get down at Sharia Aflatoun. From here the high walls of the Foreign Cemetery run south and east down long blocks shaded by banyan trees. Somewhere in this immense terrain is Cavafy's "first-class tomb."

A short way up Sharia Aflatoun is an iron gate, chained and locked. Through the palings a ramshackle house squats under acacia trees and a half dozen yellow curs sleep in the dirt. "*Alan! Alan!*" Hello! All smiles, an adolescent girl in head scarf and oversized dress appears, unlocks the gate, and shoos away the barking dogs. Her mother arrives carrying a small boy in caftan and *kofia* and from the house, disheveled and hardly awake, a thin, one-eyed man emerges, pulling on trousers.

"*Cavafis?* The tomb of *Cavafis?*" We share no language and "Cavafis" clearly means nothing to him. Together we trail down a dirt path among impressive marble monuments carved, it suddenly appears, in an unexpected script: Hebrew. The names David and Levi and Solomon appear repeatedly—"names engraved upon the stone which echoed all the melancholy of European Jewry in exile," Lawrence Durrell wrote of them in *The Alexandria Quartet*. "*Judeha,*" the one-eyed man says. "*Judeha.*" No, I explain, Greek. We get the message about the same time—I'm clearly in the wrong burial ground. He leads me back through the pack of barking dogs and points down the block: "*Greegi! Greegi!*"

It's a long walk past the Coptic cemetery, then Greek—Second Class. At last, Greek—First Class, where the gate's ajar and a uniformed attendant loafs just inside under the shade of a leafy arbor. I've hardly asked for "Cavafis" when a second man appears—Greek, from the look of him, with iron-gray hair and Peloponnesian mustache. "Cavafis, this way."

Cavafy's grave lies among marble angels along a spur of the main path, in the second row of tombs. I slide between a pair of marble markers to the waist-high fence surrounding it. An ornate column topped by a cross rises to one side, bearing a shield with the family name and the names of Cavafy's mother and infant sister. Cavafy's grave lies beside it, a simple slab of white marble with a cross in relief on its upper quarter. Below it, inlaid in weathered copper:

ΚΩΝΣΤΑΝΤΙΝΟΣ Π. ΚΑΒΑΘΗΣ

ΠοιhthΣ

ΘΑΝΩΝ ΕΝ Α Ε ΑΝΑΡΕΙΑ ΤΗΝ 29^{hn} ΑΝΡ ΙΟΥ 1933

Acacias and palms, a gravel path, a scarred bench peeling green paint. A gardener, wrapped in a *dhoti,* his scant body creased by sun and old age, fusses among the shrubbery. The brittle stalks of long-dead chrysanthemums crowd a marble vase. There's wind in the trees, and the distant clanging of a tram. A wilted rose, probably left yesterday, rests on the poet's tomb. I bend and add a branch of scarlet bougainvillea. Beyond the cemetery walls Cavafy's Alexandria, like a sleepless night in some half-remembered room, drowses in the sea-smell of a dissolving morning.

3

Looking for Sugar Street
The Cairo of Naguib Mahfouz

SHORTLY AFTER IRAN'S Ayatollah Khomeini condemned Salman Rushdie to death for alleged blasphemy in his novel *The Satanic Verses,* the press reported that a similar death threat, this time by Sheik Omar Abdel Rahman, of the Islamic Jihad, had been made against the 1988 Nobel Prize–winning Egyptian novelist Naguib Mahfouz. The Egyptian had offended Muslim zealots by his depiction of a character identifiable as the prophet Mohammed in his novel *Children of Gabalawi.* Mahfouz, one article pointed out, did not take the death threat seriously. "If they wanted to kill me, they would have done so already," Mahfouz reportedly said. He still took his early morning walk to the Aly Baba Café in downtown Cairo, the article went on; "I don't look to the right or the left," said the novelist. I was struck by Mahfouz's courage—or his faith in the will of Allah—and by his final comment: "I've done everything in my life. Whether death comes from a bullet or cancer, it doesn't really matter."

A few days later, knowing I planned a trip to Egypt, a friend sent copies of three Mahfouz novels: *The Thief and the Dogs, Miramar,* and *Midaq Alley,* set in the grim streets of al-Gamaliya, one of Cairo's oldest districts, where Mahfouz grew up and lived much of his life. I read them as novels, but also with the hope of catching a glimpse beyond the guidebook Egypt of the Sphinx and the pyramids, the living Egypt I was about to encounter. Mahfouz did not disappoint.

Born in 1912 and raised in al-Gamaliya, the Fatimid heart of Islamic Cairo, Naguib Mahfouz is regarded as Egypt's finest writer and the exemplar of Arabic literature. A student of philosophy and letters, he was influenced by several European novelists, among them Flaubert, Balzac, Zola, Camus, Proust, and Tolstoy. Variously described as the "Egyptian Dickens," the "Egyptian Balzac," or the "Egyptian Dostoevski," Mahfouz is admired for his vivid social frescoes of twentieth-century Cairo. The author of forty novels and collections of short stories and more than thirty screenplays, he is best known for his *Cairo Trilogy*—*Palace Walk, Palace of Desire*, and *Sugar Street*. Chronicling the changes in modern Egypt during the years leading toward the 1956 coup that toppled King Farouk and resulted in the rise of Colonel Gamal Abdel Nasser, the *Cairo Trilogy* traces three generations of a middle-class family from the nationalist turmoil of the First World War through the waning days of the second. After popularizing the novel and short story in the Arab literary world, Mahfouz found a worldwide audience. In awarding him the 1988 Nobel Prize, the Swedish Academy honored him as an author "who, through works rich in nuance—now clear-sightedly realistic, now evocatively ambiguous—has formed an Arabian narrative art that applies to all mankind."

———

The largest city in Africa, with a population approaching twenty million, Cairo, brown and gray from smog and desert dust, is vast, overcrowded, ugly, unbelievably dirty, and possessed of irresistible vitality. I arrived late in November, saw only the ugliness, the dirt, and crowds, and fled immediately to the port city of Alexandria, then west along the coast to Mersa Matruh and on to the Siwa Oasis, deep in the Libyan Desert. When I returned to Cairo, I was soon afflicted with a hacking cough and mild fever. The air reeked of exhaust. The wind off the Nile went to the bone. I forced myself out of the Pension Roma and into the streets, walking block after crowded block, through district after district, each dirtier and poorer than the last, dodging horn-blaring cars at every corner, and slowly the richness of Cairo's life, its incredible past and vibrant present, seeped into my blood.

One morning, while navigating narrow alleyways not far from the city's ancient bazaar, the Khan al-Khalili, I came across a smart stone facade looking onto a small square. The Naguib Mahfouz Coffee Shop, announced a sign in elegant script. Inside I discovered expensive Arabian

Nights decor and a pair of smartly dressed American women reapplying layers of lip gloss after espresso and sweets. Crystal and flatware glimmered in distant rooms, and an oil portrait of Naguib Mahfouz, his handsome, angular, aging face masked by ever-present sunglasses, graced one wall. When a waiter passed in an immaculate tuxedo, I asked if Mahfouz ever came here. Common Egyptian traits are warmth, genuine friendliness, and the enjoyment of a good joke. The waiter found my question, asked with irony, fit the latter, and laughed out loud. I suggested Mahfouz couldn't be found on the premises for he was surely drinking coffee at the Aly Baba Café. The waiter laughed even louder and agreed.

But where was the Aly Baba Café? I had long entertained a fantasy that one day I might happen on the place and find Mahfouz. I would order tea and watch quietly as he smoked, chatted with friends, and maybe even revised a manuscript. Whenever I mentioned Mahfouz to Egyptians, they brightened and spoke of him with admiration, though few, I have a hunch, had read him. After twenty years, *Children of Gabalawi* is still banned, and there were rumors that his current novel might not even be published in Arabic. Still, he had brought world attention and prestige to Egypt—important commodities in the Developing World—and for this he is much appreciated. But whenever I asked about the Aly Baba Café, though all agreed it was where Mahfouz might be found, no one seemed to know where it was.

The closest I had come was Café Riche on Sharia Talaat Harb, a literary bar where much of the 1952 revolution was plotted and where there are photos of literary figures on display, including a giant blowup of Mahfouz that hangs at the end of the dining room. But the place is too dreary and too badly run to attract even the meanest hack, and the rooms are mostly empty except for an occasional Australian backpacker or intense Egyptian lovers looking for privacy. Mahfouz and the Aly Baba, if I was ever to find them, would have to wait.

———

I had ridden over the desert on horseback to see the pyramids, seen Islamic, Coptic, and modern Cairo, and admired the breathtaking golden funerary mask of the young Pharaoh Tutankhamen in the Egyptian Museum. Now it was time to make my pilgrimage up the Nile to Luxor, Aswan, and Abu Simbel.

It was weeks before I was back in the capital. This time I had to attend to business, since my visa was about to expire. That meant a trip to the dreaded Mugamaa, a huge, gray government building facing Cairo's central square, the Midan Tahrir, and by all accounts a paper quagmire, the bureaucratic equivalent of the Vietnam War. When I mentioned my destination, the concierge at the Pension Roma said dryly that if I wasn't back within three days he'd assume I'd been mummified in paper and would let my room to someone else.

My only encouragement came from William Golding's *Egyptian Journal.* Faced with visa renewal, Golding had entered the Mugamaa expecting to spend days fencing with bureaucrats. Yet it was accomplished in no time. But then Golding, like the elusive Mahfouz, was a Nobel laureate and practically a guest of the state. Surely that accounted for the speed with which his documents were processed. Not so; I too received royal treatment from the bureaucrats. Having entered shortly after nine, it wasn't quite ten when I stepped into the winter sunlight, my officially stamped passport clutched in my fist, and made a quick getaway by joining a throng of pedestrians dashing through traffic toward the far side of the square.

With practically the whole day before me, I sauntered along the dingy street, my first thought a glass of tea to celebrate my victory over red tape. Then I found it. In the middle of the block, directly opposite the Mugamaa in the very heart of the city: a door opening into an uninviting room with orangish chairs, a dirty carpet, soiled tablecloths. Clear Roman letters over the doorway spelled "Aly Baba Café."

Instead of sweet black Egyptian tea, they served cups of hot water and bags of uninteresting Ceylon. The sugar came in small paper envelopes. The young, unsmiling waiter wore a soiled white coat. The bill was too high. When I'd finished my tea and given the waiter too much baksheesh, I asked about Mahfouz. The man's answer was matter-of-fact: "Any morning between eight and nine—he sits upstairs." I thanked him, eyed the narrow steps leading to the "dining room" above and went on my way.

The next day, Friday, I was up before daylight and in a cab bound for the Souk el Gahmell, in the distant suburb of Imbaba. Installed in a market teahouse, where a Bedouin herdsman cut the throat of a goat practically at my feet, I watched as hundreds of milling camels were bought and sold by dark men in *galabiehs* wearing oystershell Rolexes and golden cufflinks. More fascinating by far than used-car salesmen hawking dubious Fords between frames on *Bowling for Dollars.*

It was noon when I reached the Nile Hilton, drank a sour bottle of Stella beer on the shady terrace, then crossed jam-packed Midan Tahrir to the Aly Baba. There was a new waiter on the job, a toothless old man, his waiter's jacket even dirtier than that of yesterday's fellow, wheezing miserably between cigarettes. I found him chatty and warm and took a liking to him at once. We talked a long time about the joys and sorrows of being Cairene, and all the time we talked, though I didn't know it, Naguib Mahfouz was enjoying his coffee upstairs. It wasn't until he'd left, apparently down a back stairway and through the kitchen, that the waiter pulled me into the street in time to glimpse Mahfouz's thin back vanishing around a corner.

———

Next morning, a little after eight, I was on my way once again to the Aly Baba. I'd hardly entered the square when I saw Mahfouz talking intently with a man in a gray sharkskin suit at a table near the window on the mezzanine floor. If the window had been open, I could have tugged his trouser leg. My waiter greeted me with a handshake and a toothless grin, then showed me to a table downstairs. I'd brought along a copy of *Autumn Quail,* Mahfouz's 1962 novel set in Alexandria during the Egyptian Revolution. When the waiter brought our tea, I handed him the book and a pen. Would he please ask Mahfouz to sign? Everything I'd read about the author emphasized his pleasure in simple things, his strict work habits, his shyness, the anonymity he enjoyed in this labyrinthine city. Would he want to meet an admirer? I left it to him. In less than a minute the waiter was back with the book. In a thin scrawl on the first page Mahfouz had signed his name; beneath it, the date: Christmas Eve.

I had no contingency plan. What happened next was spontaneous, like an improvisation in a Method Acting class. After I'd paid and tipped the waiter, I left the Aly Baba and walked toward the Sharia Tahrir. I'd gone only a few steps when I stopped, turned back and looked up. Mahfouz was alone now, his chair drawn close to the window. He must have been watching me—maybe he'd seen the orange cover of *Autumn Quail*

33

in my hand—for when I turned, he smiled. No, *smile* doesn't describe the radiance, the warmth, the look of joy that touched his face. He shone, this man of eighty, as if gazing on the face of someone or something deeply loved. I stood transfixed—then raised my hands above my head and began silently to applaud. What Mahfouz did next seemed strange, out of context. Maybe a gesture common in the Arab world, maybe as spontaneous as my applause in the middle of the crowded sidewalk. Mahfouz suddenly raised his hands, palms outward, and salaamed in recognition of my appreciation, his head nearly touching the tablecloth as he did so. It was a gesture of joy, of humility, of acceptance of the responsibility literature had placed upon him. It went on for what seemed a long time: my applause, Mahfouz's smile and deep bows. We were strangely joined in a moving ritual at the very heart of this giant, fire-breathing city until, still applauding, I backed slowly away and was absorbed by the crowds. The last glimpse I had of Mahfouz, the smile touching his broad Egyptian mouth more radiantly than ever, was with his hands raised in farewell.

I went to the Sinai, Dahab, and St. Catherine, then came back to Cairo. I flew to Nairobi, spent a month in Kenya, and came back once again. I thought of returning to the Aly Baba, mounting the stairs, and introducing myself to Mahfouz, asking about his writing plans, the new translations of his work coming out in America. But there seemed no point. Those few minutes across from the Mugamaa on the sidewalk of the Midan Tahrir, while the notoriously shy and retiring Mahfouz salaamed and I applauded, were all I hoped for. There was nothing left to know, nothing to say. I'd found the Aly Baba Café. I'd found Naguib Mahfouz.

———

Later, after I published an account of our unusual rendezvous, people asked if I wouldn't return to Cairo and speak with the Egyptian author. When Mahfouz read the piece and wrote to thank me, a journey began to take shape. I wrote to Aleya Serour at the American University in Cairo Press, and she arranged a meeting with Mahfouz.

Meanwhile Mahfouz, already weakened by diabetes and nearly blind, was attacked by would-be assassins. When I reached Cairo he was undergoing rigorous daily sessions of physical therapy. The good news was that he was making progress. The bad news: he was too exhausted at

the end of each day to receive visitors. So I went looking for Naguib
Mahfouz in the streets and alleyways of Islamic Cairo.

———

> She got her coat and left Sugar Street with quick and agi-
> tated steps. It was cold and still quite dark, but roosters were
> defiantly crowing back and forth at each other. She shot
> down al-Ghuriya and traversed the Goldsmiths Bazaar on
> her way to al-Nahhasin.

The walk from the Pension Roma across al-Ataba Square and along
Sharia al-Azhar to the Mosque of al-Husayn is a mile over rubble-strewn
sidewalks and across three terrifying traffic circles where a pedestrian must
be quick and balletic to pass unscathed through unending streams of
smoke-spewing vehicles. For much of its length the Sharia runs beneath
the howl of an elevated highway. Here the street is devoted to string and
rope merchants, the odd shoe repair shop, and my favorite fruit stall, where
I stop for cooling glasses of fresh pomegranate juice. When he sees me
coming, the young man behind the tiled counter pops an Umm Kalthum
cassette into a decrepit boom box and the singer's voice swells over the
clamoring traffic, as pulsing and urgent as Billie Holiday or Janis Joplin.

———

> The streetcar was packed. There was not even room enough
> for riders to stand.

Ihab, waiting for a tram at Sharia Bur Said, buttonholes me as I pass.
"So you are a writer?" he says doubtfully after introducing himself and
asking my profession. Short, wiry and intense, Ihab is wearing an "American Embassy—Sofia, Bulgaria" T-shirt given him by friends in the U.S.
embassy. An economics student at Cairo University, he poses questions as
if in a classroom inquiry: What do you write? Why are you here? Do you
know Naguib Mahfouz? His eyes are lively and eager; he's both curious
and doctrinaire. I've written about Mahfouz, I explain, and hope to write
more.

"Many people in Egypt do not like him, you know?"

"How about you, Ihab?"

"I've seen movies of his books. *Sugar Street,* for instance. But I'm not interested in reading his novels. I read the books of Abas Alakaad—a much better writer than Mahfouz."

Suddenly a tram appears, and Ihab joins the throng rushing aboard. "But, Ihab," I shout into a surf of traffic and tram roar, "how do you know Alakaad is a better writer than Mahfouz if you haven't read Mahfouz?"

Ihab grins and waves as the tram slips away, leaving my unanswered question like a faded handkerchief fluttering *bon voyage* in the smoggy breeze.

———

   . . . that evening Riyad Qaldas himself had suggested going
   to the Khan al-Khalili.

Moustafa Mohammed El Sayed is a small, solemn man with a salt-and-pepper beard and a striped *galabieh*. The sign over his shop on Haret El-Wekala reads, Oriental Curiosities. Silver jewelry and semiprecious stones cram glass cases, and a dozen photographs of the legendary singer Umm Kalthum decorate a wall behind the counter. In each she wears impenetrable black sunglasses and clutches a voluminous white scarf. Naguib Mahfouz named a daughter for her. Although many years have passed since Umm Kalthum's death, she's still Egypt's preeminent star.

Moustafa has been my friend since I bought an unusual silver ring set with a Roman coin from him on my first trip to Cairo. Each time I visit, he begs me to name some impossible task he can accomplish on my behalf. This morning I offer a modest challenge. "Moustafa, can you direct me to Sugar Street?"

He lays a hand over his heart and bows his head in a Moslem gesture of humility and sincerity: "Sugar Street—*al-Sukkariyya*. Moustafa will be most happy to point the way."

Moustafa's shop is at the entrance to the Khan al-Khalili, around the corner from Sharia al-Sanadqiyyah. Before he directs me to al-Sukkariyya, he turns the shop over to Hasan, his nephew, an earnest boy of ten. Moustafa and I then begin a familiar walk that's almost a pilgrimage. First along al-Sanadqiyyah, a short, busy street crowded with shops, then into a narrow lane, the Zuqaq al-Midaq, setting for Naguib Mahfouz's chilling novel *Midaq Alley,* a grim story of life in this ancient and poor Cairene neighborhood.

36

Hardly wider than an armspan, Midaq Alley runs past a coffee house at its corner, then for twenty yards between shopfronts where men sit in the sun sipping tea. The alley jogs right, runs up a steep flight of stairs, and opens into a tiny square, where a mason, taking a break from mixing concrete, brews coffee over a kerosene burner. Strung with lines of drying clothes, the alley branches left and then dead-ends. Beyond the last tumbledown dwelling towers the magnificent six-hundred-year-old minaret of the Madrassa of Sultan Barsbey.

From this cramped geography, not a hundred yards long and a half dozen wide, Naguib Mahfouz created a metaphorical world peopled by universal characters—the barber, the café keeper, the cripple maker, the young beauty tragically turned harlot. Back at the bottom of the stairs, we discover Captain Musa and a friend drinking tea.

"Masa Awad Musa, *felluca capitain extraordinare,* down from Aswan on holiday, but always at your service."

Captain Musa's broad, mobile face gapes in a warm grin, and he laughs deeply. "My friend, Jamil," he says, slapping his companion's frail back. "Jamil is Cairene," he booms, "from right here on Midaq Alley. But me, I'm an upriver man."

The two are turned out in white from turban to shoes, contrasting Kashmiri shawls draped casually around their shoulders. We shake hands, and Captain Musa invites Moustafa and me to drink tea.

"Many thanks, but I don't have time today."

"No time for tea? You foreigners have *so* much to do. All right, suit yourself. You ever come to Aswan?"

"Sometimes."

"You know Aswan Moon?"

I swear that I eat and drink nowhere else when I'm in Aswan.

"Come see me," he booms. "You can always find me at Aswan Moon. Ask for Captain Musa. I have felluca. We'll sail together down to Luxor, maybe even Cairo—after a week on the Nile with Captain Musa, you might find time to join Jamil and me for tea in Midaq Alley."

———

The Muski was very congested. Already teeming with more than its normal pedestrian traffic, it was being flooded by currents of human beings ...

Moustafa and I turn right out of al-Sanadqiyyah into long, shop-lined Sharia al-Mu'izz li Din Allah, the main road of medieval Cairo, and after a few steps cross Cairo's busiest shopping street, the Muski. This morning the Muski is jammed, the street a jumble of shops and street vendors offering cheap plastic toys, polyester robes, tawdry underwear, rayon nighties, caftans in vile chemical colors, plastic pocketbooks, plastic shoes, plastic, plastic, plastic. A thousand cardboard belts marked "Levis." Pushcarts heaped with handkerchiefs, though Cairenes customarily blow their noses, uncovered, toward the street. Handcarts, motorcycles, trucks, and cars. Hordes of shapeless women in head scarves and shapeless gowns shuffling slowly, slowly, stopping obsessively at every shop, at every stall, to finger the finery.

> The balcony overlooked the ancient building housing a cistern downstairs and a school upstairs which was situated in the middle of Palace Walk, or Bayn-al-Qasrayn. Two roads met there: al-Nahhasin, or Coppersmiths Street, going south, and Palace Walk, which went north.

After crossing the Muski, we continue a hundred yards further along al-Mu'izz li Din Allah to a portion known as al-Nahhasin, Street of the Coppersmiths. Locals still call it by its old name—Bayn al-Qasrayn—"Between the Palaces" or "Palace Walk." Two palaces, long gone and forgotten, once stood here among the crammed shops exhibiting their profusion of antique copperware. It was *Palace Walk* that Mahfouz titled the first volume of the *Cairo Trilogy*, and it was here Ahmad Abd al-Jawad and his family, the trilogy's protagonists, lived out their lives and where Ahmad tended his store—"al-Nahhasin, which he had observed for roughly half a century from his shop."

———

> He did not return home until he had first visited Sugar Street and Palace of Desire Alley . . .

"Qasr el-Shouk, do you know it?"

"Qasr el-Shouk?"

"Palace of Desire—it's not far."

Moustafa's friend Gamal Abdel Hamid Ali is a tall, balding man with shaded glasses and a smart striped shirt. We stand outside a copper shop, and Gamal takes over as guide of my pilgrimage. About Qasr el-Shouk Moustafa was always vague, and the Palace of Desire eluded him.

Before Moustafa returns to look after his shop, we agree to meet at Fishawi's Coffee House in the afternoon, when he'll direct me to Sugar Street. Meanwhile, Gamal has drawn a map on an envelope and points the way to the Palace of Desire. His directions are anything but explicit, the map a bare sketch. I have a hunch Gamal has only a slim notion of the palace's whereabouts.

Down the Muizz toward the Bab al-Futuh and Bab al-Nasr are the Northern Gates of the old walled Fatimid city. The length of al-Mu'izz li Din Allah, from its Southern Gate of Bab Zuwella to Bab al-Futuh, is opulent with the splendid architecture of great merchants' hostels, Koranic schools or *madrassas,* mosques and mausoleums of the Fatimid and Mamluk periods from 907 to the beginning of the sixteenth century.

Just beyond the thirteenth-century Madrassa and Tomb of Sultan al-Salih Ayyub, a few steps from the old Slave Market, I turn into el-Kady, where horses and donkeys patiently graze from wagons loaded with emerald heaps of fresh parsley. From one trashy, potholed end of el-Kady to the other, scale shops line the street: produce scales, merchants' scales, scales for weighing gold, sacks of cement, slaughtered lambs, boxes of smoked fish, bales of cotton. They're stacked in pyramids along both sides of the road and down its center, hardly leaving room for the trash and mud and overflowing stream of foot traffic. I drift up the street with the crowds, then on through a tunnel hacked in a rubble wall. This is the Khan Gaffar, and on the far side, where it empties into the Atfet Ahmad Bucha Tahir, I find a newsstand. I show the vendor the map on which Gamal had thoughtfully written my destination in Arabic script. The man's English, however, is flawless: "Ah, Qasr el-Shouk, the Palace of Desire, no problem, just to next corner, turn right."

This is the heart of al-Gamaliya, the neighborhood where Mahfouz was born and raised. The street is crowded with orange sellers, their produce heaped in pyramids on ramshackle pushcarts. At the first corner, above a shop selling charcoal by the basketful, letters are scrawled across a stained wall: "Qasr el-Shook," the *u* suddenly metamorphosed to an *o.* After a few steps the street divides, each fork bearing a new name.

Somewhere in these narrow, dirty alleyways lived Yasin, Ahmad Abd al-Jawad's profligate son, though in which house on which street is impossible to tell. Down the Darb el Tablawy an arrow points to the "Palis al Musafirnana—1771–1788." Kids trail along shouting, "Hello! Hello!" A flock of goats browses outside a ravishing pink house with a forest-green door. One wall, more finished than the others, leads into an arched entry, where I meet a studious young man in mustache and glasses, his blue cardigan incongruously emblazoned with an Alpine skier.

"The Palace of Desire?"

"You have found it—the *Musafir Khanah* is the Palace of Desire."

Mahmoud Bedeir, born in the Palace of Desire, has spent his life here. While his wife, in pink satin robe and head scarf, plays with their infant son in the entrance, Mahmoud's two-year-old daughter, Aisha, tags along as he shows me through the palace—originally a merchant's palace, one of the first in Cairo in the ornate Turkish style. Here the wealthy trader Mahmud Muharram, who built the palace between 1779 and 1788, entertained colleagues who came from Persia, India, East Africa, and Indonesia. When Muharram died of sunstroke en route from the Hajj in 1794, the royal family took over the palace. Later it became a lodging house for state guests, but as Islamic Cairo grew poorer and the neighborhood slipped into decay, the Palace of Desire was nearly abandoned.

Mahmoud Bedeir works for the Ministry of Antiquities and assists in the palace's restoration. Piles of timber and cement litter the courtyard, and scaffolding conceals one wall. Mahmoud leads me through the chambers of the lower floor, the Winter and Summer houses, vast rooms rich with inlaid marble, fountains, and raised stages for musicians and dancers. The library is paneled in exotic woods, and the dining room glows with the fervent blues and greens of Iznik tile. Upstairs are the women's quarters, a domed bathing complex with colored skylights and lavish rooms sprawling beneath coffered ceilings of gilded wood. The spaces are vast and empty. As Mahmoud and I stand in the dim silence of the *qa'ah*, the great room of the harem, we seem to be waiting for something, a voice perhaps, a gesture from the past. Suddenly little Aisha dances toward us through the dust.

"Come downstairs," Mahmoud says. "We'll drink coffee." Still, neither of us moves, and as the child glides away, we stop by the tall bay windows latticed by *mashrabiyyah*, the elaborately carved wooden screens that sequester the harem from the world, gazing down onto the ragged palms in the courtyard below.

———

. . this small café, like a corridor with tables lining the two
sides . . .

Moustafa joins me at a little tin-topped table at Fishawi's on a passageway off the Midan al-Husayn. We order coffees and a *sheesha,* an Egyptian water pipe, for Moustafa. Fishawi's is open day and night, its resinous, tobacco-stained walls and gilt-framed mirrors giving some idea of its vintage; little has changed since it opened two centuries ago. Until the attempt on his life incapacitated him, Naguib Mahfouz often stopped in for coffee.

At a nearby table a young couple nuzzles in an ardent tête-à-tête. She's in wraps and head scarf; he's smart in a crisp shirt, slacks, and sunglasses. Their romance is very intense, very Egyptian—they can't take their eyes off each other as they pass the ivory mouthpiece of a *sheesha* back and forth between them. Meanwhile, a tortoiseshell cat, walking among the tables, jumps to a vacant chair and places his paws neatly on the lovers' tabletop to lap from their water glasses. With eyes only for each other, they're oblivious to their feline guest.

Among the men smoking and chatting, a handsome older woman in voluminous black shares a table with a buxom young woman in dark skirt and polka-dot blouse, a garish ceramic flower clipping her inky hair. Bursts of laughter and energetic arm-waving punctuate their talk. Only a few years ago you never saw Egyptian women enjoying themselves in public, but today it's common.

A mute salesman, wandering among the crowded tables, offers elegant leather wallets, using improvised sign language to make his pitch. Then a man selling sunglasses, a boy hawking packets of Kleenex. A murmur of Koranic recitation, peaceful and mesmerizing, croons over hidden loudspeakers. El Fishawi, "like a corridor with tables lining the two sides," is a passage for people crossing from Midan al-Husayn into the Khan al-Khalili—men in pajamas and *galabiehs*, nightshirts and caftans, secretive women in veils, bearing headloads.

————

> When his deliberate pace finally brought him to the mosque
> of al-Husayn, he removed his shoes and entered, reciting the
> opening prayer of the Qur'an.

From Fishawi's, Moustafa and I walk through a vaulted passage dense with the meaty aromas of kabob stalls and into the Square of al-Husayn. Built in 1873, the neo-Gothic Mosque of al-Husayn houses the head of Sayyidna al-Husayn, martyred grandson of the prophet Mohammed. A holy shrine and place of pilgrimage to both Sunni and Shia Muslims, al-Husayn is Egypt's most important mosque and the spiritual focus of Naguib Mahfouz' patriarchal shopkeeper, Ahmad Abd al-Jawad.

Although a strict father and stern husband, Ahmad Abd al-Jawad is a libertine who spends his nights carousing with friends and enjoying his mistresses. Noon each Friday, however, he is a devout patriarch, praying at the Mosque of al-Husayn, usually with his sons in tow. And it is to al-Husayn, when at last in middle age she is free to leave the house in Palace Walk, that his wife Amina goes each day to pray for her husband and children. The old woman's last words, spoken moments before the stroke that kills her, are of the mosque: "When I finish my visit to al-Husayn, I'll call on Khadija [at Sugar Street]."

Moustafa leads me from the mosque and across the square, then through a pedestrian underpass beneath the Sharia al-Azhar. We emerge outside the walls of the great mosque-university of al-Azhar. Founded in 970, the intellectual center of Muslim culture, it's reputedly the world's oldest university. Altered and added to over the centuries, this vast complex, like much of the city, was severely damaged by a devastating earthquake that shook Cairo in October 1992. Today reconstruction continues.

Moustafa and I stop outside al-Azhar's Bab al-Shurbah, the Soup Gate, and Moustafa points into the distance. "A hundred yards further," he says, "you'll see two mosques. Pass between them and walk toward the two towers in the distance. Sugar Street is there. Ask as you go—al-Sukkariyya. Everyone knows."

————

> "The old days!" he mused. "The days of power and strength,
> of laughter that shook the walls, of convivial evenings spent

in al-Ghuriya . . . and of people of whom nothing is left but their names . . ."

Moustafa's two mosques, acknowledged vaguely with a sweep of his hand, are part of the Ghuriya—a magnificent complex comprising a merchant's hostel, mosque-madrassa, and mausoleum built in 1505 by Sultan Qansuh al-Ghuri—the last great architectural work of the Mamluks before the Ottoman conquest. Sharia al-Mu'izz li Din Allah cuts through this complex, though here Cairenes call the street al-Ghuriya, like the district through which it passes.

This morning a construction project is under way, and al-Ghuriya is blocked by a great iron fence. Badly shaken by the earthquake, the complex of Sultan Qansuh al-Ghuri is shored and propped from every direction, and piles of sand and gravel rise like fortifications. Moustafa didn't prepare me for this. A construction foreman appears as I regard the devastation. I ask for Sugar Street.

"You must go around—another block, then turn left. Ask anyone."

His assistant guides me around the wreckage and into a dim lane no wider than a prayer carpet. From end to end it's lined with fabric shops, bolts of cotton and colorful heaps of linen stacked so deep along the street and in cramped doorways that it's nearly impossible to pass. I ask a likely shopkeeper about Sugar Street. Pointing farther along, he suggests a right turn at the next corner, where several men sip tea and gossip in front of their shops. Sugar Street? Al-Sukkariyya? Nothing but blank stares. A tea-seller passes, and someone asks him. Another blank. In turn, he asks someone else. No, no one has ever heard of Sugar Street.

After backtracking to the corner, I follow the left-hand fork where construction encompasses yet another mosque. As I pause under an awning to consult my more-than-useless map, a dark, shabby man in ragged work clothes approaches and hands me a glass of hot, sweet tea. He lounges nearby, watching as I squint over the map. When I've drunk the tea and still have no idea where to find Sugar Street, I offer the man a few coins. He looks stricken, shaking his head vehemently: "No, please, no money, you are my guest."

At last I find myself on Sharia al-Muizz il-Din Allah, al-Ghuriya, a broad street of shops overhung with grand embroidered panels in red, black, and white. Here the streets are crowded with laden donkeys and horse-drawn wagons, the last automobiles left behind. Men lounge in shopfronts, while women in caftans and head scarves go about their shopping. Fabrics and gold jewelry. Water and soda sellers. Spices in burlap bags—bay leaves from Madagascar, ginger and cardamom, cinnamon, chilies, cloves, pepper from Zanzibar and Sumatra. At the front of a dim shed a dozen women pick stones from baskets of pink and magenta lentils. A fez maker, using a huge copper contraption, presses circles of crimson felt into perfect fezes, or *tarbooshes* as the English colonials called them.

> When he drew near the store, his eyes glanced toward it involuntarily. . . . It had become a fez shop, where new ones were sold and old ones blocked. The copper forms and the heating apparatus were up in front.

———

As I leave the fez maker's shop, Rabia Mohammed Ahmed suddenly enters my life: "Can I help you find something?" He's a soldier on leave, he says. Young, handsome, full of himself, he recently completed law school. When he finishes his military service, he'll apprentice for two years with a law firm, then set up as a lawyer. He's loquacious, his English, Italian, and French fluent. His military and law stories are possibly true. More likely he's a street hustler, a freelance guide, though he insists he has no factory or shop and nothing to sell. At any rate he knows Sugar Street, and we start through the streets and alleyways of Ghuriya, where Rabia was born.

He leads me along al-Ghuriya toward the minarets of the Mosque of al-Muayyad, the twin towers that Moustafa said were to be my guides. Built atop the only surviving southern gate to the city, the massive Bab Zwayla, they rise high against the skyline. During Mamluk and Ottoman times the Bab Zwayla was a place of public executions, the heads of criminals exposed on spikes above the gate. The gate is known to locals as Bab al-Mutawalli, named for Qutb al-Mutawalli, a neighborhood saint who manifests himself to the faithful as a beam of light showing within the gatehouse.

> When the man's only response was laughter, she added, "As for the other girl, I'm imploring God's assistance with her by way of the saint at Bab al-Mutawalli."

44

Adjoining the gate is the Mosque of Sultan Mu'ayyad Shaykh, the "Red Mosque." It is built on the site of a prison where Mu'ayyad Shaykh, a freed Circassian slave, was once incarcerated. He vowed to build a magnificent mosque if he ever escaped. He became Sultan of Egypt in 1412 and completed the mosque in 1420.

Across al-Ghuriya from the mosque stands a huge old harem house, abandoned, Rabia says, since the earthquake. A crowd gathers on the corner around a sandwich stand. Nearby, in a wall of the Bab Mutawalli itself, a low arch leads east into a dim lane.

"Come," Rabia says. "We are here."

Al-Sukkariyya—Sugar Street.

———

> Was she not his girl? Of course she was. The alcoves of the
> courtyard, the stairwell, and the corner of the roof over-
> looking Sugar Street could all testify to this.

I follow Rabia into a passage so narrow that by stretching my arms I can touch both walls. Shops line the way, but most are closed, brass padlocks big as soup plates securing pulled-down shutters. The place is nearly deserted, houses empty. But at the top of a staircase two women and several children watch as we pass. Rabia calls to them, asking if we might come up. They smile in welcome, and we climb a steep stairway to join them. Pots and pans, a few makeshift toys litter the open door of a low shed. A dozen children gather, gazing up at us. The women cover their faces, giggling shyly. Rabia points out nearby rooftops where shacks and lean-tos have been built from wood, cardboard, tin. "This is where people live since the earthquake. Nothing below is safe." A few new apartment blocks are visible, rising among the dust and rubble of the medieval city. Below, Sugar Street branches into a warren of lanes edged with houses, workshops, mosques.

We wander these side streets and passageways. In dim rooms we find craftsmen manufacturing little mother-of-pearl boxes and animals carved from buffalo horn. In a courtyard, skilled young tailors embroider indigo banners with thick Koranic script in gold thread. When finished, these banners will be displayed in places of honor in the world's great mosques.

At last we're back in the deep evening shadows of the Bab Mutawalli. Here, late on a winter's afternoon in the 1930s, Ahmad Abd al-Jawad's daughter Khadija, wrapped and veiled, encountered her womanizing, wayward brother, Yasin: "I was returning to Sugar Street from al-Darb al-Ahmar when I sensed that a man was following me. Then under the vault of the old city gate he passed me and asked, 'Where are you going, beautiful?' I turned and replied, 'I'm on my way home, Mr. Yasin.'"

To the south, across the crowded road, lights are coming on in the Qasaba, the last of Cairo's spacious covered markets. Built in 1650 by Ridwan Bey, it's known to locals as Khiyamiyya, Street of the Tentmakers. Dozens of stalls display the appliquéd fabrics of reds, blacks, and whites used to make great public tents for festivals, funerals, and weddings.

"You must make your choice." Rabia points across to the Qasaba, then east down a thoroughfare packed with shoppers. "Is it to be the Street of the Tentmakers or Sharia Darb al-Ahmar?"

"It's late, Rabia—must it be either?"

"You don't wish to go on?"

"I came looking for Sugar Street."

"And thanks to me, you found it."

A woman passes, tall, sloe-eyed, statuesque, wrapped from head to foot in dark cloth. Can it be Zanuba or her daughter Karima, Ahmad Abd al-Jawad's grandchild? And the boy opposite, handsome, blue-eyed, a little dissolute, is he possibly Yasin's son Ridwan or one of his cousins, Ahmad or Abd al-Muni'm? Wherever I turn, the characters of *The Cairo Trilogy* step from doorways, cross my path, pass me in the teeming streets. "Husanayn the barber, Darwish the bean seller, al-Fuli the milkman, and Abu Sarr' who grilled snacks."

Rabia takes my arm, leads me into the crush. "Come, we will see the Sharia Darb al-Ahmar. The Street of the Tentmakers can wait—until tomorrow perhaps."

Whatever you say, Rabia. Whatever you say. It hardly matters. Wherever we go in this vast city, Naguib Mahfouz is with us. Despite his age and infirmities, he's stepping right along.

46

4

A Dangerous Man
T. E. Lawrence in the Middle East

> The dreamers of the day are dangerous men,
> for they may act out their dreams with open
> eyes, to make it possible. This I did.
>
> T. E. Lawrence, *Seven Pillars of Wisdom*

Akaba

TALAL'S FATHER HAS a prophet's face, passionate and still, that draws
to a point in a clipped silver beard. "I have land in the desert, just there,"
he says, sweeping a hand toward the east in the ambiguous way of Arabs
offering directions. "Each year the family goes there for a month, to live
as we once did in Palestine. Last year, on our way, we stopped at a black
tent to ask for water." The old man pauses to gaze out at the busy street.
It's dusk, the spice merchants doing a steady trade. "Three Toyota pickups were parked outside. Inside, the Bedu were watching CNN—the television was wired to a car battery; there was a portable satellite dish out
back."

Talal Ahmed Abdullkadir is shy, soft-spoken, middle-aged. "They
tear down Akaba every ten years," he says, taking up his father's theme.
"Then they rebuild it—everything must be *modern*. If the town changes,
the countryside changes even more. It's government policy to settle the
nomads—the Bedu, the black-tent people. From them I get my stock."
Talal indicates the merchandise amassed in his small shop: antique jewelry, exquisitely embroidered Palestinian dresses threadbare with age, tas-
seled camel packs, shelves of silver coffee pots. "It's their heritage they're

selling, their Bedouin culture. With the money, they buy their pickups and TVs."

Settling behind a massive desk, Talal takes a copy of today's *Jordan Times* from a deep drawer. The front page photo is of a small, intense man in a snowy Arabian getup, a hand gripping the hilt of a flamboyant dagger. Nearly eighty years after his triumphant entry into Akaba, and sixty-one since his death in a motorcycle accident on an English country road, here, in the morning paper, is the enigmatic and controversial T. E. Lawrence, "Lawrence of Arabia," desert fighter and author of the *Seven Pillars of Wisdom*.

I arrive in the Middle East with a copy of Lawrence's epic and a curious desire to discover its author in the landscapes he described. Saudi Arabia, where I hoped to begin, is closed to travelers. Even Lawrence was restricted to the Hejaz, the mountainous region on the Red Sea coast, and found it necessary to confer with the sherif of Mecca by telephone from the port of Jidda.*

With Arabia out, traveling in Lawrence's camel tracks means starting at Akaba, in the Hashimite Kingdom of Jordan. The capture of this key port was an early and significant victory in what became known as the Arab Revolt.

———

Thomas Edward Lawrence, born in Tremadoc, Wales, in 1888, was raised in Oxford, England, where he developed an early interest in antiquities, especially military architecture. While a student in Oxford, he bicycled through France, studying its castles and fortifications. He attended Oxford University's Jesus College and Magdalen College, and his thesis, which won first class honors in history, was published posthumously as *Crusader Castles*. Between 1910 and 1914 he was an assistant on the British Museum's archaeological digs at Carchemish, on the Euphrates River. He learned Arabic and traveled the Middle East: "I had been many years going up and down the semitic East . . . learning the manners of the villagers and tribesmen and citizens of Syria and Mesopotamia."

By 1516, Ottoman expansion made the Turks occupiers of much of the Arab world. For nearly four centuries the Arabs prospered and were

---

* Because there is no satisfactory system of transliterating Arabic into English, I have chosen to use Lawrence's sometimes eccentric, often inconsistent, spelling.

generally content, seeing in the Ottoman Empire the political embodiment of Islam. But in 1908, when the Young Turks, disgruntled army officers, took power in Constantinople, the Arabs found themselves administered by a ruthless, oppressive, and corrupt regime. In the eyes of Hussein ibn Ali, the sherif of Mecca, the Young Turks "were so many godless transgressors of their creed and their human duty—traitors of the spirit of the time, and to the highest interests of Islam." Inevitably, the cause of Arab nationalism flourished.

When Ottoman Turkey aligned itself with Germany in the First World War, "some Englishmen, of whom Kitchener was chief, believed that a rebellion of Arabs against Turks would enable England, while fighting Germany, simultaneously to defeat her ally Turkey."

Commissioned at the outbreak of the war, Lawrence was attached to the Hejaz Expeditionary Force under the command of General Sir Reginald Wingate and in 1918 transferred to the staff of the resourceful and charismatic General Sir Edmund Allenby: "What an idol the man was to us, prismatic with the . . . quality of greatness." It was Lawrence's responsibility to marshal Arab forces and channel their rebellion into effective action.

———

"This story about Lawrence," Talal explains, switching on an antique copper lamp, "also concerns Auda abu Tayi. Anthony Quinn, the American actor, is in Amman, visiting Auda and his family. He says he'll study Auda for a role in a new film."

"A *new* film?"

In David Lean's 1962 Oscar-winning *Lawrence of Arabia,* Peter O'Toole played Lawrence, with Quinn as Lawrence's ally, the old warrior-raider Auda abu Tayi. I slip a copy of *Seven Pillars of Wisdom* from my pocket and read aloud Lawrence's description of Auda: "Very simply dressed, northern fashion, in white cotton with a red Mosul head-cloth. He might be over fifty, and his black hair was streaked with white." That was in 1917, Talal. If Auda was fifty then, today he would be over 130."

"It must be so. Anthony Quinn is in Amman."

"You're sure?"

"I know it—it says so in the newspaper. When you reach Amman, you will visit Auda abu Tayi yourself. Ask any policeman—he will show you the way."

———

> We wandered into the shadowed grove of palms, at the very
> break of the splashing waves. . . . For months Akaba had been
> the horizon of our minds.

My room at the Petra Hotel overlooks the shops of the spice merchants, the produce market, the Mosque of Sharif Hussein Ben Ali. A
half dozen tramp freighters swing at anchor in the Gulf of Akaba, the
silvery finger of the Red Sea dividing Sinai from Arabia. On the opposite shore, so immaculate it appears to have been built overnight, rises the
Israeli city of Elat. To its south, beneath barren, dragon-backed mountains, is the little Egyptian port of Taba. The Saudi border lies a dozen
miles down the Hejaz coast.

In the company of an army of Arab irregulars led by Auda abu Tayi,
chief of the Eastern Howeitat, Lawrence entered Akaba on July 6, 1917:
"Our capture of Akaba closed the Hejaz war, and gave us the task of
helping the British invade Syria."

Lawrence was two months coming from Wejh in Arabia, passing
along the Nefudh's northern fringe, up Wadi Sirhan along what is now
Jordan's border with Saudi Arabia, then circling south over the Maan
plateau to enter Akaba from the mountains. The Arabs fought a bloody
battle at Aba el Lissan above the four-thousand-foot "zigzag pass of
Shtar," crossed "the green and gold Guweira plain," then descended Wadi
Itm toward the sea. Here they found the Turkish positions abandoned.
Never imagining an attack from the interior, the Turks had fixed their
batteries to repel a landing from the gulf: "Not one trench or post faced
inland . . . Through the whirling dust we perceived that Akaba was all a
ruin. Repeated bombardments by French and English warships had
degraded the place to its original rubble."

Today this modern port is prosperous and clean, with swept sidewalks and tree-lined streets. At a café on a pale curl of beach, Talal and I
sip tea and watch the morning sun warm the ridges above Wadi Itm.
Later we stroll the Corniche, where palms grow to the water's edge and
in their shade flourish gardens deep in parsley and mint. A short walk
brings us to Akaba Fort, built by the Mamluks in 1510 and restored by
the Ottoman Sultan ibn Selim Khan in 1587. After the Allied victory in

World War I, the Hashimite coat of arms went up over the fortified gate. A plaque tells us that Prince Feisal ibn al-Hussein led the Arabs. Lawrence had chosen Feisal, son of the sherif of Mecca, to lead the rebellion: "This was the man I had come to Arabia to seek—the man who would lead the Arab Revolt to full glory."

A eucalyptus tree spreads over the courtyard of the little Beau Geste fort. We sit in its shade, watching a tortoiseshell cat stalk plump pigeons before curling up on a sunny wall. An English couple prowls the fort's interior—prison cells and impressive rooms with shooting windows and tall vaulted ceilings, and a tunnel that once gave access to the sea.

Walking back, Talal points toward the Gulf and the pristine buildings clustered on its opposite shore. "I am Bedu from Palestine," he says quietly. "Someday I would like to go back. At least on a one-day visa to visit Elat. My father says even that is too dangerous. You see, my grandfather taught Palestinians to use weapons—handguns and grenades. In 1948—the year after I was born—my family fled Palestine and came here. In Israel, our family name is in the 'book.' My father says I mustn't go. I'll be arrested. There are two thousand members of our family—our clan. I tell him, 'How would they know if one of us came back?'"

Under the Sykes-Picot agreement of 1916, kept confidential until war's end, Syria and Lebanon were put under French mandate. Jordan and Palestine went to the British. The Balfour Declaration of 1917 pledged Britain's support for "a national home for the Jewish people." Though unaware of these secret documents, Lawrence was, nonetheless, skeptical of the intentions of his countrymen: "Not being a perfect fool, I could see that if we won the war the promises to the Arabs were dead paper. Had I been an honourable adviser I would have sent my men home, and not let them risk their lives for such stuff." At the 1919 Paris Peace Conference, Lawrence, the only member of the British delegation in Arab garb, swam against the colonial tide and argued for Arab independence. "I meant to make a new nation, to restore lost influence, to give twenty millions of Semites the foundations on which to build an inspired dream-palace . . . but when we won, it was charged against me that the British petrol royalties in Mesopotamia were become dubious, and French Colonial policy ruined in the Levant . . . [W]hen we achieved and the new world dawned, the old men came out again and took our victory to re-make in the likeness of the former world they knew."

Wadi Itm

After . . . came the ride up the oppressive gorge of Itm,
under the red cliffs of Nejed . . . that slow preparation for
Rumm's greatness . . .

"This car, Yusef . . . ?"

"Comes from Arabia!" Yusef shouts over the motor's roar. He's at
the wheel of his seventies-vintage Plymouth Magnum, gunning up the
gorge of Wadi Itm. A big man with a sweeping mustache and gray *gala-bieh*, Yusef has a voice thick and agreeable as Bedouin coffee. "In sixties
and seventies Saudi oil sheiks like too much big American cars. Every
year buy new ones, sell us old ones—Jordan taxi drivers."

"How do you like it?"

"Like? American car is best in world!"

The Desert Highway climbs steeply between sheer buttes flushed
pink in the morning light. Between July 1917 and August 1918,
Lawrence negotiated the gorge a score of times, often camping in steep
ravines as he rode camelback between the coast and interior. Even under
ideal conditions, it took hours to navigate Wadi Itm's "intricate rugged-
ness."

Riding in Yusef's overpowered Plymouth, we reach the top in thirty
minutes and find ourselves on a great sweep of upland desert scattered
with thorn trees and pale splashes of brush. Mountains tilt west and,
twenty miles over the Guweira plain, lift the heights of Nagb el Shtar.
"Guweira was a map of pink sand, brushed over with streaks of water-
courses, in a mantle of scrub: and out of this . . . towered islands and cliffs
of glowing sandstone."

Halfway across, at a melancholy cluster of cinder-block dwellings
and junked cars, we turn off the Desert Highway and swing east along a
narrow track toward Tuwasek and Wadi Rumm. Outfitted in dashing
khaki *galabiehs*, silver daggers, and scarlet bandoliers, a trio of Desert
Patrolmen flags us down to scrutinize my passport and Yusef's identity
card. Satisfied we aren't gun-runners or Bedouin camel thieves, they
salute crisply and wave us on toward Rumm.

Wadi Rumm

> Day was still young as we rode between two great pikes of
> sandstone to the foot of a long, soft-slope poured down
> from the doomed hills . . . the beginning of Wadi Rumm,
> they said . . .

Madela may be thirty, though he looks no older than an adolescent.
Even his sparse mustache doesn't age him. "My grandfather," he says, zip-
ping a black leather jacket over an astonishingly white *galabieh,* "my
grandfather knew Lawrence."

Is this possible? Was Madela's grandfather part of the Arab Revolt?
And "Urens"—as the Arabs pronounced Lawrence—did he know the
famous Urens? Quickly, I count the years to 1918. It's plausible.

"What did your grandfather think of Lawrence?"

Madela shades his eyes and gazes at distant Jebel Nassraniyyah rising
across the sun-washed wadi like the rusty hull of a forsaken steamer. "He
was very good for Wadi Rumm," he says. "He wrote truly about it."

At our backs Jebel Rumm rises six thousand feet, a sheer, flame-red
wall. On its lower slope, among tumbled boulders, tangled scrub marks
Lawrence's Well. "From between these trees, in hidden crannies of the
rock, issued strange cries; the echoes, turned into music, of the voices of
the Arabs watering camels at the springs."

"You've read Lawrence's book, Madela? His description of Wadi
Rumm is very beautiful."

We cross a patch of scrub to Madela's pickup. He slips behind the
wheel and starts the motor. I slide in beside him. "I have seen it," he says
shyly, putting the Toyota into gear. It suddenly dawns that Madela can
neither read nor write. "I have seen Urens' book."

We cross the valley floor among uptilts of rock like savage tents
streaming banners of crimson and scarlet, rust, copper and rose. Sage
blossoms in shallow swales of delicate pink sand. Yellow broom. A
tamarisk tree. Silence. Wind. The desert sweeps down sandy boulevards
flanked by the staggering architecture of sandstone cliffs and fallen boulders. "The Arab armies would have been lost in the length and breadth
of it, and within the walls a squadron of planes could have wheeled in
formation. Our little caravan grew self-conscious, and fell dead quiet,

ashamed and afraid to flaunt its smallness in the presence of the stupendous hills."

From Jebel Barrakh and Wadi um Ishrin, we turn west, then south toward Khazail. I'm lost. Madela expects it. A native of Rumm and an employee of the Ministry of Tourism, he knows every wadi and *jebel* in this strange and awesome terrain. "Landscapes, in childhood's dream, were so vast and silent."

At Khazail we park among dunes, then traverse a sandy slope to tamarisks growing in violet shadow. Cliffs rise thousands of feet in sheer layers of rose-colored stone. In deep shades of scarlet, umber, mahogany, rock has gushed and hardened between the layers, the way wax might, or icing between the layers of an immense cake.

At the cliff's base, where cutthroat finches breeze in and out of the trees, a chink appears in the stone. Madela leads the way up a path into a tight canyon deep in cool gloom. From somewhere in its depths a spring seeps and puddles underfoot. The walls narrow, and, brushing against the clammy stone, we slip through sideways. High above gleams a thin crack of light where the canyon's rims nearly touch. We keep on, a hundred yards, two hundred, a quarter mile, wading shallow pools, scrambling into Khazail's heart.

Back under the tamarisks, I ask Madela how far we might have gone.
"Far."

"To the other side?"

Before he can answer, the stillness is shattered by an eagle's scream, shrill and ghostly, echoing deep in the canyon from where we've come.

"No," Madela whispers, "not so far as that."

———

Late in the afternoon, we start back to the Government Rest House, where Yusef and his Plymouth wait to deliver me to Akaba. Rounding the rusty prow of Jebel Nassraniyyah, Madela wheels under a rock shelf and kills the motor. The sun edges over the dome of Jebel Rumm and we step from the pickup into a sudden chill. Silence falls in waves we can almost touch.

On the cliff's face, a few feet above our heads, someone has hewn a camel in the rock—a bas-relief a foot in height. We discover writing in strange alphabets, more camels, men herding them, and warriors wielding swords.

"How old are these carvings, Madela?"

"Eight hundred years . . . maybe more."

Lawrence surveyed the petroglyphs of Rumm: "On the rock-bulge above were clear-cut Nabathaean inscriptions. . . . Around and about were Arab scratches, including tribe-marks, some of which were witness to forgotten migrations."

The tribal markings are Thamudic, made by camel drivers from Arabia. As for the Nabathaeans, who left behind these engravings and the great carved city of "rose hued" Petra, they were nomadic Arabs who settled in the region in the sixth century B.C.E and founded a sophisticated empire that challenged invading Rome.

We prowl the cliff's face until it's too dark to see, then drive back along the margins of Nassraniyyah and across the wadi toward Jebel Rumm and the flickering lights of Madela's village.

> "Shall I ride on this time, beyond the Khazail, and know it all?" But in truth I liked Rumm too much.

Aba el Lissan, Maan, Wadi Musa, Petra

Al-Hamayma: a drab cinder-block village on the northern limits of the Guweira Plain. The minibus brakes, and a pair of soldiers in dusty fatigues swing aboard. In the grit and bush-scrabble outskirts of the village, adolescent girls, inky hair streaming against florid dresses, herd flocks of sheep and shaggy goats. Tethered among the shanties and the Toyotas, contemplative camels mouth their cuds.

From Al-Hamayma the bus growls up the sandstone heights of Nagb el Shtar, where confections of rock open to reveal Guweira fading below, miles of sun-washed desert sweeping to the fiery brink of Itm. Toward the top, where bare stone gives way to outcroppings of pine and cedar, is Ras al Yegud and, a mile beyond, in a bowl of barren hills, Aba el Lissan.

Here, on July 2, 1917, in a battle that lasted through the cruelly hot day, Lawrence and the Arabs decimated a Turkish battalion: "Our rifles grew so hot with sun and shooting that they seared our hands." With the last Turk either dead or in panicked flight, "Auda came swinging up on foot, his eyes glazed over with the rapture of battle . . . and he held up his shattered field-glasses, his pierced pistol-holder, and his leather sword-scabbard cut to ribbons. He had been the target of a volley which had killed his mare under him, but the six bullets through his clothes had left him scatheless."

When it was no longer important, the Turks retook Aba el Lissan. Then, after a winter of sporadic fighting under the command of Maulud el Mukhlus, "the Arab zealot," the Arabs regained the village, and it served as Emir Feisal's headquarters. Today, a few old men, badly in need of shaves, gaze from under checkered headcloths as our bus plows into view. On the hillside above, where Lawrence and his men "kicked our camels furiously to the edge, to see our fifty horsemen coming down the last slope," there's a sad tangle of TV antennas, mud-brick houses and dusty pickups—melancholy byproducts of settling the Bedu.

It grows cold north of Aba el Lissan, along the line of the Turkish retreat, as we cross a high, stormy plateau under slashing rain. "This plateau about Maan lay between three and five thousand feet . . . open to all winds from . . . Central Asia, or from [the] Caucasus." After rattling over the railroad crossing at Mreigha, we pick up a new highway cutting through Uheida to Maan.

> Maan was impregnable for us, so we concentrated on cutting
> its northern railway and diverting the Turkish effort to
> relieve its garrison.

A sprawling provincial market town and rail center of fifteen thousand, Maan's built of stone, cinder block, and mud. Along narrow streets, doorways open into shady courtyards. It's a busy, energetic place with crowded streetside markets overflowing with fruit and vegetables.

Though the Arabs controlled the territory around Maan, the heavily garrisoned town held out against them. Bombing in August 1917 failed to dislodge the enemy: "Two bombs into the barracks killed thirty-five . . . a bomb in the General's kitchen finished his cook and his breakfast." Maulud and Auda led a frontal attack in April of 1919, but days of fighting left Maan invincible.

Lawrence knew the capture of Maan was insignificant. A genius at hit-and-run guerilla warfare—the only fighting in which the Bedouin, practiced camel raiders, had a chance—he understood it best not to attack, but to keep Turkish troops bottled in garrisons such as Maan by harassing their only line of communication, the Hejaz Railway. For two years, using "guncotton," gelatinite, and the mobility provided by camels, he did this up and down Jordan and Syria: "Hurriedly we piled guncotton against the piers, which were about five feet thick and twenty-five feet high; a good bridge, my seventy-ninth, and strategically most critical. . . . So I determined to leave not a stone of it in place. . . . Half a minute later (my preference for six-inch fuses) just as I tumbled into the Turkish redoubt, the eight hundred pounds of stuff exploded in one burst."

I change buses in a muddy field in central Maan and set off for Wadi Musa, an hour's journey over stony, undulant desert. It's hard to imagine Lawrence traveling this harsh terrain, covering such great distances so quickly: "In the last four weeks I had ridden fourteen hundred miles by camel." The rain lets up, but clouds blacken the horizon. There are few people, almost no traffic. Sparse grazing supports a scattering of goats, the odd camel, an occasional donkey.

Then, like an artillery burst, a solitary cherry tree in full pink bloom, an olive grove, a scruffy village—Odroh. "We reached the desolate ruins of Odroh in a midday like twilight: a wind was blowing . . . and slow-moving banks of cloud and drizzle closed us about." The desert sweeps in, and the village vanishes as abruptly as it appeared. Then we're climbing through icy fog—up and over a ridge, a spiraling, perilous descent into Wadi Musa.

> We would play with them [the Turks] and provoke them to
> go for us in Wadi Musa, where the natural obstacles were so
> tremendous . . .

Wadi Musa is a shabby little town at the bottom of what might be an open-pit mine. Is this the gateway to "brilliant Petra"? After taking a frigid room at the Peace Way Hotel, I wander steep, chill streets. A few dilatory shops, a handful of cheap hotels, a warm, life-saving café where cheerful waiters dish up kebabs and mugs of sweet, scalding tea.

Next morning I discover Wadi Musa is but an interlude on the rugged gradient of Wadi Araba, a slash of the Great Rift Valley cutting south from the Dead Sea to the Gulf of Akaba. Petra, the ancient Nabathaean capital, is an hour's walk down another precipitous pitch, then on through the Siq, a mile-long canyon whose sandstone walls soar overhead. At its southern end lies rose-hued Petra, a glorious and unassailable hideaway whose temples and tombs are carved from living rock.

Too remote from their Turkish quarry, Petra was little used by the

Arabs, though in August 1917 "Maulud, the old war-horse, went up with his mule mounted regiment, and quartered himself among the famous ruins of Petra." Here he made "forays across the plateau, and to snap up by twos and threes Turkish riding or transport animals."

Shobek, Tafileh, Jurf ad Darawish

After two days tramping Petra's chasms and rock-cut palaces, I board a dawn minibus groaning out of Wadi Musa, ascending five-thousand-foot Jebel al Madhbahand, swinging north toward Shobek. A frosty wind cuts over plowed fields and clatters through olive groves at the fringes of villages. Cedars and pines line the road, and crested francolins dash across our path. The sun angles through a high, wide sky. Almonds flower. A man on a donkey. Broad fields. Junipers.

It grows hillier; spring grass carpets village orchards. At last we reach Shobek, a farm town in a steep valley—a single street, a few shops, a hundred houses scattered up a rocky hillside. On a hilltop to the north stands Monreale, a crusader fortress built in 1115 by Baldwin I. Here, in January 1918, the Arabs moved against the Turks: "Our plan . . . was to send the Arabs of Petra, under Sherif Abd el Mayin, at once up their hills into the forest towards Shobek." The Arabs took the fortress on the sixteenth and Lawrence, traveling alone aboard his fast Wodheiha camel, arrived on the snowy night of February 2: "We went over the ridge and down to the base of the shapely cone, whose mural crown was the ring-wall of the old castle of Monreale, very noble against the night sky."

The King's Highway skirts west of Monreale, then north along a rocky valley between low hills. Cairns of bleached stones rise in unkempt fields. Goats munch mouthfuls of gray, spiny scrub.

Tafileh lies deep in a steep valley. Reaching the outskirts, the bus turns west toward the center, bumping along the base of a high ridge. On the sixteenth of January 1918, Sharif Nasir "appeared at dawn on the rocky brink of the ravine in which Tafileh hid, and summoned it to surrender." The Turks, supported by the Muhaisin, a peasant clan, opened fire. "Auda, the old lion . . . raged that a mercenary village folk should dare to resist their secular masters, the Aub Tayi. So he . . . rode out plain to view . . . and shook a hand at them, booming in his wonderful voice: 'Dogs, do you not know Auda?'"

This morning Tafileh drowses in sunlight as a few peaceful locals go about their dilatory business. A scattering of trees crests the ridge—nothing more. On the twenty-fifth, Hamid Fakhri Pasha, commanding the Turkish 48th Division, brought up a thousand troops from Maan to surprise Lawrence and his Arabs. Lawrence was outraged. Allenby had just taken Jerusalem. Now it was in the Turkish interest to hold the Jordan Valley. "The Turks should never, by rules of sane generalship, have ventured back to Tafileh at all . . . it was a dog-in-the-manger attitude unworthy of a serious enemy."

Affronted by the enemy's imprudence, Lawrence wished to see them punished. He abandoned his genius for guerrilla skirmishing and lifted tactics straight from Clausewitz and Marshal Foch: the Arabs would stand and fight. With a small body of men, Lawrence mounted the ridge and laid his battle plan. Its result was a long, bloody day. At its conclusion: "Zeid beside me clapped his hands with joy at the beautiful order of our plan unrolling in the frosty redness of the setting sun. . . . It was going to be a massacre and I should have been crying-sorry for the enemy . . . the destruction of this thousand poor Turks would not affect the issue of the war."

From Tafileh we head east across the slopes of Wadi Hesa toward Jurf ad Darawish and the Desert Highway. This is high, flat, flinty desert, tough on camels and men. The barren landscape provides little to focus on, yet it holds and fascinates. Even among black flints that can lacerate the pads of a camel's feet, a tent now and then appears, a few goats, a child attending them with a sharp eye and a stick of wood.

On a hilltop to the north stand the ruins of Qasr al Basha, yet another in the chain of crusader fortresses. Then nothing until Qasr al Bint and the outskirts of Jurf ad Darawish, on the Hejaz Railway: "Jurf . . . a strong station of three stone buildings with outer-works and trenches. Behind was a low mound . . . on which the Turks had set two machine-guns and a mountain gun." This morning the bus jolts to a halt and villagers climb aboard, soldiers in limp fatigues, an old man with a silver beard, his white head scarf tucked into the throat of an embroidered cinnamon-colored cloak—the tribal garb of the Beni Sakhr.

In January 1918, on their way to capture Tafileh, Sherif Nasir and Nuri Said led a band of the Beni Sakhr against the station at Jurf. The Turks were too few to hold out. It was quick work for the Bedu. "The

Beni Sakhr mounted their camels, swearing they would charge in forthwith . . . Nuri ran down the hill. The Turkish gun was undamaged. He slewed it round and discharged it point blank into the ticket office. The Beni Sakhr mob yelled with joy . . . jumped again on their camels and loped into the station just as the enemy surrendered."

During the 110 desert miles from Jurf to Amman, Jordan's capital, I wonder if this ancient Beni Sakhr, nodding sleepily in front of me, was among the tribesmen loping their camels into the station. A satisfying image—if one can forget, for an instant, the horrified Turks receiving that point-blank discharge of their own gun.

For an hour I try to form my feeble Arabic into a question. Will the old Beni Sakhr remember that long-ago day in Jurf? We pass the station at Hesa, which Nasir dynamited in May 1918 as the Arabs began their drive to Damascus. Then I nod off. When I wake we're among fertile orchards on the outskirts of Amman. The old man has gone, got off at some desert oasis, Al Qatrana maybe, or Dhab'a. My questions about that camel charge into the station at Jurf go forever unasked.

Amman

The Bdeiwi Hotel, on Omar al-Khayyam Street, halfway up one of Amman's thirteen hills, is a classic Arab hostelry, its half dozen rooms opening onto a spacious common room thronged until dawn by card players, TV watchers, and high-spirited men shouting the gutturals of country Arabic. When I emerge from my lair to visit the bath, everything stops until I've passed through the inquisitive mob, used the facilities, and skulked back to my room. At seven the next morning I check out and wander the streets until landing a room at the Palace Hotel on King Feisal Street. Far less grand than its name, the Palace has heat, a private bath, and quiet. After sleeping an hour I set out to explore the city.

The Old Testament refers to Amman as Rabbath Ammon, capital of the Ammonites. It was besieged and destroyed by the Israelites during King David's reign, when David had its inhabitants burned alive in brick kilns (II Samuel 11–12). Later, Amman fell to the Babylonians, the Ptolemies of Egypt, then the Nabathaeans, the Romans under Herod, and eventually the Arabs. Except for its superb Roman theater, little of its past remains.

After the Arab occupation, the city declined, and when the Turks held it during World War I it was little more than a village. Allenby moved across the Jordan in the spring of 1918, intending to force the Turkish garrison from Amman before pushing on to Damascus. The English attacked on April 3, while Lawrence and the Arabs, accompanied by two thousand Sirhan camels, camped at nearby Atara, awaiting word of an English victory. Things were ripe for the advance into Syria. But Amman eluded Allenby: "At last news came that the English had taken Amman. In half an hour we were making for Themed, across the deserted line. Later messages told us that the English were falling back."

Today Jordan's capital is a city of nearly a million, sprawling chaotically over precipitous hills. Many of its residents are Palestinians who fled the West Bank during the 1948 and 1967 wars. High-spirited, generous, well educated, and friendly, they provide Amman with a positive, compelling dimension.

Typical is Abu Saleh, who runs a restaurant downtown in a warren of narrow alleyways that provide Amman's only claim to urban character. Just a few steps from the Palace Hotel, Abu Saleh provides plentiful, cheap, delicious food, and I take my meals in his spacious, low-ceilinged dining room. Bearded, handsome, Saleh presides from behind a vast paper-laden desk. When I've eaten, he invites me to join him for coffee and sweets. Saleh and his wife are informed and well-traveled, and we swap yarns about Bombay and Bali, Nairobi, Kathmandu, San Francisco.

Not until my last evening does he speak of his family and past. "I'm Palestinian," he says in clear, dispassionate English. "My family comes from Haifa. I have aunts, uncles, and cousins there I've never met. My mother hasn't seen her brothers since 1948. Maybe this year the road between Jordan and Israel will open and I can take her to see them. Maybe not. She's afraid she'll die before they let her go. But this is not *her* problem, not *my* problem—this is the problem of the sixty percent of Jordanians who are Palestinian."

> The hills of the west and the plains of the east were the parts
> of Arabia always most populous and active. In particular on
> the west, the mountains of Syria and Palestine . . . entered
> time and again into the current of our European life.

Muaggar, Kharaneh, Amra

Basan pilots the Mercedes through heavy morning traffic and on into the greenness east of Amman. Tall and lean, with a slow grin, he drives with skill and a heavy foot. Soon we're among the olive groves of Muaggar, where, on August 20, 1918, Lawrence, accompanied by Colonel Buxton and the Imperial Camel Corps, on an expedition to dynamite the bridge at Kissir, "hid in the sub-structures of the Roman temple-platform." They'd discovered Turkish tax collectors visiting neighboring villages and, with secrecy of movement impossible, aborted their plan to blow the bridge. Instead, they "waited till dark was thick, and then rode off for Azrak, fifty miles away."

Beyond Muaggar the landscape gives way to the pale grays of sterile scrub, then bleak expanses of stone. Nothing but undulant space and tall skies—the desert tableland reaching east to Baghdad. The Mercedes gathers speed, and soon the golden walls of Kusair al Kharaneh rise from a flat and treeless plain. "We [passed] the lone palace of Kharaneh about midnight, too careless to turn aside and see its strangeness."

The *kusairs* of the eastern desert are the ruins of Ghassanide hunting palaces, built by seventh-century Omayyed princes. Bedouins at heart, with a passion for the desert, they journeyed to these palaces for a few weeks each year. Once this desolate country teemed with ibex and gazelle, deer, cheetah, even bear, and these early Arabs took pleasure in their ancient pastimes of hunting, hawking, horse racing, and evenings of poetry and music.

This morning Italian tourists snap photos in a stiff, cold wind. I turn up my collar, wrap a *kefiyah* tightly around my head, and follow them over the stones. Built in 711 C.E. on possibly Byzantine foundations, Kusair al Kharaneh is tall and austere, its unadorned walls and stately towers laid out on a perfect square. Maybe it was Kharaneh's formality that Lawrence found "strange" on that moonlit night. It's the only example of a desert *kusair* built strictly for defense—though in this wasteland, under a sky massing with glowering cumulus, what it defended and against whom beggars the imagination.

Lawrence passed Kharaneh at midnight, and the next day, "in the afternoon, tired, we came to Kusair el Amra, the little hunting lodge of Harith, the Shepherd King, a patron of poets; it stood beautifully against its background of bosky rustling trees." Basan and his Mercedes need only minutes to cover the ground, but the Italians have gotten the jump and are already struggling over the desert when we arrive. It's years since Lawrence's "bosky rustling trees" went up in flames to grill the desert's last gazelle, though wild dogs snap and growl beneath a tamarisk at the bottom of a nearby wadi. Even in wind-driven grit Kusair el Amra is lovely: where Kharaneh was dominant masculine angles, Amra's feminine domes harmonize with the terrain as agreeably as Bedouin tents.

A step into the eighth-century halls is like plunging from the Arab East into medieval Europe, the walls frescoed with scenes of hawkers, hunters, men driving gazelle and oryx into nets, and the foes of Islam: Roderick, king of the Visigoths; Chosroes of Persia; the emperor of Byzantium. Bare-breasted dancers adorn supporting arches, and down a serpentine corridor are bathing rooms ornamented with an *oud*-strumming bear, a dancing monkey, and the domed steam room itself mapped with the night sky. "Buxton put headquarters in the cool dusk of its hall, and we lay there puzzling out the worn frescoes of the wall, with more laughter than moral profit . . .

> Meanwhile, Amruh was wonderful. They asked me with astonishment who were these Kings of Ghassan with the unfamiliar halls and pictures. I could tell them vague tales of their poetry, and cruel wars; but it seemed so distant and tinseled an age.

Kusair al Azrak

At the northern end of Wadi Sirhan, the great drainage system extending along the Saudi-Jordanian border south to the Nefudh, are the pools and swamps of the Azrak oasis. Once a major caravan route, Wadi Sirhan afforded Lawrence a secure and watered road for his continual journeys up and down the country, and Azrak became his northern base.

Today, eighteen-wheelers, transporting goods over the H5 between Akaba and Baghdad, highball through Azrak or pull in at garages, gas pumps, and shabby cafés strung along the roadside under windblown palms. The pools and swamps in which Lawrence "promised everyone a bathe; the Englishmen, not washed since Akaba," are the products of underground rivers filtering water from the Syrian highlands. Today, nearly pumped dry, "these shining springs" supply drinking water to Amman. Still, palms crowd the broad swale of the oasis, and a pale band of vegetation reaches south into stone-scrabble desert.

Beyond the Al Sayyam Rest House, on a ledge at the edge of town, the Kusair al Azrak stands beneath a sky piled with cloud. Lawrence, in the company of Ali ibn el Hussein, Feisal's brother, arrived on November 4, 1917. "It was to be Ali's first view of Azrak, and . . . the blue fort on its rock above the rustling palms, with the fresh meadows and shining springs of water, broke on our sight . . . Azrak's unfathomable silence was steeped in knowledge of wandering poets."

Though now beset by the threadbare town, the Kusair possesses something of Lawrence's haunting magic. Its towers and walls of black basalt surround a parade ground whose small mosque stands just off-center like an architectural afterthought: "The little mosque in the square . . . had been half unroofed and the Arabs had penned sheep within the walls. [Hassan Shah] set his twenty men to dig out the filth, and wash the pavement clean." Around the parade ground the buildings are little more than stone husks, roofless, vacant, their ponderous blocks tumbled down. On a corner stands Lawrence's Tower, its massive doors, weighty basalt slabs "turning on pivots of itself." Lawrence took up quarters in the, "southern gate-tower, and set my six Hurani boys . . . to cover with brushwood, palm-branches, and clay the ancient split stone rafters." Outside is a plaque carved from black stone:

Built by the Romans: rebuilt by Arabs during the Crusades
and used by Lawrence.

The English are here—a handful of cultured Brits guided by a dogged Jordanian woman. A gangling young Englishman appears to have replaced her. A graduate student from Lawrence's Oxford, probably, homely, soft-spoken, diffident behind horn-rims and a slow smile. In tweeds, with shooting sticks and stout shoes, the troop obediently follows him beyond the little mosque to visit distant stones.

I wander the opposite way, through roofless rooms along the western walls, where I discover another of the great basalt doors, a foot thick, weighing tons. Heaving tentatively, I find to my astonishment that it swings easily. Outside, beneath a sweep of palms, graze a flock of bleating goats.

According to Lawrence, "Azrak lay favorably for us, and the old fort would be convenient headquarters if we made it habitable, no matter how severe the winter." It was an ideal hideout, too remote to attract the attention of the enemy. From here Lawrence might keep an eye on the disposition of Turkish troops while preaching the word of the Revolt among the tribes and enlisting fighters in the Arab cause.

As the summer of 1918 wore on, Lawrence and the Arabs planned their attack across the Syrian border on the vital rail center at Deraa. "We would march a camel column of one thousand men to Azrak where their concentration must be complete on September the thirteenth. On the sixteenth we would envelop Deraa, and cut its railways. Two days later we would fall back east of the Hejaz Railway and wait events with Allenby."

On his arrival with Ali ibn el Hussein in the autumn of 1917, however, Lawrence was less sanguine. The war was going badly in Europe, and "Allenby had failed in his weather, and there would be no great advance this year." Nearer home were the failure in mining a bridge over the Yarmuk gorge and chances missed in destroying trains. Arriving at Azrak, Lawrence found that Abed el Kader el Jezairi, the crazed Algerian patriot, had turned spy and gone over to the Turks. Then the weather turned foul.

At the top of the gate tower Lawrence's room occupies a twenty-by-thirty-foot cell of black stone. A ceiling of interlocking stones rests upon a graceful supporting arch. Two shooting windows pierce massive walls, while a third, framed by a Gothic arch, looks onto the parade ground below. A trio of doorways completes the set. Here Lawrence met the great chieftains of the Sherarat, Serahin, the Ruala, and Beni Sakhr, as well as Druses, Syrian politicians, Armenians fleeing the Turks, and well-mounted Arab officers deserting from the Turkish forces. "Three guest-masters . . . received the rising tide of these newcomers, sorted worshipful from curious, and marshalled them in due time before him [Ali ibn el Hussein] or me."

Today, the English crowd Lawrence's chamber, for it is Lawrence they've come to find. Their Jordanian guide finds herself on shaky ground, overshadowed by the shy student. Lawrence, apparently, has been written out of Arab history. He might be heartened: "My proper share was a minor one, but because of a fluent pen, a free speech, and a certain adroitness of brain, I took upon myself, as I describe it, a mock primacy. In reality I never had any office among the Arabs."

Ignoring Lawrence's humbler side, the graduate student places him at Azrak. His flock nods approval at his apt descriptions, keen observations. Among the sites they've visited, he tells them, this room is least changed since Lawrence's day. "In every respect, it's just as he found it. And if today seems blustery and chill, I thought it might cheer you if I read a few lines from Lawrence about this room in that disagreeable winter of 1917."

Holding his book to the light, he begins:

> In the evening, when we had shut-to the gate, all guests would assemble, either in my room or Ali's, and coffee and stories would go round until the last meal, and after it, till sleep came. On stormy nights we brought in brushwood and dung and lit a great fire in the middle of the floor. About it would be drawn carpets and saddle-sheep-skins, and in its light we would tell over our own battles, or hear the visitors' traditions. The leaping flames chased our smoke-ruffled shadows strangely about the rough stone wall behind us.
>
> At last the sky turned solidly to rain, and no man could approach us. In loneliness we learned the full disadvantages of imprisonment within such gloomy ancient unmortared places. The rain guttered down within the walls' thickness and spouted into the rooms from their chinks . . . It was icy cold, as we hid there, motionless, from the murky daylight until dark, our minds seeming suspended within these massive walls, through whose every shot-window the piercing mist streamed like a white pennant. Past and future flowed over us like an uneddying river. We dreamed ourselves into the spirit of the place; sieges and feasting, raids, murders, love-singing in the night.

Amman, Cairo, Damascus: A Bureaucratic Interlude

The young woman behind the counter wears a head scarf of virginal white, intricately and tightly tied. Her prim expression is equally

taut. When I present my passport through the porthole in the glass sep-
arating us, it hangs like an unshaken hand.

"I'd like to apply for a visa to visit Syria, if I may?"

She jerks a thumb toward her colleague at the next window, a bland
young man in a colorless shirt, then gazes sourly into space.

I switch lines. An attractive blond New Zealander speaks to the
bland man. Her voice shrills: "I've waited a week for an answer—are you
giving me a visa or not?"

The young man shakes his head.

"Why not? Can you give me a reason?"

Again, the head shakes.

"I want a reason. If you give visas to other people, you have to give
me one or deny them to everyone else."

A vacant look.

"You're not going to help me, are you? I've got a plane to catch in
Istanbul. I must cross Syria to get there. But you don't care, do you?"

An empty pause before the young man says: "Fly."

"Fly? I can't *afford* to fly!"

"Fly . . . or don't go."

Lawrence made peace between a dozen Arab tribes rumbling with
ancient feuds. He found fodder for two thousand animals and provisions
for his men. There were a hundred other essentials. He secured arms and
ammunition, cable, detonators and explosives for dynamiting trains, and
coordinated bombing runs for the R.A.F.'s Bristols and Handley-Pages.
And on September 13, 1918, as planned, he set out from Azrak: "Just at
dawn our column marched. Of them one thousand were the Aba el Lissan contingent: three hundred were Nuri Shaalan's nomad horse. He had
also two thousand Rualla camel-riders."

In view of his expedition, my own, a fifty-mile bus ride to Irbid, a
change for Ramleh, and then a hike over the Syrian border into Deraa,
seems modest enough. The Syrian embassy in Amman, however, may not
prove a beacon of cooperation.

The New Zealander, sobbing, goes out the door. A second young
woman approaches, handing over a royal blue passport imprinted with
the golden seal of Her Britannic Majesty. The bland man thumbs its
pages, then tosses it back.

"Why didn't you get a visa in London?"

"I'm not in London, I'm in Amman. I wish to visit family friends in Lebanon. To do that I must pass through Syria."

"You're English . . . you should have gotten your visa there."

"I've tried to explain . . ."

"You want a visa, you'll have to go to London."

"You're not making sense . . . England is over two thousand miles away."

The young man motions me to the counter. Dismissed, the Englishwoman brushes past, trembling with rage. My instinct is to smash the glass, take the man by the throat, and rip out his windpipe. Instead, I offer too big a grin and stupidly confess that a visit to Syria is the dream of a lifetime.

Whatever his reasons, after flipping the pages of my passport, he passes a visa application through the porthole.

"You ever visited Occupied Palestine?"

"Israel? No."

"You can fill this out . . ."

"Thank you, I will."

"No promises. Pay thirty-five dollars for the visa, another twenty dollars for the application fee. If you don't get the visa, you get the thirty-five back . . . we keep the twenty."

"When?"

"Tomorrow—nine."

———

The big, low-ceilinged dining room at Abu Saleh's is crowded with familiar faces—a meeting of conspirators. The New Zealand blonde, the young Englishwoman, a half dozen others from this morning's visa session. Over platters of grilled chicken and heaps of flat bread, we spend a few gratifying hours uttering unpleasantries about the bland young man and his virginal associate.

"Isn't *anyone* getting through?" I ask around a mouthful of *baba ghanouj*.

"A Dutchman," answers an Australian with an earful of gold. "That was a week ago."

"Then it's *arbitrary* . . . a lottery!" I feel a spark of hope. "Anyone *might* get through."

"Dutchman had a flight booked out of Damascus—Syrian Air to Rotterdam. They gave him a transit visa to the airport."

"Then, there are *no* travelers in Syria?"

"Oh, plenty, mate. People who got visas back home . . . or knew the score and picked them up in Cairo."

"Cairo?"

"Syrian embassy in Cairo . . . no problem. Give visas away like they were popcorn. You want to go so bad, fly down to Cairo."

"Cairo? You're sure?"

"Too expensive or we'd all do it. As is, most of us are busing to Israel."

"But I've *got* to see Deraa, Damascus . . . Aleppo."

"Who knows, mate, maybe you'll be one of the lucky ones."

———

Nine sharp, and of course, the young woman behind the counter, wearing yet another head scarf, as intricate and taut as yesterday's, knows nothing of luck. "I cannot give you a visa to enter Syria." No explanation, no apology. The bland young man, busy rifling through a filing cabinet, glances over as the young woman dishes my passport through the porthole, counts out my thirty-five dollars, then, to my surprise, adds the twenty-dollar application fee.

I tip my imaginary hat. "Thanks so much, you've been *terribly* helpful."

She is not amused—for all her grim complexity, there's no irony in this woman.

———

At the Intercontinental on Zahran Street, I call the Syrian embassy in Cairo, saying only that I'm an American, have never visited Israel, and wish to go to Syria.

"We're open all morning, won't you please come in."

"Is this the Syrian embassy? You're sure they'll be no problem."

"None that I can foresee."

"It may be a few days before I can get there."

"Whenever it's convenient . . . we'll be most happy to see you."

———

> In Cairo, where I spent four days, our affairs were now far
> from haphazard. Allenby's smile had given us Staff. We had
> supply officers, a shipping expert, an ordnance expert, an
> intelligence branch . . .

I spend five days sleeping at the Pensione Roma, hanging out at the
Hilton, site of the old British barracks on the Nile, drinking soapy Stella
beer at the Windsor Hotel.

If there's a place in Cairo that's unchanged since Lawrence's day, it's
the Windsor. Once a British officers' mess, the upstairs bar is as threadbare as an over-the-hill Pall Mall club, with overstuffed chairs and worn
leather couches, relics of the Raj. Brown with pipe smoke, the walls bris-
tle with the horns of ibex and gazelle. Antique waiters pass among the
patrons, offering felicitations: Mister Abdul, in his legendary *dishdasha* and
shabby fez; the ex-weightlifter Mahmoud Soliman, still possessing a
bone-crushing grip.

A desk-bound intelligence officer stationed in Cairo during the
war's early stages, Lawrence may or may not have visited the Windsor—
though Churchill and, more recently, Michael Palen, were guests. It's easy
to imagine Lawrence sipping pink gins and debating strategy at the bar
with Allenby and Ronald Storrs, Hogarth, Captain Hornby, and Colonel
Joyce. "Now I had been four months in Arabia continually on the move
. . . I wanted a bath, and something with ice in it to drink."

When I'm not at the Hilton or drinking Stella, I bide my time in a
bungalow across the river in Doqqi, deep in the gardens of the Syrian
embassy. The shadowy grounds are cool, the porter all smiles, and the visa
consul, a handsome Circassian in a well-cut suit, a Countess Mara neck-
tie draped around his heavy neck, helpful. The torpid wheels of bureau-
cracy turn slowly, but turn they do. At last, on a morning late in March,
a Syrian visa, baroque as the Circassian's tie, is stamped into my passport,
and by midnight I'm aboard a Syrian Air 737 bound for Damascus—the
once-forbidden city.

Bosra and Deraa

> Allenby had appointed us watchmen of the [Turkish]
> Fourth Army. We had just seen its disordered flight. Our

duty was completed; we might honourably fall back to
Bosra.

"Ah, so you're staying a few days in Deraa . . . must be for Lawrence
. . . all that *mystery?*" Elizabeth Todd knows a lot about Lawrence but isn't
saying much. A stout, jolly lady from Cambridge, she works in a college
there. We share a table in the shade of a Coca-Cola awning at the edge
of a vast, echoing square. Elizabeth is waiting for the last bus to Damascus; I'll take any ride I can find to Deraa.

We're the only two at Bosra's only café. Bosra's not really a town,
though families live in makeshift houses built from blocks pilfered from
the ruins. Once the northern capital of the Nabathean kingdom, Bosra
became Roman in 106 C.E.—Nova Trajana Bostra, capital of the province
of Arabia. It was an important seat of a Christian primate by the time
Mohammed met the Nestorian monk Boheira outside the fourth-cen-
tury monastery and was told of his impending vocation as prophet. Later
it became a Muslim holy place and, for centuries, it prospered as a stop
on the pilgrimage to Mecca. Its fortified citadel encloses a Roman theater as intact as the day the last actor took his final curtain call. It with-
stood two twelfth-century crusader sieges and another by the Mongols
in 1261. When raiding tribes made the pilgrimage route unsafe in the
seventeenth century, the road shifted west. Bosra declined and was abandoned.

By September 1918, with the Turkish army in retreat all across the
Eastern Front, the Arabs might have honorably fallen back to Bosra. But
Lawrence wouldn't hear of it. If they were to have a say in negotiations
at war's end, the Arabs had to press on to Deraa, then Damascus. "They
had joined the war to win freedom, and the recovery of their old capital [Damascus] by force of their own arms was the sign they would best
understand."

Still, you can imagine Arab tents pitched in Bosra's columned streets,
the camels grazing in the sanctuary of the ruined cathedral. Today a pony
and a pair of ragged donkeys forage grass among the black stones of a
fallen wall.

"That's the thing about Lawrence," Elizabeth Todd says, sipping juice,
"one is so often at sixes and sevens with him, isn't one? He's so ambivalent, so torn between the Arabs and the English . . . not feeling himself

71

quite either . . . despising first one, then the other . . . despising himself most of all, don't you think? Yearning for the greens of England one minute, ardent about the desert the next. Then this other business . . ."

"By which you mean . . ."

"Well, yes, Deraa . . . what *is* one to think of Deraa? Can this beastly story possibly be true? Did anything at all happen? Did it happen somewhere else . . . with someone else? Possibly it was fantasy from beginning to end. *Mysterious* . . . know what I mean?"

November 1, 1917, nearly a year before the Arab forces stormed Deraa, Lawrence, disguised as a Circassian peasant, slipped into the enemy-held town. The plan: to explore the place with his companion Faris, then meet Halim with the ponies at Nisib, a village to the south. Ostensibly Lawrence was to take stock of Turkish defenses and discover a route of attack. It was just minutes, however, before he was accosted by Turkish soldiers: "A sergeant came after, and took me roughly by the arm, saying 'The Bey wants you.'"

He'd nearly been caught in Amman, masquerading as a Gypsy girl. This time he was grabbed and taken before the garrison commander. The bey quickly made his desires known: "He flung himself back on the bed, and dragged me down with him in his arms." When the bey fondled him, Lawrence "bore it for a little, till he got too beastly; and then jerked my knee into him."

Outraged, the bey called the corporal of the guard and, while Lawrence was held, "leaned forward, fixed his teeth in my neck and bit till the blood came. Then he kissed me." The bey gazed into Lawrence's face: "You must understand that I know: and it will be easier if you do as I wish."

Lawrence writes that he was "dumbfounded." Did the Turkish officer suspect his guest's identity? Capture of the famous Urens would have been a plum for the bey. Lawrence believed the bey's remark was "evidently a chance shot, by which he himself did not, or would not, mean what I feared." A moment later, the bey "half-whispered to the corporal to take me out and teach me everything."

For the next hour Lawrence was lashed with "a whip of the Circassian sort, a thong of supple black hide." The lengthy and detailed description of this beating, the blood and pain of the flogging itself, the kicks and blows and arm-twisting that accompanied it, has the ring of the connoisseur. Elsewhere he wrote of his abhorrence of physical contact: "The disgust of being touched revolted me more than the thought of death and defeat . . . I so reverenced my wits and despised my body." At the hands of a half dozen sadistic enemy conscripts, he seems in his element. At last, covered in filth and blood, he was thrown to the floor and the corporal lashed out at him with his nailed boot. Ribs cracked. Lawrence's reaction was candid: "I remember smiling idly at him, for a delicious warmth, probably sexual, was swelling through me: and then that he flung up his arm and hacked with the full of his whip into my groin."

Lawrence was dragged into the bey's presence, only to be rejected "as a thing too torn and bloody for his bed." Locked in a shed for the night, he escaped and made his painful way from town. "Deraa felt inhuman with vice and cruelty, and it shocked me like cold water when a soldier laughed behind me in the street. . . . [T]he passing days confirmed: how in Deraa that night the citadel of my integrity had been irrevocably lost."

Elizabeth Todd finishes her drink as a bus arrives. We cross the square and I see her aboard. It's a big air-conditioned Karnak coach, the sort never bound in my direction. Elizabeth pauses at the top of the steps and waves goodbye.

"Don't suppose you'll find much, will you, in Deraa?" she calls down. "But do please be careful. One never knows, does one, who may be lurking about."

———

"Your Mister T. S. Eliot, please, in which poem does he ask many questions?"

"Questions?"

"You must know of Mister T. S. Eliot?"

"Yes, of course, questions: 'The Love Song of J. Alfred Prufrock,' you mean. 'Shall I part my hair behind? Do I dare to eat a peach?' That what you have in mind?"

"Yes, Mister Alfred Prufrock is exactly the one. But what of Ernest Hemingway? How could the man who wrote *The Old Man and the Sea*, the story of an individual's perseverance against great odds, commit suicide? It seems writers create one thing and live quite another."

Elizabeth Todd is right, you never know whom you'll find lurking on Syrian street corners. In this case Abdullah Hassan Abud, a high school English teacher, has found me, hopelessly lost, at a midtown intersection.*

In his early thirties, with pale eyes and clipped hair, Abdullah wears the stubble beard that seems obligatory for young Syrian males. "May I be of assistance?" he asks, before touring me through Deraa's three equally shabby hotels. I choose the Al Salam for no other reason than it's the last I've seen and won't have to traipse back to the others. Next, Abdullah treats me to Nescafé and condensed milk, a Syrian cappuccino, at a café on the town square.

In the funk of late afternoon, after a day's hard traveling, I fail to take Abdullah up on Hemingway's self-destruction. Undismayed, he pursues his hypothesis: writers create one thing, live another. "Take Lawrence, for instance."

"D. H. Lawrence? Lawrence Durrell?"

"Colonel Lawrence . . . what of him? Was he living one thing, writing another? Did he not know that when the Turks were beaten, the British and French would divide Arabia as if it were theirs to divide?"

"He didn't know."

"You're quite sure?"

"The Sykes-Picot Treaty established English and French hegemony in the Middle East. It was kept secret until war's end. Lawrence knew nothing of it. Nonetheless, he suspected Britain's motives and urged the Arabs to rush into Damascus ahead of the English troops. The Arabs would then be seen as victors who'd earned the right to govern themselves."

"Did he honestly believe they would?"

"Hoped . . . but, no, he didn't honestly believe. It was a deep problem for him—part of his self-hatred—deceiving the Arabs so they'd follow him and help the English win the war."

"Forgive me, please, but I do not like the English, do not like what they have done to people all over the world."

---

* I have changed the names of Syrians to protect them from possible harassment. Amnesty International claims that at least eight internal intelligence organizations operate in the country.

Junction of the Jerusalem-Haifa-Damascus-Medina railways and axis of Turkish communications, Deraa was an Arab objective from the start. Just as they'd softened Maan in the south, Arab dynamiting of bridges and rail lines around Deraa weakened the town to near-collapse. When Trad and his brother Khalid led in the first Arab detachment, the Turks were in retreat. Khalid charged "through and over several detachments of Turks . . . to find Trad in secure possession. He had won through in the later twilight, taking the station at a gallop." Lawrence arrived next morning, November 28, 1918: "I gave liberty to my camel—the grand, rebellious Baha—and she stretched herself out against the field . . . so that I entered Deraa quite alone in the full dawn."

The station stands at the very center of town. It's two stories of painted brick, vaguely European, possibly even German, with peaked Bavarian roofs and an odd assortment of picturesque chimneys. A brass bell, green with age, and an old-fashioned clock cling like limpets to the wall outside the stationmaster's office; a Syrian flag hangs above the door. Nearby, swags of bunting bear the likeness of President Assad. When Lawrence entered Deraa, he sent word of victory to Feisal, who "drove in a day later, our string of armoured cars following his Vauxhall. He installed himself in the station. I called with my record of stewardship."

This morning three dozen wooden freight cars string through the marshaling yards. Wildflowers blossom between the rails. A pair of women in violet caftans and trailing head scarves squat outside the waiting room, nursing babies. A rusty sign swings above a door: "Information."

Inside, a withered little man in a large visored cap, possibly a hand-me-down from a Luftwaffe officer, peers over a high counter. To my surprise, in a country where the lingua franca is home-grown French, he speaks clipped English: "May I help you, sir?"

"A train to Damascus . . . is such a thing possible?"

"One train each week, and today, dear friend, today is the day. Noon. Four hours to Damascus. You will arrive at teatime."

"May I purchase a ticket?"

"Ticket? Ticket? Dear friend, is still early. Plenty time for ticket."

> In the square I showed [General Barrow] Nasir's little silk
> pennon, propped on the balcony of the charred Govern-
> ment office, with a yawning sentry underneath.

Sherif Nasir's silk pennon was soon purloined by Indian troops who fancied its silver knob and exquisite staff. Then they pilfered every chicken in town. Today, the old government office is gone, and Deraa's central square bordered by nondescript buildings painted in mind-numbing pastels. At the square's heart, guarded by triple swags of heavy chain, stands a fountain of monstrous modernity in which a few gallons of swampwater steep beneath primordial scum. On its sad perimeter ragged shoeshine boys scuttle after clients and adolescent girls beg coins.

"Young boys shining the shoes, they are Kurds," Abdullah says, dropping into a chair at the outdoor café.

"How do you know, Abdullah?"

"They are speaking Kurdish language, though I cannot understand what they say."

A trio of girls sidle up to our table with outstretched hands. They have dark, flowing hair and wear tiers of neon-colored garments: chrome yellow, scalding pink, effervescent violet. "And these?" I ask, reaching for a coin.

"Gypsies." Abdullah shakes his head in warning. "Give them nothing. Be watchful. They will steal everything."

The girls move in, whining, wheedling, reaching for my pockets, the change from my coffee. I press coins into a small hand but they're thrust back. Not enough. More. Money. Real money. The smallest and bravest grabs for my camera. Before she can wrap her fingers around it, the waiter moves in and cracks her sharply over the skull with bared knuckles. She drops, stunned. He boots her in the ribs before she drags herself away, howling.

"Is Deraa always like this?" I ask Abdullah. "Lawrence, on one famous occasion, had an experience not unlike this Gypsy girl's. It doesn't seem a happy place."

Abdullah blinks with incomprehension. "How could it be different? I have lived here all my life. It has always been this way." He catches his breath, then begins a rapid string of disconnected inquiries. Half the night, he lay awake, thinking what to ask. But they are not questions, for he doesn't expect answers. In a burst, he asserts that it is inconceivable there is anyone who doesn't believe in God, that reckless sex is rapidly destroying western civilization, that every member of the United States Congress is Jewish. "How else can you explain America's Middle East policy?"

His misconceptions of the West only illuminate my own misguided notions of Islam and Arabs. To show that I know something of his country, I ask about Syrian support for Iran in the Iran-Iraq war. "Isn't it true that Iran still gives Syria two thousand barrels of free oil a day for providing that support?"

Abdullah glances nervously around. Talking Syrian politics is not a popular Syrian pastime. Abdullah leans nearer, whispering: "These things we must not know. They are military secrets. Please, speak of something else."

We speak of the bill: who will pay? I press money into the waiter's hand. Abdullah snatches it back. "This is not possible," he says, sharply. "You are guest in my country."

"Abdullah, you've paid for *everything.*"

"It is as it must be."

The waiter understands. Only Abdullah's money is acceptable. This generous, decent, hard-working young teacher pays our bill, then apologizes for not coming to see me off at the station. His school opens in just minutes. There are children waiting. He clutches me, kisses me on both cheeks. "*Ma'asalaama,* my friend. You will write to me soon. I await your letter. You will explain all things about Mister Hemingway."

———

The train crew, a trio in checked *kefiyahs,* sprawl on a meadow of spring grass among the rails. It's minutes before our scheduled departure, but there's no train and no one's in a hurry. The women in the violet caftans move onto the platform, still nursing their babies. A man in a suit and tie clutches an attache case and paces nervously beside an ancient couple lugging cardboard boxes bound with string. The little man in the Luftwaffe cap glances at the antique clock. It's three twenty-three—just as it was at seven A.M.

"Ticket? Ticket?" he shouts cheerfully when I offer him a wad of Syrian pounds. "Plenty time for ticket."

Finally the train arrives, rumbling through the marketplace, scattering chickens, fruit vendors, and old men on bicycles before sliding into the marshaling yards, a sleek pumpkin-colored Jordan Railways diesel drawing a caboose and a pair of wooden passenger carriages so old I'm surprised they eluded Lawrence's dynamite.

The diesel is uncoupled, shunted, sent solo back to Amman. Then a Syrian Railways engine is nursed, coughing dryly, out of a locomotive shed. The crew couples it to the antique cars, and the man in the Luftwaffe cap issues me a cardboard ticket—Deraa-Damas—then punches it with a toy conductor's punch. At last I'm aboard the Hejaz Railway, focus of so much of Lawrence's energy: "Traveling became an uncertain terror. . . At Damascus people scrambled for the back seats in trains, even paid extra for them. The engine-drivers struck. Civilian traffic nearly ceased; and we extended our threat to Aleppo by . . . posting a notice one night on Damascus Town Hall, that good Arabs would henceforward travel by the Syrian railway at their own risk."

I pass along grim rows of slat benches in the vacant third-class carriage, then cross the open vestibule to first class. After stowing my bag in a seedy compartment, I settle onto a threadbare seat. As the train lurches forward and picks up speed, a voice across the compartment reflects my thoughts: "Quite a nice train, actually."

"Seems so."

"Splendid trip up from Amman."

"You're . . . ?"

"English . . . Devon, actually."

"And you've come from Amman? Got your Syrian visa there?"

"London, before I left. Only spending a fortnight. Bit of a dustup at the Syrian embassy in Amman, I'm told."

"Ah, yes, bit of a dustup . . ."

By now, the Englishman and I realize that the train has slowed noticeably. In fact, it's stopped. Through the smudged window is a road rapidly filling with traffic—heavy trucks, bicycles, donkey carts, taxis, vintage Fords and Chevys I haven't seen since high school.

"I say, what do you suppose . . . ?"

"Bit of a dustup with the train, I should imagine."

The corridor quickly fills, and passengers step down from the carriage onto the road. A driver abandons his '57 Impala and advances on the train. Others follow. Soon a crowd gathers around the engine, and the train crew, spirits vanished, head miserably back to the station.

"Problem?" I ask as they shuffle past.

One glances warily from under his headcloth and shrugs. "Big problem."

"How big? We'll be going soon?"

"Not going soon."

A young man whisks us off the train and into a taxi, then joins the driver up front. The Englishman and I speed across town to the "meecro" station and are put aboard a minibus departing for Damascus. This happens so swiftly that not until we're underway do we realize the young man isn't with us. A perfect stranger, whose name we haven't gotten, whose face we can't remember, has paid the taxi and our fare to the capital as well.

Tafas, Sheikh Miskin, Ezraa, Khirbet el Ghazala

The mass rising we had so long prepared was now in flood, rising higher as each success armed more rebels. In two days' time we might have sixty thousand armed men in movement.

Across the Yarmuk River north of Deraa we roll over the wide level of the southern Hauran—the lush greens of spring wheat punctuated by the silver of olives, the pinks of blossoming cherries. Workers, farmers, students, old men in the garb of Sherarat and Rualla double up in cramped seats or stand, bent-necked, in the narrow aisle. In towns and villages the bus empties and refills. Tafas, Sheikh Miskin, Sheikh Saad, Khirbet el Ghazala.

In late September 1918, as thousands of Turkish troops fled across fields and through these village streets, the peasants rose against them, and the Arabs pursued with terrible doggedness. In the distance, at Ezraa, where grain elevators tower above the plain, Talal el Hareidhin destroyed the garrison. Auda stormed Khirbet el Ghazala, captured a train and two hundred prisoners. Nuri Shaalan took four hundred, with mules and machine guns, then cut the road from the Hauran to Deraa.

The panicked Turks raped and slaughtered as they ran. At Tafas, where the bus sighs to a stop long enough for an ancient in the robes of the Beni Sakhr to scramble aboard, they murdered everyone—old people, children, babies. It was Talal's village. He arrived as the Turks retreated toward Sheikh Miskin. Lawrence and Auda rode with him. The women, some pregnant, had been horribly mutilated. A little girl of Talal's family, a lance driven through her neck, died in his arms.

When the three caught up with the Turks, Talal mounted a low hill and looked down at their troops. Then he spurred his mare "and galloped headlong, bending low and swaying in the saddle, right at the main body of the enemy . . . we had stopped shooting, and the Turks had stopped. Both armies waited for him; and he rocked on in the hushed evening till only a few lengths from the enemy. Then he sat up in the saddle and cried his war-cry, 'Tallal, Tallal,' twice in a tremendous shout. Instantly their rifles and machine-guns crashed out . . . Auda looked very cold and grim. 'God give him mercy; we will take his price.'" The price was high; the Arabs flamed with vengeance. Lawrence, always remorseful over the deaths of hapless Turks, now felt none: "I said, 'The best of you brings me the most Turkish dead,' and we turned after the fading enemy . . . By my order we took no prisoners, for the only time in our war."

Damascus

> A galloping horseman checked at our head-cloths in the car,
> with a merry salutation, holding out a bunch of yellow
> grapes. "Good news: Damascus salutes you."

Wahid. Itheen. Talata. Arba'a. Seven A.M. and downstairs, in a courtyard shaded by poplar trees, a company of Syrian soldiers does jumping jacks around a babbling marble fountain. One. Two. Three. Four. Apparently, calisthenics aren't a military secret in the Syrian Arab Republic, as these young troopers, successors to Auda, Tallal, Nasir, Nuri Shaalan, are exercising just beneath my third-floor window.

The Barada Hotel backs against the faded walls of the old barracks, faces the central post office across the traffic of Said el Jabri Avenue. A block west, where Said el Jabri ends, stands the colossal relic of the Hejaz Railway Station. Like this whole turn-of-the-century neighborhood, it bears the sober look of central Europe—Bucharest maybe, or Maribor—touched by whimsical flourishes of carved stone and Arabic arches. Front and center over the great portal hangs a grandiose portrait of Hafez

Assad. Damascus is rife with likenesses of the avuncular president with the toothbrush mustache and thinning hair. History, however, cautions against self-glorification.

Damascus, the world's oldest continuously inhabited city, has been fought over and conquered too many times. Here, where the apostle Paul was converted to Christianity, the head of John the Baptist lies entombed in the majestic Omayyed mosque at the city's heart. In its courtyard archaeologists have unearthed relics dating to the third millennium B.C.E. According to the biblical book of Kings, an Aramaean temple dedicated to the god Hadad once stood here. Next came the Romans' Temple of Jupiter and the Christians' Church of St. John the Baptist, and, in 705, the Omayyed caliph Alwalid built his mosque. Conquerors and occupiers are legion: King David of Israel, Assyrians and Persians, Nebuchadnezzar, Alexander the Great, Nabathaeans, Romans under Hadrian and Alexander Severus, Omayyeds and Seljuk Turks, Nureddin the Egyptian, Mongols and Mamelukes, Saladin, Tamerlaine, and the Ottomans of Suleiman the Magnificent.

On September 30, 1918, it was the turn of the Turks and Germans to abandon Damascus—but not before firing their stores of ammunition. The city rocked with explosions. As the last German troops departed, the Arab flag snapped over Town Hall. At dawn the next day Lawrence rode in aboard the Blue Mist, his Rolls-Royce tender, and the city's quarter million citizens turned out to cheer his triumphal tour, chanting, "Feisal, Nasir, Shukri, Urens, in waves which . . . rolled along the squares, through the market down long streets to East gate, round the wall, back up the Meidan; and grew to a wall of shouts around us by the citadel."

This morning vendors chant, hawking spices, luggage, sweets, carpets, spitted chickens, gowns shimmering with sequins. Lawrence's quarter million has grown tenfold, but the press of two and a half million Damascenes hasn't extinguished the city's spirit. When I pass the barracks behind the Barada, a soldier steps smartly from a sentry box and salutes: "*Marhaba, monsieur.* Welcome to Damascus."

———

In an alleyway behind a nondescript modern block off Aththawra Street, the arched portal of the Historical Museum, once an eighteenth-century pasha's palace, opens into a courtyard dripping with spring's first wisteria. It seems a good place to begin—I'm looking for photos, maps, memorabilia, someone to show me the way "up the long street to the Government buildings on the bank of the Barada," and to the Town Hall, where Lawrence found the "steps and stairs were packed with a swaying mob: yelling, embracing, dancing, singing."

It was at Town Hall, in his capacity as deputy for Feisal, that Lawrence established a civil government to administer a city littered with the tragic debris of three years of war. By the first evening policemen and firemen were on duty, the water was running, streetlights were working. Next morning Lawrence dealt with the spy Abd el Kadir—the Algerian had stuck by the Turks until the end, then swapped sides and put himself in charge. At Town Hall, with Nuri Shaalan's Rualla massed outside and Lawrence's "reckless guardsmen lounging in the antechamber," Abd el Kadir was summoned and deposed. With the support of the Druses, he staged a halfhearted rebellion, but by noon the Algerian and his henchmen had fled. It was the closing skirmish of Lawrence's war.

The old man shuffling from the museum to greet me is nearly ancient enough to have fought in that war. But the language barrier, bogus French on both sides, villainous Arabic on mine, prevents a real exchange. He bows me into the courtyard, which is lulled by lapping fountains and rife with flowers. We cross the garden and pass through a half dozen rooms, each more opulent than the last, as florid and dream-like as gilded gesso, mother-of-pearl, colored glass, and inlaid everything can make them. But it proves less a history museum than a glimpse into the immoderate life of a Damascene aristocrat. Where are the Germans and the Turks? Lawrence? Auda? John the Baptist and the electric tram-cars that once clattered through town?

The last room, a reception hall as elegant and stiff as a powdered wig, contains, curiously, a collection of postcards, faded sepia images of genteel mustachioed notables of the twenties in fezes and morning coats—possibly King Feisal and his courtiers with their French overlords. There's nothing to identify them. The old man and I are at a loss.

Sensing my predicament, he sends for the curator, a tall, smartly dressed woman with flaming hair and dazed, preoccupied eyes. Her smattering of English, coupled with my French, allows a conversation of sorts. But a veil of perplexity descends at the mention of Lawrence. Why is this nosy stranger asking *her* about an unknown Englishman? Auda? Abd el Kadir? Town Hall? Mysteries all—as if the places and players of the Arab Revolt never existed.

———

The Souk al Hamadiyeh is the great market of the old walled city, a web of dim, covered, crowded passageways where storekeepers offer brass and copperware, jewelry, silks and carpets, sweets, nuts and spices, wedding gowns, *kefiyahs,* perfumes, coffee, leather, gold. Shoppers pass munching *booza booza* ices, while in echoing halls families gather at trestle tables to gobble bowls of *mahalabiyya,* milk pudding crusted with almonds and pistachios.

At its far end, the souk's vaulted roof gives way to what's left of the western gate of the Roman Temple of Jupiter: a pair of Corinthian columns supporting a decorated lintel. In the space beyond rises the Omayyed Mosque with its spacious courtyard and three minarets, and on the southeastern corner the lofty Minaret of Jesus, where, legend says, Jesus will appear on Judgment Day.

The Souks al Hamadiyeh and Madhat Pasha are the "markets" of Lawrence's triumphal tour. From the souks, thronged alleyways lead into a long street running to East Gate, the Street Called Straight, where the sudden roar of trucks and taxis is a blow. It was through East Gate and along the old Roman road, the Street Called Straight, that the Blue Mist roared and crowds cheered.

After a few blocks, a Roman arch soars over a small garden, complete with rosebush and bench, and I rest as traffic fumes past. This is the boundary of the Christian quarter. On a nearby corner stands St. Mary's Church, and not far, at Bab Kisan, the Chapel of St. Paul, built on the spot where the saint was lowered from a window in a basket to escape Jews angered by his preaching in the synagogues.

———

During the past two thousand years, the walls of Damascus were flattened and rebuilt a dozen times. The one standing today went up in the thirteenth century, but Bab Sharqi, a single utilitarian arch of pale stone big enough to drive a bus through, survives from Roman times.

The great Rolls-Roycean bulk of the Blue Mist, Lawrence waving from high on the back, his silken robes flying, would enliven the scene. Otherwise, Bab Sharqi is a prosaic chunk of municipal architecture.

Lawrence's route around the walls, down Ibn Assaker Avenue and the river to the citadel is too terrifyingly dense with smoking traffic to walk. Instead, I circle through the Christian neighborhoods of the old city, where the upper floors of houses nearly touch over narrow, twisting lanes, and shops and teahouses border little tree-shaded squares. At Bab as-Salam and Bab al-Faraj, bridges cross the green Barada tumbling down from the snows of the Anti-Lebanons.

The medieval citadel, part of the western wall, faces a continuing assault by vehicles circling Lawrence's Meidan along An Nasr Avenue. In the process of reconstruction, the old fortress, a tidy package of cautiously hewn, uniformly gray stone, has the look and feel of an attraction in a California theme park. An epic equestrian statue bestrides the pavement out front: Sal al-Din, Saladin, scourge of Christian crusaders, Arab hero—proving again the stale but apt adage that one man's terrorist is another's freedom fighter. Lawrence, the hit-and-run desert soldier who dynamited trains almost at will, was a terrorist to Turkish troops serving a long way from their Anatolian villages. But in England, to his ultimate regret, he became a legend.

It is less clear what Lawrence means to Arabs. In Akaba, where *Revolt in the Desert* and *Crusader Castles* were on display, and Talal Ahmed Abdullkadir showed me Lawrence's photo in the *Jordan Times,* Lawrence seems a popular hero. At Wadi Rumm, when Madela told me his grandfather had known Lawrence, I was convinced of this. Then the evidence grew thin. At Petra and Wadi Musa, not a sign. In Amman, when I asked a policeman for the home of Auda abu Tayi, he shrugged with incomprehension. The mention of Lawrence drew an empty gaze.

The plaque at the entrance to the Kusair al Azrak said "used by Lawrence," but the Jordanian guide hardly knew of him. Then surprisingly, at Deraa, his name came unbidden—Abdullah Hassan Abud asking point-blank if Lawrence knew the British and French would dominate the Middle East when war ended.

Of Damascus Lawrence wrote: "To my mind, the Arab Movement would not justify its creation if the enthusiasm of it did not carry the Arabs into Damascus . . . the capture of Damascus—which was what I expected from the Arabs, the reason why I had joined with them in the field, taken ten thousand pains, and spent my wit and strength."

Today, Hafez Assad is the man of the hour, Sal al-Din yesterday's hero. There are no portraits, no statues of Lawrence, no books in shops, no photos in the press. He is erased from history, a nonperson. Abdullah's question partially explains it—if he's recognized at all, he's an English-man who led the Arabs down the garden path of colonialism and set the stage for a Jewish state in Palestine. Hardly the stuff of Arab heros. None of this would surprise Lawrence, who was excruciatingly aware of both his role and his Englishness: "About the [English] soldiers hung the Arabs: gravely-gazing men from another sphere. My crooked duty had banished me among them for two years. To-night I was nearer to them than to the troops, and I resented it, as shameful . . . mixed with longing for home . . . to make fertile my distaste, till not merely did I see the unlike-ness of race, and hear the unlikeness of language, but I learned to pick between their smells: the heavy, standing, curdled sourness of dried sweat in cotton, over the Arab crowds; and the feral smell of English soldiers: that hot pissy aura of thronged men in woollen clothes."

———

An icy wind blows down from the Anti-Lebanons and citizens nav-igate the Meidan, bundled in sweaters and jackets, the men's *kefiyahs* tugged about their ears. Evening traffic streams along Khalid Ibn al-Waldi, then vanishes in a crimson river of taillights up Moussallam Baroudy Road. Corner teahouses are packed, and gangs of young men in headcloths and stubble beards hang around outside, watching me pass. Now and then, one squints through the smoke of a smoldering cigarette and shoots a comment in my direction. Nothing more sinister than "Welcome to Syria."

Where Said el Jabri Avenue intersects the Meidan, traffic circles the roundabout fronting the Hejaz Station. The floodlit portrait of the ubiq-uitous Hafaz Assad surmounts the station's columned porch, and to the right stands a green locomotive with red wheels—a 1908 French-built coal-burner that once towed carloads of pilgrims to the holy city of Medina. A survivor of Lawrence's dynamiting raids, it's plastered with pictures of the president—in the event one forgets the appearance of that venerable gentleman.

Stepping into the old station is like entering the lobby of a fanciful Arabian Nights movie palace of the twenties, one in which a picture hasn't shown in decades. Beneath a soaring coffered ceiling, Turkish tiles ring under the shoes of occasional passersby. A feeling of damp abandonment pervades: ticket windows are shut, offices closed. A light burns down a long corridor where a woman wearing a paisley head scarf passes time in a gloomy waiting room. Trains no longer run from the Hejaz Station, she explains. There's a new terminus in the distant suburbs for arrivals and departures. "Aleppo, Deir Ez-Zor, Qamishle, Latakia, Tartus, even Deraa—go wherever you like."

"No trains at all from Hejaz?"

"On Fridays, yes, in summer, an old steam train to the valley—to Ain el Fijah and Sarghya. People carry food in baskets and sit all day beside the river. It's shady there and cool—but not for some months yet."

The platform lies beyond tall oaken doors lit by panels of beveled glass. A string of ghostly freight cars rests along an abandoned siding and a half dozen passenger coaches from Lawrence's time, classic wooden cars with curtained windows and polished brass, stand to forlorn attention along the main line. Above the entrance to the first car projects a marquee of fading red canvas lettered in white: "Hejaz Bar."

Inside, solitary drinkers hunch over small tables in the long car while a bartender in a crisp tuxedo smiles expectantly, cramming ice into a silver cocktail shaker. "Something to drink, monsieur? Tom Collins? Whiskey sour?"

Hejaz Bar—a strange and unexpected end to a railway that once sped *hajjis* to the sacred cities of Arabia. In their white, seamless robes, they'd circled seven times Islam's Holy Stone, the black-cloaked Kabaa, and assured their entry into Paradise. Of October 3, 1918, his last day of command, Lawrence wrote, "Damascus was normal, the shops open, street merchants trading, the electric tramcars restored, grain and vegetables and fruits coming in well." Can he have imagined it so normal as this?

Tom Collins? Whiskey sour? I apologize and back away. Maybe later. Tomorrow, possibly. Another time. I stand on the platform in the shadow of the old station. Traffic beats around me in great waves; wind streams off the mountains. At a little curtained window, the bartender's face appears, trying to see where I've gone. A wave goodbye and I'm off. Of that final day, Lawrence wrote, "When Feisal had gone, I made to Allenby the last (and also I think the first) request I ever made him for myself—the leave to go away . . . In the end he agreed; and then at once I knew how much I was sorry."

Aleppo—Epilogue

I reach Aleppo through the eastern desert by way of Palmyra, where Roman columns march in flawless pink rows down sandy avenues. Here the English, by planting faked documents avowing eminent attack, kept the Turks "chained up in an unfortunate garrison . . . till the end of the war, much to our advantage." From Palmyra I head east to Albukamal, where the Euphrates flows into Iraq, then west again by way of Mari, Doura Europos, Deir Ez-Zur, and on through the lush Euphrates Valley.

An important trading center since Roman times and once the terminus of the Orient Express, Aleppo lies on the edge of a cultivated steppe, 230 miles north of Damascus. Its two million citizens are Palestinians and Circassians, Arabs, Jews, Iraqis, Uzbeks and Kazakhs, Kurds, Azerbaijanis, Turks, Chechens, Persians. Its roofed souks cover acres, and in the narrow lanes around Bab al Faraj are the shops of Armenian traders.

Here, in outfits of ersatz leather, their hair fried crisply golden or baked brittle yellow, broad-shouldered women from Georgia and the Ukraine, Byelorussians, Serbs and Croats, Slovaks, Hungarians, Russians, Rumanians, Bulgarians drag sad Brobdingnagian suitcases bulging with cheap baby clothes, cheap shoes, sleazy underwear, bolts of tiger-striped rayon and glittering imitation silks in and out of bargain hotels and aboard buses chartered for quickie shopping excursions. The same buses will carry them long miles back to melancholy homelands where they'll hawk their shoddy goods in street fairs and weekend markets. Yet there's a tough, good-natured camaraderie among these women, an abiding humor that gives this old quarter a sense of spirit and change.

———

The Baron Hotel is ten minutes from Bab al Faraj, along streets where cigarette hawkers wade through snarled traffic chanting, "Marlporoo! Marl-poroo!" and roving shoeshine boys sing out "Shine, monsieur

...shine!" Opened in 1909 by the Mazloumian brothers, a pair of quick-witted Armenians, the Baron was soon among the most popular hotels in the Middle East. In the days when Aleppo was the end of the line for the Orient Express, the Baron was a stopping place for such luminaries as Agatha Christie, Charles Lindbergh, Theodore Roosevelt, and Lady Mountbatten. Between 1910 and 1914, when he assisted in the British Museum's digs at Carchemish, Lawrence, too, frequently put up here.

The Baron's a handsome four-story place with iron grillwork and tall arched windows. The high-ceilinged halls and reception rooms are paneled in murky wood, hung with frayed engravings. Hardly luxurious, it needs paint; the plumbing's archaic, the furniture tattered and uncomfortable. But the Baron has that romantic patina of the Raj, suggesting intrigue and corruption, that should never be scrubbed away.

The downstairs lounge is crowded with buttoned couches, leather armchairs, a dozen low tables bearing shaded lamps. It's dim, silent, solemn on this cool April morning. In a case against a distant wall, a light glows softly over books arranged on glass shelves. One is propped open: *The Collected Letters of T. E. Lawrence*. It's easy to imagine Lawrence on a spring day, tea tray on the table beside him, letter paper braced against his knee. He writes his mother:

> Baron's Hotel, Aleppo
>
> 1 April 1914
>
> Another letter from this beautiful hotel, whose face you
> must be getting to know by heart.

On the shelf below, framed under glass, is "Mouricir Laurence's" unpaid bill:

> Baron's Hotel
> Mazloumian Frères, Alep (Syrie)
>
> Alep (Syrie) 8/6/1914
> Mouricir Laurence

March 6	4 jour pension	32–
April 1	. . . champagne	16–
	2 jour pension	16–
		64–
	. . . 2 Repas	3–
		61–

June 8	4 jour . . . dejour	30.50
	2 limonato	1.20
		92.70
		16–
		76.70

On those spring and summer days of 1914, the twenty-six-year-old Lawrence could not have foreseen the figure he would cut across the world's imagination. Though, perhaps he had an inkling, for he wrote, "I had dreamed, at the City School in Oxford, of hustling into form, while I lived, the new Asia which time was inexorably bringing upon us."

By October 3, 1918, it was over. With Feisal and Allenby in Damascus, Lawrence submitted his report and was relieved of duty. The white silks and Meccan headropes were put away, Lawrence of Arabia gone. The following year he turned up as a delegate at the peace conference and was later adviser on Arab affairs in the Colonial Office. The first draft of *Seven Pillars of Wisdom* was written in Paris in the winter and spring of 1919; then, near Christmas, while changing trains at Reading Station, Lawrence lost the 250,000-word manuscript. The following year he rewrote the book, using his memory and "two diaries and some of my surviving field-notes." The final 330,000-word book was printed in a small, private edition in 1926 and offered to subscribers. Not until his death was *Seven Pillars of Wisdom* published by Jonathan Cape in London and Doubleday in New York.

Lawrence, however, prepared *Revolt in the Desert,* a 130,000-word abridgment of *Seven Pillars of Wisdom,* serialized in the *Daily Telegraph* in 1926 and published the following year by Jonathan Cape, and George Doran in the United States. He later wrote *The Odyssey of Homer,* a prose translation, and *The Mint,* a controversial novel of military life, which appeared twenty years after his death.

Back in England, with his role in the Middle East behind him, Lawrence became an aircraftsman in the Royal Air Force, then a regular soldier in the army. In 1927, embarrassed by the "Lawrence of Arabia" legend, he changed his name to Shaw. There is much that is unexplained, contradictory, strange about this many-sided genius who lived on the masochistic side of asceticism—his conflicting and dissimilar selves, his need of punishment, his craving for fame and desire of obscurity, a fascination with disguise, and his symbolic suicides, taking up new lives and new names. Even the motorcycle crash that killed him is puzzling. A thread of evidence suggests there was foul play—a mysterious black car seen along the back lanes near his Dorset cottage the day he died. But then most cars were black in 1935.

—

If anything's changed since 1914, it's the Baron's wine list. The champagne that "Mouricir Laurence" drank and failed to pay for on that first of April more than eighty years ago is no longer on ice. The over-stuffed chairs, the tall barstools, the pale spring light seeping through shutters are doubtless the same. A fitting place for a last drink.

Across the room a familiar silver-haired man and his silver-haired wife sip pink gins. They were among the British travelers in Azrak the day the horn-rimmed scholar read Lawrence's narrative of the icy winter of 1917. Now, the silver-haired gent flourishes a copy of *The Times* at his wife.

"Seems Wilfred Thesiger's given up on Kenya . . . settled in London."

"Poor old dear, I'm sure he wanted to die out there . . . be eaten by the baboons . . . or whatever they are."

"Gotten a knighthood out of it, anyway . . . Sir Wilfred . . . must be some compensation."

"Compensation? For *not* being eaten by baboons?"

Though the Baron is steeped in the Lawrence legend and the young Lawrence spent hours in this high-ceilinged room, it's Thesiger they speak of—Thesiger for whom Lawrence was hero, role model, a standard by which the desert traveler forever measured himself and his achievements. Michael Asher, Thesiger's biographer, wrote of the World War II British army major, "The idea of fighting among the Arabs, with his Lawrentian images of camels and deserts, had fired his imagination."

In December 1946, Thesiger completed his most memorable journey: "I had crossed the Empty Quarter. It was fourteen days since we had left the last well at Khaur bin Atarit. To others my journey would have little importance. It would produce nothing except a rather inaccurate map that no-one was likely to use. It was a personal experience and the reward had been a drink of clean, tasteless water. I was content with that."

On this April afternoon in the Baron's bar, at the end of the line in Aleppo, with the silver-haired couple and Ahmed the barman for company, I doff my imaginary hat to Thesiger and toast the troubled, brilliant, enigmatic Lawrence: traveler, soldier, writer—my quarry since Akaba. I drink a tepid glass of Al Chark, Syria's thin, flavorless beer. I'm content with that.

5

The Pagan Soul

Lawrence Durrell and the Marine Venus

> Among the note-books of Gideon I once found . . . the
> word *Islomania*. There are people, Gideon used to say . . . who
> find islands somehow irresistible. The mere knowledge that
> they are on an island, a little world surrounded by the sea,
> fills them with an indescribable intoxication.
>
> Lawrence Durrell, *Reflections on a Marine Venus*

NOTHING SPILLS THE romantic wind from an islomane's sails more
than landing at the little port of Mandraki toward the end of the tourist
season. Yes, the crusader castle soars like a dream above the old town of
Rhodes, St. Nicholas's Lighthouse suns its medieval stones on the end of
the quay, and the Greek sea and sky are scrubbed the lucid blue of delft-
ware. But with the diesel stench of the hydrofoil from Turkey still in my
nose, it's hard to appreciate. There are taxis and tour buses to dodge,
sponge vendors, café touts, cruise operators, disco barkers, proprietors of
jewelry, fur, and leather boutiques, and their pastel prey: legions of sightseers, sporting water bottles and fanny packs, sunscreen and beach hats,
trooping over the obligatory stones in the wake of baying guides.

I arrive on the eve of the Little Summer of Saint Demetrius, the
limpid last two weeks of October when sightseers begin to fade. With
the tourist machinery shutting down and the pilgrims who feed it wing-
ing back to Liverpool, Stockholm, and Oshkosh, I'll search out the quiet
corners of this island Lawrence Durrell described so powerfully in *Reflections on a Marine Venus: A Companion to the Landscape of Rhodes*. If quiet
corners still exist. Can the Marine Venus possibly survive among the lan-
guishing glitz? And the Turkish Cemetery, with its oleander screen and

sun-bleached tombstones? Too much to expect: the abode of the Villa Cleoboulos and the banner-draped Tomb of Murad Reis.

———

The curator of the Archeological Museum, a buoyant young woman in plaid shirt and blue jeans, leads me from the archives in the Inn of France and over the cobbles of the Street of the Knights, assuring me I'll find what I'm after. We navigate historical stones: the Street of the Knights leads from the Palace of the Grand Masters, past the "Inns of the Tongues" to Alexander the Great Square. The curator is in a hurry. We race under a soaring arch of ginger-colored rock and dash around a corner.

There is no making sense of these medieval streets without appealing to history. The old town of Rhodes was built in the fourteenth century by the Order of the Knights of St. John. Members of a quasi-religious, quasi-military fraternity, the knights were among the crusader forces who stormed Jerusalem on a sweltering summer afternoon in 1099. Their tenancy in the Holy Land lasted until 1291, when Muslim soldiers turned them out and they retreated to Cyprus. To protect their western flank and keep communications open to Europe, they needed Rhodes. In the summer of 1309 they captured the island from the Emperor of Constantinople. The knights ruled until December 1522, when they were driven out by a Turkish army commanded by Suleiman the Magnificent. After gathering their possessions and embarking for Malta, the knights left behind some of the finest medieval fortifications in existence.

The poet, novelist, and travel writer Lawrence Durrell often prowled this old city. Born February 27, 1912, in Julundur, India, Durrell grew up in India, spent his young adult years in England, and later lived on the Mediterranean islands of Cyprus, Corfu, and Rhodes. He was with the British Occupying Forces when they arrived on Rhodes in the spring of 1945. In *Reflections on a Marine Venus,* he describes an afternoon carouse with his drinking companion Gideon: "We pursued our way across the deserted market-place and entered the old walled town of the Crusaders . . . At the spur of a gentle incline we turned into the famous Street of the Knights at the top of which lay the Castello." He enjoyed rambling the narrow lanes and drinking in shady *tavernas,* but scorned restorations undertaken by the Italians during their occupation from 1912 to 1943, calling the Castello "that monument to bad taste."

Durrell had little sympathy for the crusaders or their legacy of fortifications. Divided into national alliances, or "tongues," the knights were, after all, western European, not Greek. Describing the Acropolis hovering above the Rhodian village of Lindos, he wrote: "Here one regrets the intrusion of Byzantines and knights—everything sweaty-Christian should be scraped off, so that the pagan soul of the place can float free."

The "pagan soul" of Durrell's Rhodes was embodied in the Marine Venus, a first-century remodeling of an Aphrodite by the sculptor Diodalsa. To save her from the depredations of the Second World War, she had been hidden in a "damp crypt." Durrell was present when they winched her out. "When the pulleys finally raised her out of the darkness, slowly twisting on the end of her cable—why, which of us could fail to recognize the presiding genius of the place?"

Across the courtyard of what was once the Infirmary of the Knights, a broad staircase leads to the Archeological Museum. The curator steers me to the top and down a long room of saffron-colored stone flanked by Grecian marbles. She waves toward an object on a distant pedestal. "Just as I promised," she says. And with a quick goodbye she's off to her next appointment.

Until now I secretly believed Durrell imagined the Marine Venus, as if she were a fanciful prop around which he built his book. Even if he'd glimpsed her once, would I be so fortunate? I doubted it. But now we are alone in this golden room—just the two of us.

Today they call her "Aphrodite of Rhodes." She's smaller than I'd pictured, hardly two feet high, more lifelike, lovelier. Bent down on one knee, her upper body turns toward me as if in motion. Just bathed, she dries her hair, holding marble tresses to the sun. "The ripeness of her body was offset by the face, not of a Greek matron, but of a young girl."

We spend the morning together, the Marine Venus and I, watching the sun advance across the high windows, hearing the distant gossip of the museum guards. Now and then, to savor my good fortune in finding her, I step onto a terrace dense with bougainvillaea amid broken chunks of ancient marble. When I return I'm stunned to discover her still there. "It is as if our thoughts must be forever stained by some of her own dark illumination—the preoccupation of a stone woman inherited from a past whose greatest hopes and ideals fell to ruins. Behind and through her the whole idea of Greece glows sadly, like some broken capital, like the shattered pieces of a graceful jar, like the torso of a statue to hope."

———

On the marble steps of the *entrata grande* rest a tired transistor spluttering *bouzoúki* music and a watchman sunning himself. Sporting a tweed jacket and clipped mustache, he assumes a military air. The Albergo della Rosa, built by the Italians in the 1930s, is an immense Mussolinian cake of pink stone, a monstrous accretion of bombastic angles and rhetorical planes. The shut-up building has been unoccupied for years. When I rattle the door the watchman shakes his head in warning. Then, suddenly inspired, he asks in Tuscan sibilations if I speak Italian. "*Si, lo parlo.*" And Giovanni Zaneto unfolds like a deck chair and extends his hand.

On a spring night in 1945, after a stormy crossing from Alexandria, Lawrence Durrell mounted the Albergo's entrance. The hotel first billeted Italian, then German troops. Now, the English arrived. "At the end of the long corridor of darkness two tall gates rose up, and behind them the once famous *Albergo della Rosa,* showing here and there a point of light, weak and diffuse. The steps seemed endless—it was like climbing into the sky." Durrell napped on a sofa in the once-fashionable lobby, then was shown to a room upstairs. In the morning, before breakfast, he "burst into the Aegean water, clear and cold as wine. . . the blue race of the sea . . . deployed crisply across what must be one of the finest shingle beaches in the world."

Durrell was information officer with the British Occupying Forces, his task to produce three daily newspapers: Greek, Italian, Turkish. That first morning he went to work, plunging into the old town to hunt down printing presses. Rhodes was chaos. German forces had only recently surrendered, and wreckage littered the town. "The esplanade along Mandraccio, the ancient harbour, is studded with pill-boxes and long rows of iron staples from which grave Indian infantrymen are unwinding the barbed wire. Groups of German prisoners . . . are busy filling in the bomb-craters."

"Up there!" Giovanni Zanetos waves six floors up toward a sundeck surmounting the roof. "Italian artillerymen fired on the Turkish coast." Now sunlit Anatolian mountains rise a dozen miles across the straits. Easy to imagine bored soldiers taking potshots at distant crags.

Inside the Albergo the proportions are staggering, as if it had been built for indoor sport, skeet shooting and lacrosse, or Mussolini himself, chest barnacled in medals, haranguing noisy, black-shirted mobs. Beneath ceilings high as Olympian skies, Giovanni proudly points out huge, splashy paintings: the sylvan splendor of fascist gods—fawns and satyrs guzzling wine under the voluptuous gaze of acquiescent nymphs. The pictures are signed, "Afro—1938." In these vast rooms the Praetorian Guard had taken up quarters.

The forsaken, spacious old hotel hasn't changed much since Durrell's midnight arrival. Track lighting, installed during a television studio's fleeting tenancy, disfigures a few rooms. Foes of fresh air, the TV people glazed the great outdoor cafés facing Durrell's shingle beach. Upstairs, Giovanni warns, things have gone to ruin. "Masons imported from Italy built the place, but now it's not safe. The walls are crumbling." He sleeps somewhere below, cooks his frugal meals in immense basement kitchens originally built to feed hundreds.

With his transistor radio and collapsible chair, Giovanni poses for my camera at the top of the steps. His antique Vespa is parked on the drive. When the shutter clicks, he's a shadow in the Albergo's great, sun-drenched facade.

"Come back," he says. "It will be like old times. The Italians are coming—big investors with millions to spend. They'll redo the Albergo, make a casino—the best in Greece." We shake hands and I start toward Durrell's two tall gates. "It's true," Giovanni calls. "Just like old times!"

———

Prowling the island in a rented car, I find many of Durrell's rural haunts cemented over. At Mount Phileremo, where once "the Hellenic fountain breathed quietly, half asleep," there isn't a slot for my toy car among the tour buses. In Soroni, during the Festival of St. Saul, Durrell joined in dancing and feasting under the shade of pines. I discover pastel curio stalls and a dearth of trees. Rodini is now suburban. From Paradissi on the west to Archangelos on the east, the beaches, bordered by soulless hotels, are engulfed each summer with topless sunbathers.

———

Whitewashed Lindos lies on a pair of peacock-blue bays thirty-five miles south of Rhodes, along the island's rugged eastern coast. Durrell called it "the official beauty-spot of Rhodes." The house where I'm staying belongs to friends of friends. With rosy sandstone arches and mosaic floors, it was built in 1620, the year our Pilgrim forebears set their buckled shoes on Plymouth Rock.

The Acropolis soars overhead—sheer cliffs crowned by a medieval tonsure of crusader walls and the Doric columns of the Temple of Athena Lindia. Late on a summer afternoon Durrell peered over the edge into the sea, six hundred feet below. "Down there on the darkening water lay a tiny fishing-boat like a model. 'Listen,' said E. In the silence, like the voice of an insect, came the strains of a fisherman singing. The sound slanted up at us through the canyons of coloured rock."

Today Lindos is awash with T-shirt emporiums and English disco devotees. Durrell's singing fisherman, if he dares lift his voice, goes quite unheard. In his travel guide *The Greek Islands* Durrell said, "Only brisk tourism will keep the island's economy balanced." Earlier, he had written: "I am a romantic in the French sense" (*Réalités,* November 1960). Durrell the romantic cannot have foreseen that supreme destroyer of romance, the packaged tour.

———

The gravel road climbs a dozen miles through pine forests, crosses tilled upland valleys where families harvest olives among silvery trees, then mounts steeply into Laerma. My hike from the coast has taken a long December afternoon. There are twenty houses, a new church with an antique tower, and a *taverna* where a suave old waiter serves coffee under a sycamore tree. Inside, backgammon players argue and rattle dice. Otherwise, silence. Everyone's in the fields. It's dark when the mayor finally comes from his groves to give his approval: I can bed down for the night in the Town Hall.

It's consoling to discover that the southern half of the island and the barren ridges radiating from Mount Attaviros remain as Durrell found them. "[We] turned right, to circle the great charred butt of Atabyron, whose stony ramps of black rock made it seem more than ever medieval. . . . We pushed on across this razor-back landscape of rock and thistle."

In the morning chill, steam rising from gardens on the outskirts of town, I leave Laerma for Agios Isodoros. The road ascends switchbacks through pine woods. Once or twice cars pass, now and then a garden

tractor on which farmers ride to their fields. Two hours of steady climbing bring me into a high valley. The whitewashed walls of the Monastery
of Artamitou gleam in distant sunlight. As I round a low hill purple with
heather, the clustered houses of faraway Agios Isodoro hang on a rocky
shelf beneath the summit of Mount Attaviros.

"It is partly poverty that keeps the Greeks so happy, so spare and in
tune with things," Durrell wrote in *The Greek Islands*. The sentiments,
clearly, of a well-heeled dreamer. Yet in these mountain valleys, where
families offer rides aboard rattling tractors or pause in the olive harvest to
shout hello, *Kahleemerah,* and wave from windy trees, I want to agree.
How unlike the sour tycoons of the coast growing fat off the tourist
boom.

After a late lunch of wild greens, olives, *feta* cheese and a flask of
retsina at the Taverna Isodoros, I relax in a field of clover beside the
Chapel of St. George. Far to the southwest gleams an azure slice of the
Aegean Sea, to the northeast fertile valleys and distant indigo ridges. A
chill edges into my bones as the afternoon sun slips behind the mountain.

All evening a fire blazes in the potbellied stove at the Taverna
Isodoros. Shouts of card players fill the room. Beside me the village
priest, a white bearded ancient in cassock and stovepipe hat, deaf as one
of Attaviros' stones, sips sweet Greek coffee and smiles benignly. The
room, once white, is tarred caramel with cigarette smoke, and generations
of hand-tinted photos embellish resinous walls.

This village atop the island's spine is Durrell's Greece. These are the
landscapes and people he wrote of in his stunning "island trilogy." The
first of these books, about Corfu, was *Prospero's Cell*. Next came *Reflections on a Marine Venus,* followed by his volume on Cyprus, *Bitter Lemons*.

In the warmth and noise of the *taverna,* I buy the priest another coffee, order *ouzo* for myself. Beyond the open door a full moon hangs
above the valley. The weather's turned bitter, and a pale scarf of cloud
flies from the shoulders of Attaviros. I toss back the first drink, then
another. Clear and strong, a product of the village still, seasoned with a
suspicion of wild anise, the *ouzo* seems a fitting libation to honor
Lawrence Durrell's paean to the island of Rhodes.

———

Monte Smith rises over the city of Rhodes, its lower slopes dense with suburbs. Near the top, posh condominiums give way to fields, cypresses, lovely old farmhouses dripping vines. From a distant pasture a white mare and her black colt watch as I plod toward the summit. In transparent winter air the slender columns of the Temple of Apollo rise above dense pines. The colt nickers, then canters after me.

Durrell often watched the sunset from the temple. "Today, after lunch we walked, the four of us, up the gentle slopes of Monte Smith, past the little light-house where the Indians are quartered, and along the broad and lovely road which leads to Trianda. Beneath us the blue carpet of sea stretched away to Anatolia."

I've come to see the sun mirrored on Turkey's snows. Rhodes lies below: the walled crusader fortress, the tree-lined avenues of the new town. From up here Mandraki Harbor bursts with the blues and whites of the Greek flag. When we pass under the trees to the temple steps, the colt whinnies and gallops back to his dam.

There is no ticket kiosk, no asphalt path. I wander alone among Doric columns erected in the second century B.C.E. Underfoot, the pale lavender of wildflowers fades among stones. Down the slope a stadium is dug into a hillside, five tiers of ancient stone seats shaded by olive and cypress trees. "In this green and sleepy hollow an old shepherd kept his flock of sheep, standing under the great oak-tree which crowns the amphitheatre. Descending the terraces slowly, Sand points out all that remains of the ancient city—a few outcrops of stone-carved tombs."

———

I cross the old town from Koskinou to St. Paul's Gate, then exit onto the harborfront. Along the outer jetty, yachts are moored under a trio of Byzantine windmills; tour boats, gangways stowed for the winter, crowd the seawall. In January sunlight I pass the post office, the Church of Evangelismos, the Gothic porch of the Archbishop's Palace, the pastel Mussolinian block of the National Theater.

The Moslem Cemetery continues to elude me. Durrell wrote: "It is buried in overhanging trees, and hidden in a triple circle of oleanders and rhododendrons." If it survives, it must be near the Albergo della Rosa. Maybe Giovanni Zanetos will know. I'm on my way to ask but mistakenly turn into an unfamiliar street. It's like a country lane in the heart of the city, dim and overgrown. Soon I'm among lemon and eucalyptus trees. Above a fence and an oleander hedge, I glimpse the peaked cap of a squat minaret.

The street leads to an iron gate. I push through and walk beneath shaggy trees, among Turkish tombstones. A crumbling wall lies ahead. When I peer over—it's like looking into an old black-and-white photo: the frontispiece of *Reflections on a Marine Venus*. Here at last is the Villa Cleobolus, the flag-draped Tomb of Murad Reis. "We stumbled upon the little garden which encircles the Mosque of Murad Reis—a garden at whose heart I was later to find the Villa Cleobolus; and here we sat for a while perched upon Turkish tombstones, smoking and enjoying the darkness."

Sabak Kororo, a tiny, alert woman of eighty-three, carefully sweeps the mosaicked courtyard. She wears a shapeless blue smock, a pink bandanna bound over crimped hair, and a look of cheerful determination. A fire smolders against a garden wall. She sweeps leaves into a basket, tosses them onto the blaze. The sharp smell of winter smoke fills the air. When I speak, Sabak Kororo turns from the fire, smiling.

The old woman leads me over a pebbled path, through a low doorway, and into a dim, circular room. "Murad Reis," she whispers, pointing beneath a blue dome daubed with stars to the holy man's catafalque smothered in emerald silk. Through a haze of incense, pale light falls from a low window. In the dimness I admire an etching of the bearded, hawk-nosed divine. His searching eyes probe from beneath a turbaned brow like the gaze of the prophet Ezekiel turned toward Babylon.

Farther along, beneath its minaret, is the little Mosque of Murad Reis, and opposite it a whitewashed cottage with green shutters, the Villa Cleobolus, hardly larger than a doll's house. "A tiny studio, bedroom and bathroom. That is all. A coloured table built around the trunk of a baobab-tree makes a shady dining room." Sabak Kororo points to herself, then to the cottage. "*Casa mia.*" She rests her head on folded arms to mimic sleeping. *Casa mia*? Is it possible she speaks Italian? When I ask, she taps her chest: "Tuuur-kish." I wish her, "*Günaydin.*" Good morning. "*Günaydin,*" she responds, and her smile broadens.

Inside, despite the villa's opened shutters, it's dim as a cave, so small that light can't enter—everything in miniature. I duck to clear the door-way, crouch beneath low beams. "It is simply a match-box of a house, but its situation is more beautiful than anything." In this womblike cell I pic-ture Durrell writing the poems of *On Seeming to Presume* and *A Land-mark Gone,* as well as gestating the complex novels of *The Alexandria Quartet: Justine, Balthazar, Mountolive, Clea.* Pursewarden and Scobie, Melissa, Justine, Clea, Narouz and Nessim, Mountolive and Balthazar surely drew their first fictional breath in this toy house.

Durrell summed it up in a passage from *The Greek Islands:* "For two lucky years I was able, by virtue of my job with the occupying force, to swim at the *Albergo Della Rosa* beach and to inhabit a tiny studio buried in flowering hibiscus hard by—at the shrine of Murad Reis which still exists, though the old Mufti is dead."

For an hour I relax in the little garden beneath the baobab tree. The chairs pulled close to a small table are made of bent wire, the kind of chairs you find in old-fashioned ice cream parlors. When she's finished sweeping, Sabek Kororo vanishes into the Villa Cleobolus and, after a few minutes, returns with a copper beaker of steaming coffee. She carefully arranges a pair of thimble-sized cups on the table, then tall glasses of cold water. This was Durrell's "shady dining room," where he and his friend "E." were often joined by Gideon and Sand, sometimes even by the mufti himself. This morning the old Turkish woman fills the cups, then sits across the table. The coffee is sweet, black, and strong, thick with the bit-ter grounds that Turks favor in their brew. When I've finished, the old woman, suddenly turned fortune-teller, upturns my cup on its saucer and peers into the dregs for a sign of my future.

I'm too content with the present to give it much thought. Durrell lived two years in this garden with its diminutive house—packed, creative years during which he must have planned much of his future writing. Would that Sabek Kororo, studying the coffee grounds, might find that I could stay so long—and so profitably.

6

Where the Tigers Were
Thomas Mann's Venice

Very well then, he would travel. Not all that far, not quite to
where the tigers were . . .

Thomas Mann, *Death in Venice*

DRAPED IN THE shabby robe in which he had sewn a fortune in jew-
els, Marco Polo stepped ashore in his native Venice after twenty-four
years traveling in Cathay. The explorer's tales of the rich life, the luxurious hunting parties, the sumptuous golden palaces in the fabled land of
Kubla Kahn, soon made him the laughingstock of the Rialto. Riding a
vaporetto down the Grand Canal on a drizzly May morning seven hundred years later, I wonder what the notables of the court of the Great
Kahn made of Polo's account of his birthplace?

It's hard to imagine a city as romantic, as magical, or as beautifully
bizarre as Venice. Glowing sensually along myriad canals, it's as luminous
as a pocketful of Marco Polo's gems strewn along the rim of its velvet
lagoon. It was here Thomas Mann set *Death in Venice,* his haunting
novella of art and self-destruction. The 1929 Nobel laureate could not
have chosen better than *La serenissima,* "the most Serene City," as Venetians like to call it, to work out his struggle between order and passion in
the story of Gustav von Aschenbach's obsession with the Polish boy
Tadzio.

But *La serenissima* chose Mann. In May 1911, with his wife, Katia,
and his brother Heinrich, he traveled to the Istrian Peninsula, where the
trio relaxed for a week on the island of Brioni, then sailed for Venice. In
A Sketch of My Life Mann describes the journey's serendipitous events:
"Nothing is invented: . . . the gloomy ship from Pola . . . the suspect gon-

dolier, Tadzio and his family, the departure prevented by a muddle with the luggage, the cholera, the honest clerk at the travel agency." The somber masterpiece of passion and death that resulted is perhaps the most perfect of the German novelist's shorter works.

The morning train rolls across the causeway and glides to a stop at Venice's Stazione Santa Lucia. It's early May, misty and cool—more than eighty years after the doomed Aschenbach arrived so splendidly by sea: "Thus it was that he saw it once more, that most astonishing of all landing places, that dazzling composition of fantastic architecture which the Republic presented to the admiring gaze of approaching seafarers: the unburdened splendor of the Ducal Palace, the Bridge of Sighs, the lion and the saint on their two columns at the water's edge, the magnificently projecting side wing of the fabulous basilica . . . and as he contemplated it all he reflected that to arrive in Venice by land, at the station, was like entering a palace by the back door."

Yet the back door presents its own splendor: the dome of the Church of San Simone Piccolo shimmering across a dark sweep of the Grand Canal, the Scalzi Bridge, the gilded facades of sixteenth-century palaces. Drizzle turns to chilling rain as the *vaporetto* churns from Santa Lucia toward San Marco. Among a flotilla of cargo boats navigating toward the public market, the damp crew of a passing barge squat amid a glorious cargo of blossoming geraniums. Halfway into the first bend of the Grand Canal the boat nudges a pier: Cá D'Oro. I leap ashore beneath the gilt facade of the old *palazzo*, hurry across the Campo and the Strada Nuova and lose myself in a warren of dim lanes.

The Hotel Bernardi-Sermenzato, on Calle dell'Oca—Street of the Goose—is smaller than its name. My whitewashed room boasts antique beams and views of tiled rooftops. Across the tight canyon of the Calle I discover a nameless café serving flasks of wine, heaping platters of *pasta al vongole,* and the delectable bite-size squids Venetians call *calamaretti*. Up the street, where feral cats haunt dim doorways, I enter the Campo Apostoli, with its neighborhood church and little forest of plane trees. A ten-minute walk takes me into Piazza San Marco: "That most astonishing of . . . places, that dazzling composition of fantastic architecture."

The great Byzantine basilica is golden, the Doge's Palace a stunning pink, both magnificent confections floating airily against a gauzy sky, dazzling displays of Venetian pride, wealth, and power. This morning the piazza is nearly submerged—not by the Adriatic but by a tide of milling tourists. Yet it's still Venice. Still exciting. After taking a table in an elaborate little cabinet at Florian's, I order an espresso, feeling exactly like a character from *Don Giovanni*. A favorite subject for writers and painters since it opened in 1720, Florian's is still as ornate and elegant as a Baroque stage setting. Both Mann and Aschenbach frequented the place: "In mid-afternoon [Aschenbach] took the vaporetto across the stale-smelling lagoon to Venice. He got out at San Marco, took tea on the Piazza, and then . . . set off on a walk through the streets." Not in the pursuits of the sightseer but in pursuit of the beautiful boy Tadzio: "On Sunday . . . the Poles never appeared on the beach; he rightly guessed that they were attending mass in San Marco, and hastened to the church himself. There, stepping from the fiery heat of the Piazza into the golden twilight of the sanctuary, he would find him whom he had missed . . . Then he would stand in the background, on the cracked mosaic floor . . . and the massive magnificence of the oriental temple would weigh sumptuously on his senses."

———

Sunday morning I cross the Campo Apostoli and find my way along the Marzaria to San Marco. Sunlight gleams from the dome of the great basilica. For a while, I stand in the golden light beneath mosaicked arches, watching the mass unfold through candle smoke and incense. When the priest turns from the altar to bless the congregation, I slip quickly back into the piazza. "Then, when the great doors were opened and the crowd streamed out into the shining Piazza swarming with pigeons, the beguiled lover would hide in the antebasilica, he would lurk and lie in wait . . . he would observe the boy, the cloistral sisters and the governess turn right and walk through the clock tower gateway into the Merceria, and after letting them get a little way ahead he would follow them—follow them furtively on their walk through Venice."

———

Each day I cross the piazza and make my way through the gateway of the fifteenth-century clock tower where two mechanical bronze Moors hammer out the hours on a great brass bell. Here, where Aschenbach trailed "that noble figure . . . beauty itself," I begin my walk. The city unpeels from the core of the piazza like an onion.

Sightseers vanish into shops peddling Marco Polo T-shirts and gaudy Murano glass, or drain Cokes at restaurant tables forested with pastel napkins fashioned into Gothic cathedrals. Tourist traps give way to hardware stores, neighborhood cafés, *alimentari* where cheeses and lengths of salami swing from shadowy rafters. *Calles* open into *campos,* little squares surrounded by tall, shuttered houses, or cross humpbacked bridges over shady canals.

Here, in Venice's out-of-the-way corners, Mann's symbols of eros and death weave patterns in the sensuous luxuriance of the tale. "This was Venice, the flattering and suspect beauty—this city, half fairy tale and half tourist trap, in whose insalubrious air the arts once rankly and voluptuously blossomed . . . Gripped by his adventure, the traveler felt his eyes drinking in this sumptuousness."

Out beyond the Jewish Ghetto, Murano and Burano lie across the silvery lagoon and, in the misty distance, low-lying Torcello with its ghostly medieval cathedral. Just offshore, outlined in the gloom by black ramparts of cypress trees, floats San Michele, the cemetery island.

Narrow canals lead toward the broad sweep of the Rio della Misericordia, where lopsided old *palazzi* of ocher and faded maroon look about to topple into their own reflections. I turn into a lane, mount a bridge, and find myself in a deserted *campo.*

Although I've come across it by accident, the place is hauntingly familiar, as if I'd spent a childhood summer here. Thumbing open *Death in Venice,* I discover the *campo's* description: "A little square, one that seemed to have been abandoned, to have been put under a spell, opened up in front of him . . . On the steps of the well in its center he sat down and leaned his head against the stone rim. The place was silent, grass grew between the cobblestones . . . Among the dilapidated houses of uneven height all round him there was one that looked like a *palazzo,* with Gothic windows that now had nothing behind them, and little lion balconies. On the ground floor of another there was a chemist's shop. From time to time warm gusts of wind blew the stench of carbolic across to him." There, at its end, where the *campo* branches into an alleyway, is the

Gothic *palazzo* with its lion balconies. Nearby are the well and the chemist's shop. Clumps of grass sprout between cobblestones and a faded sign stenciled across a wall of worn stones reads, "Campo dei Mori"— Square of the Dead.

For a moment I stand with my back to the city, gazing into eerie and empty space, this place of death, astonished that the feverish Aschenbach is not here but has somehow picked himself from the well's stone rim and found his way back into the ailing heart of *La serenissima*.

In a setting steeped in exoticism and sensuality, where "out of little overhead gardens umbelliferous blossoms spilled over and hung down the crumbling masonry," Mann introduced a permeating sickness. The year of his visit a cholera epidemic ravaged Palermo, not Venice, but Mann used the contagion to heighten his mood of doomed eroticism: "Sitting at his round wrought-iron table on the shady side of the Piazza, [Aschenbach] suddenly scented in the air a peculiar aroma, one which it now seemed to him he had been noticing for days . . . a sweetish, medicinal smell that suggested squalor and wounds and suspect cleanliness."

Fearful of harming the tourist trade, authorities suppressed the truth of the epidemic. Aschenbach pressed a British travel agent for details: "Asiatic cholera had been showing an increased tendency to spread . . . Originating in the sultry morasses of the Ganges delta, rising with the mephitic exhalations of that wilderness of rank useless luxuriance, that primitive island jungle shunned by man, where tigers crouch in the bamboo thickets."

Aschenbach had not gone "quite to where the tigers were." The tigers came to him. His obsession with Tadzio left him powerless. Plague-stricken Venice would have its say: "Tadzio stayed on; and to Aschenbach, in his beleaguered state, it sometimes seemed that all these unwanted people all round him might flee from the place or die, that every living being might disappear and leave him alone on this island with the beautiful boy."

———

On a chill, showery morning, tossed about in a motor launch, we cross from the Molo at San Marco to Giudecca, then to the island church of San Giorgio Maggiore, and at last navigate the broad lagoon to the Lido. It was on the Lido, in a reception room of the Hotel des

Bains, that Aschenbach first saw Tadzio: "A long-haired boy of about fourteen. With astonishment Aschenbach noticed that the boy was entirely beautiful."

It's a short walk from the landing to the Gran Viale S. M. Elisabetta, "that white-blossoming avenue, bordered on either side by taverns and bazaars and guesthouses, which runs straight across the island to the beach." After a block of pink marble sidewalks, I duck out of the cold into a quiet café. The boulevard outside, flanked by shade trees and blooming oleander, is nearly deserted. A clairvoyant waiter in a trim white jacket brings the steaming cappuccino I haven't yet ordered but which is exactly what I crave. "Grazie! Il Hotel des Bains, dove?"

His English is precise, though heavily accented, as if he's rehearsed his answer. "The viale to the beach—two hundred meters—turn right. The *signore* can't miss it."

The viale intersects the Lungomare Marconi. A bus hisses past, a shock after a week of gondolas and *vaporetti*. Across the Lungomare, over gloomy dunes, lies a gloomier sea flat and opaque as iron. Down the broad boulevard lifts a screen of emerald pines and the dove-gray wing of a great hotel. "What a place this was indeed, combining the charms of a cultivated seaside resort in the south with the familiar ever-ready proximity of the strange and wonderful city!"

Beyond wrought-iron gates and a graveled drive, marble steps mount to a veranda strewn with urns of yellow pansies. Tall glass doors frame a pair of wicker armchairs flanking a table covered by white linen. Over high columns bearing ironwork sconces, gaunt letters span the entablature:

HOTEL DES BAINS

Time has stopped, the clock turned back. The great sweep of the veranda lies empty, a stage setting awaiting the first actor. Aschenbach might emerge at any moment, settle on the white cushions of an armchair. "He took tea on the front terrace, then went down to the esplanade and walked some way along it."

In the hushed entry a placard announces a seminar for British computer engineers. There's not a sign of them, not a sound. Possibly, they're locked away somewhere dreaming of mysterious software or brooding over keyboards. Except for a porter and a clerk in green livery motionless behind an oaken reception desk, the lobby is empty. "The kind of ceremonious silence prevailed here which a large hotel always aims to achieve."

From distant reception halls, burnished and gleaming with fresh paint of luscious peach and deep cream, comes the subdued glow of shaded lamps. Can Aschenbach be far? Will Tadzio "in his striped linen suit with the red breast knot [come] from the sea, through the beach barrier and along the boarded walks back to the hotel?"

———

"A waiter circulated and announced in English that dinner was served. Gradually the company disappeared through the glass door into the dining room." This morning the dining room is empty, silent, vast, its unlit chandeliers of Murano glass floating beneath a high coffered ceiling. Light from the garden spills through French doors and exquisitely molded fanlights to shimmer on a score of tables set with goblets, heavy silver, napkins of ivory damask. Suddenly, I'm faint with hunger. What delicacies might be served? What gastronomic abundance? Now, breakfast completed, there's no sign of lunch, not a whiff of cooking. It's as if the Hotel des Bains exists in a state of suspended animation, as if everything hinges on Aschenbach and the boy. When will they appear?

On the evening of Aschenbach's arrival, the great writer sat in the reception hall reading a newspaper and watching the boy. "The young Poles were still waiting round their cane chair, and Aschenbach . . . having the spectacle of beauty before his eyes, waited with them." Soon, the Polish children were joined by their mother and followed her in to dinner: "The girls in order of age, after them the governess, finally the boy. For some reason or other he turned round before crossing the threshold . . . his strangely twilight-gray eyes met those of Aschenbach . . ." Thus begins one of the most remarkable facets of this remarkable story, Mann's subtle observation of the act of falling in love.

It is a love inherently tragic, self-destructive, unrequitable, doomed at the outset by Mann's ambivalence between sensuality and morality, an ambivalence that tightens the spring of dramatic tension. Aschenbach, an artist dedicated to order, form, dignity, is overthrown by beauty and its erotic implications. In the dining room of the Hotel des Bains, beneath the dazzling Venetian chandeliers, Aschenbach's metamorphosis begins: "He lingered for another few minutes, then he too crossed into the dining rooms and had himself shown to his table—which, as he noticed with a brief stirring of regret, was at some distance from that of the Polish family."

———

Aschenbach "went through the hall accompanied by the courteous attentions of the hotel staff, went down over the great terrace and straight along the wooden passageway to the enclosed beach reserved for hotel guests."

This morning the beach is empty, the sand damp from a week's rain. A gaunt pier of crumbling concrete reaches into a leaden sea. Before one of the conical-roofed bathing huts, shut now against the weather, Aschenbach had settled beneath a brown awning. "Three or four hours were then his, hours in which the sun would rise to its zenith . . . hours in which the sea would turn a deeper and deeper blue, hours in which he would be able to watch Tadzio."

At the water's edge small waves draw away the sand, leaving shells and pebbles behind, a swatch of color in a world gone monotonously gray. I walk for a while, skipping stones across the drab surface of the water. It's warmer now, a damp, cloying warmth dashed by sudden splashes of rain. Offshore, below a bruised sky, a fishing boat navigates from left to right like a cursor across a dimmed screen. Here along this stretch of beach the Polish boy was often found "in the blue and white bathing costume which now on the beach was his sole attire—this charmingly trivial, idle yet ever-active life . . . a life of sauntering, wading, digging, snatching, lying about and swimming, under the watchful eyes . . . of the women on their platform, who with their high-pitched voices would cry out his name: 'Tadziu! Tadziu!'"

On this sodden beach at the Hotel des Bains, in this small corner of the world remarkably unaltered in ninety years, *Death in Venice* worked out its final struggle between dignity and passion. Aschenbach's ardor for the Polish boy stripped him of his self-protective will to flee the epidemic. At the novella's end, while reclining in his accustomed chair, Aschenbach, "the master, the artist who had achieved dignity, he who in such paradigmatically pure form had repudiated . . . the murky depths, who had proclaimed his renunciation of all sympathy with the abyss," succumbed to the contagion as the boy turned from the sea's edge and looked back: "Resting his head on the back of his chair, [Aschenbach] had slowly turned it to follow the movements of the walking figure in the distance; now he lifted it toward this last look; then it sank down on his breast . . . while his face wore the inert, deep-sunken expression of profound slumber. But to him it was as if the pale and lovely soul-summoner out there were smiling to him, beckoning to him; as if he loosed his hand from his hip and pointed outward . . . into an immensity rich with unutterable expectation. And as so often, he set out to follow him."

———

It's late when the launch leaves the pier at the Lido and crosses toward the classical towers and domes of Palladio's San Giorgio Maggiore, then crescent-shaped Giudecca with its surreal villas and shadowy little squares. At last Venice, the light over the lagoon turning solid stone translucent, as intangible as a reflection on water, the city's domes and spires, its grand *palazzi* awash in colored light reflected, refracted, and repeated between sea and sky.

Other cities rich in art and architecture are built on islands threaded by canals, but there is only one Venice. No other city has so forcefully appealed to the romantic imagination, an appeal not without peril, a peril Thomas Mann clearly understood. For it was here he explored his themes of the precariousness of Western bourgeois culture, the tragic dilemma of the artist, and the seductions of eros, spirituality, and death. Mann's great writer Gustave von Aschenbach and the boy Tadzio are a part of the pervasive atmosphere of the city, an atmosphere that sets *La serenissima* apart not only from all other cities of the world but from the tangible world itself.

7

Le Mura degli Angeli
Giorgio Bassani on the Walls of the Angels

SIGNORA COLLEVATTI, THE AGED concierge, opened the door on the second ring, then stepped aside for me to pass. The small house at the end of Via delle Vigne stood against a high wall lined with ancient trees. Three padlocked gates stood in the wall, one a broad central gate through which a hearse could pass, narrow gates on either side for mourners on foot. "Benvenuto, Signor," the old woman exclaimed with a sharp Ferrarese accent. Wearing a dowdy housedress, she crossed a small room as gray as her chignon, then bent to take something from a cupboard. The cry of a child came from the back of the house, along with the savory aroma of simmering stew. The woman lay the object on a table—a yarmulke of black cloth that perched unsteadily on my head when I put it on. I found myself postured like a student in an old-fashioned finishing school balancing a book. Although I'd never worn one before, the signora smiled her approval, then waved me toward a door opening onto a meadow shaded by plane trees, ginkgoes, white candelabra of flowering ash. I readjusted the yarmulke, then stepped into Ferrara's Cimitero Ebraico, the opening scene of Giorgio Bassani's *The Garden of the Finzi-Continis.*

This haunting, elegiac novel renders the lives of a rich, reclusive Jewish family living in the Barchetto del Duca with its great house, "the *magna domus* . . . isolated down there among the mosquitoes and frogs" in Ferrara's northeastern corner. The unnamed narrator is a young, middle-class Jew intrigued by the Finzi-Contini family since childhood, especially the two children, Alberto and Micòl. In the autumn of 1938, at the age of twenty-two, the narrator, like other Jewish members of the

Eleonora d'Este Tennis Club, had been forced to resign. He and a small group were invited by the Finzi-Continis to play on their private court. From the moment he entered the garden, "to be more precise, the vast park that surrounded the Finzi-Contini house before the war, and spread over almost twenty-five acres," he became emotionally involved with the family. The story follows this growing intimacy and especially his infatuation with Micòl, the daughter. At the same time it portrays the crisis of Ferrara's Jews, targeted for deportation to Germany.

———

I came on the morning train from Venice's Santa Lucia station, crossing the causeway to Mestre, then on to Padua. After Padua the train gathered speed. Beyond windows tinted a faded sea green, the flat farmland of the Po Valley swept to the horizon. Tile-roofed houses of lion-colored stone stood along dusty, poplar-lined roads bordering fields of young wheat, corn, and vegetables, and orchards of espaliered trees— pears, peaches, apricots—their carefully tended limbs supported by lattices. We sped through Rovigo and after twenty minutes crossed the Po, broad and slow, a ribbon of chased silver sliding between tree-lined banks. We passed from the Veneto into Emilia-Romagna, and ten minutes later rolled into the old brick-and-steel station at Ferrara.

Under the dynasty of the Este dukes, a political force throughout the Renaissance, Ferrara became a haven for many painters of the day: Francesco Cossa and Cosimo Tura, Dosso Dossi, Jacopo Bellini, Pisanello, and Andrea Mantegna. "The Duke desires . . . every day to decorate and magnify this his city of Ferrara with new edifices and palaces," wrote a contemporary of Ercole I, a fifteenth-century scion of the Este family. Encouraged by his wife, Leonora d'Aragona, Ercole imported architects, scholars, and musicians. Theater flourished, the Renaissance poet Lodovico Ariosto wrote his epic *Orlando Furioso,* artists built and embellished the Castello Estense, which, behind its moat, still dominates the city center. From Nicolò II, who commissioned the castle, through Ercole, his grandson Alfonso I who married Lucrezia Borgia, and the last Este duke, Nicolò II, who brought Tasso and Guarini to his court, the Este dynasty made Ferrara one of the most splendid urban centers of the time.

From the Middle Ages to the present, Ferrara has been a center of

Italian Jewry. Under the protection of the Este family, Jewish immigrants came from Spain, Portugal, and Germany. By the sixteenth century the Jewish community numbered two thousand, with ten synagogues and a rabbinical court. In 1598, when Nicolò II failed to produce an heir, Ferrara passed under papal sovereignty and Jews were forced to wear yellow shawls and forbidden to own property. In 1627 Ferrara's ghetto was isolated from the city, its five gates locked from sunset to daybreak. Briefly, during the Napoleonic occupation, Jews regained their civil rights, but the reestablishment of papal rule saw them herded again into the ghetto. Not until the Risorgimento, the fall of the Papal States and the founding of the Kingdom of Italy in 1861, did they achieve their freedom and begin to assimilate, culturally and economically, into the nation's fabric. Ferrara then saw the rise of a well-to-do Jewish bourgeoisie, to which the Bassani family belonged.

Born in Bologna, Giorgio Bassani (1916–2000) came to Ferrara as a small child to live at number 1 Via Cisterna del Follo, near the Punta della Giovecca. With his grandparents, parents, and younger brother and sister, Paolo and Jenny, he spent an untroubled childhood and adolescence in the serene atmosphere of the old dwelling.

Tranquil existence ended abruptly in 1938, when Mussolini aligned himself with Hitler's anti-Semitism and instituted the racial laws. Jews faced a new wave of discrimination that eventually, with German occupation, propelled them into Nazi death camps. The unanticipated moment of betrayal, when Jews were first excluded from the Fascist Party, then from the social and economic life of the nation, absorbed Bassani. This theme runs through his fiction: *The Goldrimmed Eyeglasses, The Heron, Behind the Door, The Smell of Hay,* and *Five Stories of Ferrara.* Nowhere is it more fully explored than in the Viareggio Prize–winning novel *The Garden of the Finzi-Continis,* which captures Ferrara's doom-laden atmosphere in the final year of the decade: "The fatal last days of August '39—till the eve of the Nazi invasion of Poland and the *drôle de guerre.*"

———

> The tomb was big, massive, really imposing: a kind of half-ancient, half-Oriental temple of the sort seen in the sets of Aïda . . .

113

Commissioned by Moisè Finzi-Contini, paternal great-grandfather of Alberto and Micòl, the tomb is described as an "incredible pastiche" of architectural styles, a "real horror," according to the mother of Bassani's unnamed narrator. I set off under the trees among chaste headstones of white marble and a single row of neat sepulchers hardly bigger than dollhouses: Hanau, Levi, Fink, Rotstein. Here were Finzi, Finzi-Teddeschi, Finzi-Ascoli, and the graves of Giorgio Bassani's mother and father. Then in the distance, "at the end of an abandoned field . . . it stood out, it was immediately noticeable." The field was dense with spring daisies, bordered by rows of dark cypress trees—the tomb, yes, like something you would see in the last act of *Aïda*.

Yet it didn't match Bassani's description. Where he noted "marble . . . snow-white Carrara, flesh-pink Verona," I found a severe fifty-by-fifty-foot edifice of austere dark stone. Under a columned portico, double iron doors bore stars of David. To one side a bronze plaque:

CIRO CONTINI

ING. ARCHITETTO

ide ó e diresse con amor

le Opere di Questo Cimitero

Ferrara 1873—Los Angeles 1952

Ciro Contini, far away in California. Was he related to the cultivated, one might say slightly decadent, family of the thirties who spoke "finzi-continian," their private language? To Professor Ermanno, his wife, Signora Olga, and her mother, Signora Regina Herrera, with her "intense" white hair? To young Alberto and Micòl? And what of the epigraph dedicated to little Guido, Professor Ermanno and Olga's firstborn, who had died of "infantile paralysis, the American kind, galloping . . ."?

Mourn

Guido Finzi-Contini

(1908–1914)

of exceptional form and spirit

your parents thought

to love you always more

not to mourn you

It was "dedicated to the dead child," Bassani wrote, "on the monumental tomb of the Jewish cemetery (seven lines only carved and inked in a humble rectangle of white marble)." The humble rectangle didn't exist, any more than did the colorful marbles of the crypt or, for that matter, the hyphenated Finzi in the surname of the émigré Ciro Contini. In a novel that, on its surface, seems so thoroughly autobiographical, I expected to find things as Bassani described them. Now, I wondered. Would I find the Barchetto del Duca and the *magna domus* along the Corso Ercole I d'Este? And beyond the high walls the seductive garden of the Finzi-Continis? There are writers who create worlds, *creatori di mondi,* places so real, peopled by characters you've known forever, that at times you grow forgetful that you're reading fiction at all. I was reminded of William Faulkner, who said that his fiction elevated "the actual into the apocryphal." Had Bassani done something similar? Did he produce in the flatlands of the Po River valley a Ferrarese version of Faulkner's Yoknapatawpha County? A place half-real, half-imagined?

———

It was late afternoon when I left the cemetery. Signora Collevatti was nowhere around, so I signed the guest book, left the yarmulke on the table, and reached the broad, arrow-straight Via Montebello, which leads to Ferrara's heart.

Two- and three-storied brick buildings, plastered in ocher and burnt sienna, flanked cobblestoned streets. A city of pleasant cafés, well-stocked book stalls, bicycles, and trees, the "great trees of the Ferrara walls laden with leaves." To a pedestrian unaccustomed to scores of bicycles careering around corners, wheeling two and three abreast along narrow lanes, they're something of a menace. Cycling schoolboys, hellbent for a scratch soccer match in the Piazza Arostea, nearly ran me down as I crossed the Piazza Trento e Trieste, beside the arcade of rickety-looking shops ranged along the soaring walls of the Gothic-Romanesque cathedral. Around the corner, across from the cathedral's carved twelfth-century portal, stands the Palazzo Municipio, a handsome wing of Castello Estense, whose great battlemented towers rise beyond a moat aswarm with mauve carp swimming furtively in its shadows.

Handsome as Ferrara is on a soft spring evening, in winter it turns icy, somber, fogbound: "The severe, grim winter of the Po Valley." Even now I feel a touch of gloom, a hint of menace. Perhaps it's the dark spirit of Ferrara's most famous son, the Dominican friar Giralamo Savonarola, born here in 1452. At thirty-seven Savonarola went to Florence, where

115

his hellfire preaching caused paintings, books of poetry, cosmetics, and other "vanities" to perish on great bonfires. Botticelli stopped painting Venuses; Pico della Mirandola gave up verse. In 1492 Lorenzo the Magnificent, tormented by Savonarola's bullying sermons, died at forty-three, and within two years the last Medici had fled. The golden age was over. Charles VIII of France governed the fading flower of the Italian Renaissance. Florentines, sickened by Savonarola's "puritanical republic," sent the Dominican friar to the gibbet and flames. Here in Ferrara, outside the Castello on the Piazza Savonarola, an ice-white statue of the cowled, gesticulating puritan stands atop a stone plinth, offering passersby a baleful benediction.

———

Morning was cool and drizzly, though I felt more cheerful. I left the Hotel San Paolo and dodged bicycles along Corso Porta Reno, where Bassani's protagonist and his Marxist companion Giampi Malnate, the young Milanese chemist and friend of Alberto Finzi-Contini, often ate dinner at "I Voltini, a little restaurant beyond Porta Reno." I had a cappuccino and brioche at a standup bar, then turned down the Via delle Volte. This medieval lane, bridged every few dozen yards by ancient houses, is said to be Ferrara's red-light district, a district where Malnate and the narrator spent an evening carousing with prostitutes. Leaving the "refined looking blond" Gisella, they crossed the city, talking of the narrator's unrequited passion for Micòl Finzi-Contini: "Gripping the handlebars of our bicycles, we walked up Via Scienze to the corner of Via Mazzini. Arriving there, we turned right, along Via Saraceno."

I followed the route of the two companions across Via San Ramano and Via Vittoria, then turned into Via Scienze. A short way along on my right, I discovered the Palazzo Paradiso, where the Biblioteca Comunale Ariostea was established in 1747, a tall, elegant building with a broad stone entrance and oaken doors swung wide. I checked my shoulder bag, then mounted a wide Renaissance staircase. On the second and third floors I found long, book-lined rooms arranged with tables and chairs, the place packed with university students bent assiduously over their books. On a morning in 1938, soon after the promulgation of the racial laws, the narrator of *The Garden of the Finzi-Continis* came here with "the fine idea . . . of settling down with my books." The Biblioteca Comunale

116

had long been a "refuge . . . a second home for me." But on this particular morning an attendant approached who ordered him to leave: "The
librarian had given explicit instructions . . . I would please get up and
clear out." This actually happened to Bassani. Today, however, I was
relieved to discover the library contained all the author's works in their
various editions and translations.

I sat in the courtyard of the Palazzo Paradiso, scanning yesterday's
Corriere della Serra while watching students come and go along the central hallway. The place too cool and damp to linger, I collected my bag
and, instead of following the path of Malnate and the narrator, headed
toward Piazza Trento e Trieste. Here Via Mazzini forms the northeastern
boundary of the ghetto that runs in a triangle along Via Vignatagliata and
Via Vittoria to Via delle Volte. At 95 Via Mazzini stands the tall shuttered
building housing Ferrara's three synagogues.

Listed beside the door on a slab of white stone are the names of the
Jews who vanished in Nazi concentration camps. I rang the bell and followed Signorina Martina, a pretty, doe-eyed young woman in flared
jacket and pleated skirt, down a damp passageway into a courtyard, where
I donned a yarmulke, then joined a dozen twelve-year-old schoolboys on
a tour of the building.

Following the students up the stairs to the Scola Tedesca, the German synagogue on the second floor, I realized they were about the age
of Bassani's protagonist when he came here "twice a year at least, at
Passover and Kippur." Entering the German synagogue I was dazzled by
its ornateness: silk draperies, polished woodwork, and elaborate stucco
decorations ablaze under crystal chandeliers: "The German one . . . [a]
severe, almost Lutheran assemblage of wealthy, bourgeois bowler hats."

This building has been the center of Jewish life in Ferrara since
1485, the signorina explained in Ferrarese Italian as we climbed to the
third floor. Willed "forever for the common use of the Jews" by Samuel
Ser Melli, whose father, Salomone, had come from Mantua to the Estense
court as a financier. As she spoke the students scribbled notes, though I
guessed none were Jewish, any more than was I or the signorina.

Upstairs we stepped into the Scola Italiana, the Italian synagogue,
with its decoratively painted ceiling, twin chandeliers, and a "resounding
pavement of white and pink rhombohedrons," although still gutted since
its desecration by the fascists in 1941. Here the narrator, his father, and

his brother worshiped on a bench at the front. Sitting behind them were the Finzi-Contini men: Professor Ermanno, Alberto, and Signora Olga's two brothers, the Herreras from Venice. The mothers, daughters, sisters, and aunts sat upstairs in the women's gallery, watching through grillwork. It was at the moment of the *berahà* and the rabbi's intoning of "*Jevare-hehà Adonài veiishmeréha . . .*" that the boys gathered under their father's tentlike *talèds,* and Micòl Finzi-Contini "rushed down from the women's section" to join Alberto under Professor Ermanno's shawl. The *talèds* were old, handed down through generations, filled with holes and tears. The children took advantage of the ancient fabric: "For the entire duration of the blessing, Alberto and Micòl never stopped exploring, they too, the gaps in their tent. And they smiled at me and winked at me, both curiously inviting: especially Micòl."

After the Scola Italiana we saw a small museum with a collection of silver Torah decorations, menorah, prayer books, and shawls, then ducked into the Scola Fanese. Founded by the De Fano family, this tiny synagogue is used strictly for Seder. For artistic purposes Bassani placed the Scola Fanese in a house on Via Vittoria, exchanging it for the Spanish synagogue which in his imagination he ferried here, creatively establishing a degree of geographic unity.

The Finzi-Contini children, raised in virtual isolation, were schooled by tutors at home in the *magna domus* and appeared at the *ginnasio* only at examination time, "which at least once a year brought us in direct contact with Alberto and Micòl." In the mid-thirties, when the two began the university, Alberto chose engineering at Milan Polytechnic and Micòl English in Venice, while the narrator, like Bassani himself, studied literature at Bologna. At this time Professor Ermanno got permission "to restore 'for the use of his family and anyone interested' the former Spanish synagogue incorporated in the temple building on Via Mazzini." By this move, in protest against the Fascist Party's admission of Jews, the hermetic Finzi-Continis withdrew even further from the community and were seen "only rarely and fleetingly, those few times, at a distance."

———

I took up the trail of Malnate and the narrator and entered the narrow, twisty Via Saraceno that eventually runs into Via Borgo di Sotto. I walked as far as the little square before Santa Maria in Vado, where the companions, still talking of the narrator's futile infatuation with Micòl

Finzi-Contini, paused in their 2 A.M. wandering to drink from the foun-
tain. Down the street, where it turns into Via Scandiana, stands the
Palazzo Schifanoia—the "Palace of Joy," once the summer residence of
Borso d'Este, the boisterous younger brother of Ercole. Bassani set the
house of his protagonist in this short street. After their late-night walk
Malnate left the narrator at his door, then rode away on his bicycle.

After a brief imprisonment for antifascist activities in 1943, Bassani
fled to Rome, leaving Ferrara and the house where he had spent his
youth. It's around the corner on Via Cisterna dell Follo, a quiet street
nearly deserted on this cool spring morning. A few doors away, beside a
walled garden spilling over with copper-colored lantana and creamy frax-
inus, stands the two-story Bassani house. Plastered a pale ocher, with traditional Ferrarese green shutters, a tall, arched doorway, and handsome
Baroque grilles shielding ground-floor windows, it has the look of solid
bourgeois comfort: large, traditional, sedate. Today it's hard to conceive
that anything so horrific as fascism ever intruded.

At first, fascist interference into the life of Bassani's protagonist seems
only slight: a letter from Marchese Ippolito Barbacinti "that 'accepted' my
resignation as a member of the Eleonora d'Este Tennis Club." This and
his expulsion from the Municipal Library were the opening salvos.
Meanwhile the young man's father was ousted from the Fascist Party, and
then the Merchants Club.

The narrator's dismissal from the tennis club thrust him into the
Finzi-Contini orbit. I walked from the Bassani house around the corner
to see "the red courts of the Eleonora d'Este," once popular with Bassani, as well as his Ferrarese contemporary, film director Michelangelo
Antonioni. I quickly discovered the club was named for Marfisa d'Este,
not Eleonora, but otherwise was exactly as the author described. A notice
on the brick wall beside a wrought-iron gate read:

T. C. Marfisa
vietta l'entrate
ai non soci

Ignoring the warning that nonmembers were forbidden, I pushed open
the gate and walked under an arbor smothered in pink roses. Four courts
of red clay, impeccably maintained, surrounded by a clipped lawn. A

119

rose-covered colonnade sheltered the terrace fronting the low brick clubhouse. An appealing place, as tranquil, solidly bourgeois, and traditional as the Bassani house, which, it appeared, almost backed against the clubhouse wall. To my surprise no one was on the courts. I and a gardener mowing the grass had it to ourselves. Alone among the flowers and colonnades, I found it hard to remember that beyond the walls once existed a world rife with racism and fascists. Though I took warning: "*non soci,*" "beware."

———

I was already speeding on my bicycle along the Mura degli Angeli, my eyes fixed on the motionless, flourishing vegetation of the Barchetto del Duca . . .

A short walk from the tennis club brought me to Pinzaali Medagli d'Oro and the Walls of the Angels. Bassani's descriptions of the walls confused me. How does one bicycle along a wall? What I discovered when I climbed the fortifications was a huge earthen berm backing the fifteenth-century bastions and atop it a broad path lined by towering poplar trees. If no one played tennis at Marfisa d'Este, here I found joggers, dog walkers, cyclists. On my right, beyond the sharp drop of the walls, stretched the countryside: meadows, trees, farmhouses and, not far off, a modern *superstrada*.

Ferrara lay to my left, the battlemented towers of Castello Estense and the spire of the Duomo in the distance. Below spread the old Hospital of Saint Anna, where Elia Corcos, a character based on Bassani's maternal grandfather, Cesare Minerbi, was chief physician for forty years. It was Dr. Corcos whom Professor Ermanno summoned when little Guido Finzi-Contini was stricken with polio. I walked past small factories, brickmakers, glaziers, manufacturers of garden implements, old workplaces resembling weathered remnants of the Industrial Revolution.

From the walls I looked down into the Cimitero Ebraico, snowy tombstones in ranks among the greenery. Sequestered in its lonely field stood the gray hulk of the Contini tomb. I hiked to the northeast quadrant of the city. If Bassani's description was dependable, I should pass above the garden of the Finzi-Continis. By the time I reached the Punta della Montagnola and looked down into a dense wood of tangled trees— oriental plane and flowering ash, oaks, horse chestnuts, elms, hawthorns, lindens, Aleppo pines—I knew my search to find one of Italy's most famous gardens was futile. No sign of the *magna domus* below, nor the "vast park" planted with specimen trees, not even the "tan patch of the tennis court." The *magna domus* was a product of Bassani's imagination, the garden inspired by a park of the Dukes Caetani di Sermoneta at Ninfa near Rome—the trees so dear to Micòl studied precisely by Bassani in the botanical gardens at Rome's Palazzo Corsini.

Descending a steep path, I entered the Corso Ercole I d'Este, the famous Renaissance street running "straight as a sword from the Castle to the Mura degli Angeli, its entire length flanked by the dark forms of patrician dwellings." Although I knew it would never appear, I found myself looking for the "door of dark oak" that led into the garden of the Finzi-Continis. "The garden of the Finzi-Contini," Bassani once said, "has never existed at the end of Corso Ercole I d'Este, the most beautiful and celebrated street in the city. However, on the left, just on this side of the wall, there was the green space which I wrote about, the area which could have contained it."

If the garden was imaginary, I wondered about Micòl—Bassani's creation of the beguiling blue-eyed Jewish girl with "the blond hair, that special blond, streaked with Nordic locks." It is said she was an enchanting combination of various women Bassani knew in his youth: "There are at least three Micòls around." For Professor Ermanno, Micòl's father, Bassani drew on Silvio Magrini, president of the Jewish community, whose son died of an incurable illness. The son served as a model for Micòl's brother Alberto. In the novel, Alberto died of cancer in 1942. The others, Professor Ermanno and Signora Olga, Micòl and her grandmother Signora Regina Herrera, were arrested by the fascists and "sent off . . . to the concentration camp of Fòssoli, near Capri, and from there, later, to Germany." Of the 150 Ferrarese Jews deported to Nazi death camps, just five returned. As I reached the city I grieved for this fictional family, this small clutch of Finzi-Continis, *rarae aves* even here in their native Ferrara, who did not survive. Perhaps Alberto was the lucky one.

———

The morning drizzle gave way to an afternoon of high skies, followed by a limpid moonlit evening. After a dinner of *bolito misto* and a bottle of Cagnina de Romagna at Osteria degli Angeli, I had coffee at a café under the porticoes along Corso Martiri della Libertà. In the thirties this was the Corso Roma, heart of the city's social life. On its far side the floodlit towers of the Castello and the chilling statue of Savonarola. A few doors from where I sat, next to the Farmacia Navarra, was the F.I.S. Café, which Bassani had transformed into the "Caffè della Borsa," a meeting place of Ferrara's gentry and a principal hangout for fascist bigwigs.

The *farmacia* is still there. That afternoon I tested my vision on an electronic ophthalmic device. Everything was starkly modern except the baroque eighteenth- century ceiling, painted as though for a performance of *The Magic Flute*. In *A Night of '43,* which closed the cycle of Bassani's *Ferrara Stories,* the pharmacist Pino Barilari peered through the window looking for proof that his wife was unfaithful and witnessed the fascists who mercilessly shot down eleven antifascists.

Historically the event took place on the night of November 14, 1943, when the men, taken from their homes and the prison on Via Piangipane, were murdered to avenge the killing of the federal secretary, Igino Ghisellini. Those shot included well-known lawyers, trade unionists, and Jews. As a warning to citizens, Prefect Enrico Vezzalini ordered the bodies left where they fell. Across the Corso Martiri della Libertà, the Street of the Martyrs for Liberty, the place of execution is marked by two marble plaques on the castle wall.

———

Following a thread of memory, Giorgio Bassani pieced together a world where past impinged on present, bringing to life the tragic years from the promulgation of the racial laws to the massacre of the antifascists. Cyclical in nature and reinforced by the continuity of its characters and settings, his work created a panorama of the life of his city and times.

Finishing my coffee, I stroll past the cathedral to the Via San Romano. "My greatest ambition as a writer," Bassani stated, "has always been to appear reliable and trustworthy, to give the reader the assurance that the Ferrara I depict in my stories is an actual city which really existed." In order to get closer to what "really existed," I realize that Bassani had fabricated the city's most famous landmark: the garden of the Finzi-Continis, a product of pure invention that enriched the city, enlarged its history. The actual became the apocryphal. Giorgio Bassani's Ferrara was a place half-real, half-imagined in the ghostly light of an April moon.

Lake Filled with Light

E. M. Forster in Tuscany

> . . . at Lugano the sun was setting, and the whole lake filled
> with light. Everything began to look like Italy.
>
> E. M. Forster, *Diaries*

"THE ENGLISH COUNTRYSIDE may be pretty," an Italian
friend remarks, "but there is no *light* in England." He is not being smug.
He's half Sicilian, half Tuscan—smugness isn't in him. Typically, he's
impatient, pessimistic, paranoiac. But he knows what makes a pleasant
landscape and what makes a landscape great.

Every generation of travelers rediscovers the great landscapes,
panoramas they pursue, meditate upon, paint and photograph. It's not
only scale and drama that make them so but a quality of atmosphere that
virtuosos of light like Turner and Monet spent their lives refining in
paint. One thinks of thunderheads building and rebuilding over the San-
gre de Cristo, of immense azure skies piled above the Masai Steppe, the
mists of Ladakh, and the high-pitched blues of Greece.

San Gimignano

Tuscan light is subtle, its sources indirect, though at times, especially
in winter, so dense you can stir it with a spoon. For E. M. Forster the light
of Tuscany was both deep and revealing, a benediction offering illumination and self-knowledge. *Where Angels Fear to Tread,* a slim tragicom-
edy that's the first of Forster's Italian novels, is an easel on which he
displays his veneration of Italy, as when the English author celebrates the
light of summer: "Italy . . . is only her true self in the height of summer

. . . her soul awakes under the beams of a vertical sun . . . in the terrific blue sky . . . in the whitened plain which gripped life tighter than frost, in the exhausted reaches of the Arno, in the ruins of brown castles which stood quivering on the hills."

In the spring of 1901, Forster visited San Gimignano—*delle Belle Torri*—twenty miles northwest of Siena. The town became his fictional Monteriano, the setting of *Where Angels Fear to Tread.* Nearly a century later, a few days after Easter, Guido Ottaviani and I cross the Tuscan countryside toward the twelfth-century hilltown, traversing ridges touched by mauve clouds, hillsides awash with yellow oceans of blossoming rape. Guido, small, spare, with intense blue eyes set in a face honed by aestheticism, remarks upon the first shoots emerging from gnarled vines and violets blanketing embankments. As far as we can see are "vast slopes of olives and vineyards, with chalk-white farms and in the distance other slopes, with more olives and more farms, and more little towns outlined against the . . . sky." A countryside little altered, Guido says, since 1338, when the Sienese artist Ambrogio Lorenzetti brought it to life in *Good Government,* frescoed on the walls of the Palazzo Pubblico.

———

While sightseeing in Tuscany with Miss Abbot, her young companion, the good-natured widow Lilia Herriton falls for a local ne'er-do-well, the handsome Gino Carella. Back in England's suburban Sawston, Lilia's in-laws are scandalized. Philip Herriton, the hero of *Where Angels Fear to Tread,* hurries to Monteriano but arrives too late—Lilia and Gino are wed.

Months later Lilia dies giving birth to Gino's child. Accompanied by his sister Harriet, Philip returns to "buy" the baby from his father and bring the boy to England—a scheme hatched by Harriet and Philip's conniving mother: "If I can rescue poor Lilia's baby from that horrible man, who will bring it up either as Papist or infidel . . . I shall do it."

———

Nowhere is Forster's homage to Tuscany more apparent than in his depiction of gray, colorless Sawston as contrasted with Monteriano, which floats "in isolation between trees and sky, like some fantastic ship city in a dream." Approaching San Gimignano across the cloud-touched hills, I recognize Forster's "narrow circle of the walls, and behind them

125

seventeen towers . . . Some were only stumps, some were inclining stiffly to their fall, some were still erect, piercing like masts into the blue."

Little has changed inside that "narrow circle of the walls" since Forster's day. Guido guides me through shady alleyways and along the brick pavements of Via San Matteo. We pass through the Arco dei Becci, part of the town's original bastions, into the Piazza della Cisterna, where pale stone steps encircle the still functioning thirteenth-century cistern. Anarchic clusters of rugged *palazzi* and fortified towers of rock and brick mount skyward, built for defense and prestige in the days of the Guelphs and Ghibellines by the feuding Ardinghelli and Salvucci families, who made fortunes in the saffron trade and warred upon each other. Seventy-two towers stood against the skyline when Dante visited San Gimignano in 1300. Today, fifteen remain.

We wait in shadow beneath the crenellated walls of the Palazzo del Popolo, San Gimignano's town hall. The Torre Grossa, the tallest and best preserved of the towers, rises above us. Guido's eyes narrow as he assays a pair of young locals striding our way. Nervously, he sweeps a hand to his hip as if expecting to find a dagger. A scene from Verona, another city rocked by feuding Guelphs and Ghibellines, flashes through my mind and I fear one of these fiery young Tybalts will challenge my wary friend: "Turn thee, Benvolio! look upon thy death." "*Stronzi*"—Guido whispers the expletive only half in jest as we watch the *condottiere* swagger past. In the shadow of Torre della Rognosa they turn into Palazzo del Podestà and vanish. We then step peacefully into the town hall to view the *Maesta,* Lippo Memmi's masterpiece in the Sala di Dante.

However tangible the quarrels between Guelphs and Ghibellines may be to today's sardonic Tuscans, these medieval spires and light-filled spaces charmed Philip Herriton, though they had no impact on some of Forster's other well-bred English characters. Philip's sister Harriet, inoculated against foreign places by England and her waspish mother, remains untouched by Monteriano. "She was curiously virulent about Italy." It is Philip and Miss Abbott whom Tuscany illuminates in this graceful story of self-discovery. "I tell you, Miss Abbott, it's one thing for England and another for Italy. There we plan and get on high moral horses. Here we find what asses we are . . . My hat, what a night! Did you ever see a really purple sky and really silver stars before?"

Italian luminescence has done its work. Like Lilia before her, Miss

Abbott falls for Gino, though she'll never see him again: "I'm in love with Gino—don't pass it off—I mean it crudely—you know what I mean." Coming at the novel's end, this confession draws Philip and Miss Abbott together, perhaps more closely than love.

Guido and I share a bottle of Vernaccia, San Gimingano's choice white wine, at a café in a corner of the Piazza Duomo, a sunny space at the hub of ancient streets, weathered towers, palaces. Beyond the walls the Tuscan hills ride against a lush vault of untroubled blue. It's easy to see how: "After long estrangement, after much tragedy, the South had brought [Philip and Miss Abbott] together in the end . . . those silver stars in a purple sky, even the violets of a departed spring . . ."

———

Beyond the Porta alle Fonti the road winds in dizzying turns down a hillside. At the bottom, where it strikes eastward toward Poggibonsi, Forster found violets blooming in deep woods: "The trees of the wood are small and leafless, but . . . stood in violets as rocks stand in the summer sea." Now they're gone, both flowers and woods, vanished beneath vineyards, olive groves, fields of blossoming rape that spread in flaxen waves across the Chianti country toward Radda, Greve, and finally Florence.

Firenze

"These *stones!*" Guido says with scorn, heartened by the perfidiousness of his fellows. "They're shabby substitutes—not genuine at all." The venerable stones that once paved Florence's Piazza della Signoria were taken up a few years ago to repair underground water and electric lines, then stacked in neat tiers around the piazza's perimeter. One morning workers arrived to discover the stones had vanished, neatly stolen during the night. Eventually they were replaced by stones Guido considers cheap substitutes, stones of no historical consequence—those unstained by the blood of the man Miss Lucy Honeychurch, heroine of Forster's *A Room with a View,* saw murdered on the square.

Longing for something interesting to happen, the innocent Lucy stood on the piazza admiring the Palazzo Vecchio. Tuscan light again played its role: "She fixed her eyes wistfully on the tower of the palace, which rose out of the lower darkness like a pillar of roughened gold. It seemed no longer a tower, no longer supported by earth, but some unattainable treasure throbbing in the tranquil sky."

Then, "something did happen." Near the Loggia dei Lanzi, as if to substantiate Guido's trepidations, a pair of Italians argued over a debt. One was stabbed and died at Lucy's feet. As any well-bred Victorian might, Lucy swooned. When she came round she gazed into the eyes of George Emerson, the young man who had given up his room with a view so that Lucy might have it. "She had complained of dullness, and lo! one man was stabbed, and another held her in his arms."

From a table at Rivoire, on the piazza, Guido and I look across the square to where the Italian was murdered. Here too, in 1498, the Dominican prior and mystic-reformer Savonarola was burned at the stake. The Piazza della Signoria was always witness to Florence's brawls, festivals, and executions. When we've finished our drinks, we stroll among sightseers gathered for the Easter holidays: Japanese snapping photos, Germans counting stones, Italian students dancing around the Great Fountain with its heroic figure of Neptune. The few remaining horse cabs clatter through the city carrying Americans. The loggia that "showed as the triple entrance of a cave, wherein dwelt many a deity, shadowy but immortal" has been enclosed by an iron barrier. Through the palings one can't reach the sculpted deities within the vaulted hall, but the piazza is much as Forster and Lucy found it: "Here, not only in the solitude of Nature, might a hero meet a goddess, or a heroine a god."

———

It's early. The bells of Santa Maria della Fiori peal over the city. Guido has returned to Podere Sasso, his farm near Serre di Rapolano, and I'm on my own. Upstream from the Ponte alle Grazie, a pair of men in a two-oared scull sever the Arno's sunlit surface. The river slides like an ivory comb over the Pescala di San Niccolo. Somewhere on the right bank, on her first morning at the Pensione Bertolini, Lucy woke in a room with a view: "It was pleasant to wake up in Florence . . . to fling wide the windows . . . to lean out into sunshine with beautiful hills and trees and marble churches opposite, and close below, the Arno, gurgling against the embankment of the road."

Soon after breakfast, while the tedious Charlotte Bartlett, Lucy's cousin and chaperon, "settles in," Lucy sets out for the Church of Santa

Croce—one of several walks in which Forster, while illuminating the city, develops both theme and character. Lucy, under the wing of the eccentric Miss Lavish, "turned to the right along the sunny Lungarno." Miss Lavish, a Florentine aficionado, highlights the sights: "Ponte alle Grazie—particularly interesting, mentioned by Dante. San Miniato—beautiful as well as interesting."

Today the old Ponte alle Grazie is gone, mined by the Germans in the Second World War and replaced by a graceless modern span. Miss Lavish was right about San Miniato, however. The clarity and restraint of the Tuscan Romanesque church, rising across the Arno among olive and cypress trees, deserves all the Englishwoman's praise.

After leaving the river I wander through narrow lanes into Florence's oldest neighborhood, Santa Croce. Though only a block from the church, it's here Lucy and Miss Lavish become lost. "Lost! Lost! My dear Miss Lucy . . . Two lone females in an unknown town. Now, this is what *I* call an adventure." They float "through a series of gray-brown streets" and stumble upon Piazza Santisima Annunciata—where I stumble upon the equestrian statue of Grand Duke Ferdinando I. Lucy exclaims over "those divine babies," Luca della Robbia's fourteen terracotta infants ornamenting Brunelleschi's Spedale degli Innocenti. The two tourists meander on, then "drift into another piazza, large and dusty, on the further side of which rose a black-and-white facade of surpassing ugliness . . . it was Santa Croce. The adventure was over."

Turned out in laurel wreath and stone toga, Dante Alighieri scowls down from his stone pedestal outside Santa Croce's north door as though passing judgment on the tourists and junketing students swarming over the "large and dusty" piazza. I join the mob sweeping toward the great church, recalling a freezing January afternoon years before when I stood here among a shivering Florentine crowd enjoying a one-man circus: fire-eater, magician, juggler, clown. Do I find Santa Croce "of surpassing ugliness"? It's a matter of taste and time. To modern visitors, reared on architecture that is often truly ugly, Santa Croce, its well-proportioned facade of pale gray and deep green marble highlighted in pink, seems quite beautiful.

Jilted on that spring morning by Miss Lavish, Lucy enters the church alone: "Of course, it must be a wonderful building. But how like a barn! And how very cold! Of course, it contained frescoes by Giotto . . . but who was to tell her which they were? . . . Then the pernicious charm of Italy worked on her, and, instead of acquiring information, she began to be happy."

Lucy soon meets Mr. Emerson and his son George, who take her into the Perruzi Chapel to view Giotto's great frescoes. Then as now, the church is jammed. On the day of Lucy's visit the unctuous Reverend Eager, resident chaplain of Florence's English Church, lectured a tour group, "directing them how to worship Giotto." Using Eager as a foil, Forster lampoons the theory of "the tactile values of Giotto" advanced by art-philosopher Bernard Berenson, and remarks on the battle then raging over the need to *de*-restore the badly restored frescoes. De-restoration won out in the 1950s. Today bald patches of plaster appear where Giotto's work was once clumsily retouched. As for Berenson, in the Easter swarm amid the babble of a dozen languages, I encounter guides broadcasting "the tactile values of Giotto" as if they, not Berenson, had first proclaimed them.

———

A long established hilltop retreat, Fiesole rises above the heat and noise of Florence. After coffee at a café on the precipitous Via San Francesco, I pass the Church of Sant'Alessandro, then the first-century Teatro Romano, and begin the trek to Settignano. The road winds across the steep face of hills, through olive groves and vineyards. Below, the towers and domes of Florence rise above the lush tapestry of the Val d'Arno. Along this road Mr. Eager organized "a drive in the hills" for the crew at the Pensione Bertolini. "We might go up by Fiesole and back by Settignano . . . and have an hour's ramble on the hillside." The carriages stop above "a great ampitheatre, full of terraced steps and misty olives . . . It was a promontory, uncultivated, wet, covered with bushes and occasional trees."

In his notes to the 1990 Penguin edition of *A Room with a View,* Oliver Stallybrass points out that a setting such as Forster describes can be found a quarter mile above the Castello di Vincigliata, "shortly after successive hairpin bends . . . But the terrain is not, today, uncultivated."

A few hundred yards above the Castello, I turn between shady cypress trees and take my own ramble on the hill. It's cool and wet from last night's rain. The wild cry of a hoopoe sounds among the olives.

Although there is no "promontory . . . covered with bushes and occasional trees," this is Forster's Italy with its profound color and space where Tuscan light comes into play. For it's Lucy's illumination, the waking of "an undeveloped heart, not a cold one," that is Forster's theme: "Italy worked some marvel in her. It gave her light and . . . it gave her shadow." Where better to develop this theme than on a Tuscan hillside where the "vast slopes of olives and vineyards" so affected Philip Herriton in *Where Angels Fear to Tread*?

When Mr. Eager's party alights from the carriages they spring "about from tuft to tuft of grass, their anxiety to keep together being only equalled by their desire to go in different directions." Soon the clergymen, Mr. Eager and Mr. Beebe, have gone in one direction, the Emersons in a second, the women in a third. Cousin Charlotte and Miss Lavish want to gossip about the young George Emerson. Not wishing the innocent Lucy to overhear, they encourage her to search out the Reverends Eager and Beebe. Reluctantly, Lucy agrees and asks the Italian driver where she might find the "*buoni uomini,*" the "good men" of the church. "Italians are born knowing the way . . . Anyone can find places, but the finding of people is a gift from God." The driver leads the way, understanding the emotions Lucy fails to comprehend. She is in what Forster calls "a muddle," her mind and "undeveloped heart" at odds. Then "the view was forming at last; she could discern the river, the golden plain, other hills. 'Eccolo!' he [the driver] exclaimed. 'There he is!'"

"At the same moment the ground gave way, and with a cry she fell out of the wood. Light and beauty enveloped her. She had fallen onto a little open terrace, which was covered with violets from end to end." Violets are the modus of illumination: "From her feet the ground sloped sharply into the view, and violets ran down in rivulets and streams and cataracts, irrigating the hillside with blue."

The "good man" she finds is not the good man she expected. George Emerson stands at the brink, "like a swimmer who prepares." He turns "at the sound of her arrival. For a moment he contemplated her, as one who has fallen out of heaven. He saw radiant joy in her face, he saw the flowers beat against her dress in blue waves . . . He stepped quickly forward and kissed her."

Tuscan light has done its work, but there's a long summer of "muddle" in England before Lucy allows herself to see it. In the rectory at

Sawston, the philosophical Mr. Emerson tells her: "Now it is all dark. Now Beauty and Passion seem never to have existed. I know. But remember the mountains over Florence and the view."

———

But what of the room with a view? In his essay "A Room without a View," in the 1990 Penguin edition of his novel, Forster speculated on his characters in the intervening years. George, a prisoner of war in Mussolini's Italy, went to Florence after the fascist collapse. "And George set out . . . to locate the particular building. He failed. For though nothing is damaged all is changed. The houses on that stretch of the Lungarno have been renumbered and remodelled and, as it were, remelted . . . so that it is impossible to decide which room was romantic half a century ago."

Oliver Stallybrass concludes that in 1901 Forster stayed at the Pensione Simi, Number 2 Lungarno delle Grazie. The Simi was Forster's Pensione Bertolini. Stallybrass writes that the Pensione Simi had "occupied the ground and first floors, below the then Pensione Jennings-Riccioli, by which around 1930 it was absorbed."

The Lungarno late on a Sunday afternoon. Wisteria blossoms hover in dense purple clusters on overhead colonnades, and anglers casting for carp crowd the parapet near the Ponte delle Grazie. I join a group of habitués sipping Campari at a small café. As the river slides quietly past, the sun slips into the trees above San Miniato, bathing the valley in Tuscan light.

A few steps from the bridge the Lungarno crosses the Via Tintori, Street of the Wool Dyers, then runs to the Piazza dei Cavalleggeri. Near the piazza, I discover a four-story structure of stone and stucco encased in scaffolding. A number 2 is stenciled beside tall doors. To the left is a plaque:

HOTEL

JENNINGS

RICCIOLI

Borne high in the scaffolding a sign announces that the old hotel will soon become the Palazzo Jennings Riccioli: *Apartamenti, Uffici e Negozi*— apartments, offices, and shops.

On the embankment a young Englishman in tan corduroy and a

young woman in a spring dress of palest pink are deep in a romantic tête-à-tête. As he leans near her, she slips her hand into his, rests her head against his chest. Just here, after the murder on the piazza, George and Lucy paused. "They were close to their pension. She stopped and leant her elbows against the parapet of the embankment. He did likewise. There is at times a magic in identity of position; it is one of the things that have suggested to us eternal comradeship."

Overhead the empty windows of the old hotel stare down upon the river. The oarsmen have gone, leaving the Arno to fishermen dozing over bamboo poles. Below the ivory sluice of the Pescala di San Niccolo the stream mirrors the fading lavender *palazzi* on the distant bank. The Pensione Bertolini may have gone, but behind one of those windows is the room with a view where one can imagine George and Lucy, at last united, in each other's arms.

9

The Nine Dragons of Cochin China
In the Vietnam of Marguerite Duras

MARGUERITE DURAS WAS a political opportunist who, with apparent callousness, navigated the extremes of right and left as political currents changed. She remains a controversial figure in France, where she is not universally admired. Since I am no authority on modern French history or Marguerite Duras' role in it, I have omitted references to her political life. "The Nine Dragons of Cochin China" concentrates solely on her novels The Lover *and* The North China Lover *and their effect on my travels in Vietnam.*

"The French names of Saigon's streets? No one remembers them. Not since independence."

The French consulate lies along tree-shaded Duòng Nguyên Thi Minh Khai, behind Notre Dame Cathedral, near the heart of Ho Chi Minh City—still widely known as Saigon. The consulate is a cluster of freshly whitewashed buildings behind spic-and-span walls. The Vietnamese soldier at the gate barely glances up from his morning paper as I pass through into a shady garden, modestly cool in the hundred-degree heat. Another Vietnamese in a crisp white suit and open collar escorts me past several Europeans waiting in the alcove of an outbuilding, then through tall, open doors into the consulate itself, a splendid colonial relic, the foyer a deep space of polished hardwoods and high ceilings. The woman behind the reception desk is the only other person in the room.

Slim and stately, she's exquisitely turned out in an *ao dai*—the classic dress of Vietnam, a fragilely colored silk tunic over flowing white silk trousers.

"I'm sorry, I really can't help you," she continues, in the weightless music of Saigon English. "We have no *plan de ville* with the old names."

Masking disappointment, I open my notebook. "Does this mean anything to you?"

"The Lyautey Boarding School. No, it means nothing." She runs a fair, finely-boned finger down the page, then stops at the words: Chasseloup-Laubat Secondary School. "This one I know. I remember it from the time I was a girl. But the name is changed now. It's not far, just a few blocks along Thi Minh Khai, on the corner of Nam Ky Khoi Nghia."

I'm looking for the world of the French novelist Marguerite Duras—the Cochin China of the 1920s. Saigon. Cholon. Sadec. The Mekong: "The fabulous, silken flatness of the delta." Have I found a piece of the puzzle? "You're *sure* it's the same . . .?"

"How could it not be?" she asks, gazing through tall open doors into the lush garden. "I was a child here. I remember everything."

In the film, here in this book, we will call her the Child.

The child: Marguerite Duras. Born Marguerite Donnadieu in Indochina, April 4, 1914. She left for France in 1931, sailing from the docks of the Messageries Maritimes aboard "an ocean liner with three classes of service." Educated in Paris, she began writing neorealist novels in 1942, then turned to more abstract literary forms, her later work characterized by an increasing detachment from the narration. Though most famous in America for her screenplay of Alain Resnais' 1959 award-winning film *Hiroshima Mon Amour,* she wrote several novels, many set in the Indochina of her youth. These included her first success, *Un Barrage contre le Pacifique,* published in 1951 and issued as *The Sea Wall* in a 1952 English translation, and *L'Amant, The Lover,* 1984 winner of the Prix Goncourt. She died in Paris in March 1996.

In May 1990 she learned that the Chinese lover of *L'Amant* was dead, buried at Sadec, that the blue house on the banks of the Mekong River where he'd lived still stood. "I stopped the work I was doing. I wrote the story of the North China lover and the child: it wasn't quite there in *The Lover,* I hadn't given them enough time." Consequently, *The North China Lover* was born. *Amant de la Chine du Nord.* A poignant retelling of the relationship, drawn from Duras' adolescence, between two outcasts, a French schoolgirl and her Chinese lover.

Whereas *The Lover* is a nostalgic, lyrical story filtered through the recollections of an "already old" woman, *The North China Lover,* though no less exquisitely written, is much tougher, deeper. Set in the late 1920s and early 1930s, the twilight of colonialism in Indochina, the two novels perform with the finesse of a sonata: *The Lover* fashioning the opening statement, *The North China Lover* a reiteration of themes with variations. Refraining from the romantic uses of the past, *The North China Lover* confronts the desire, love, and pain of the relationship between the child and an older rich Chinese, the poverty-ridden lives of poor whites under colonialism, the passion and cruelty of their tragically flawed family: the child's diabolic older brother Pierre, "the killer," an opium addict; the little brother Paulo, who is "different," who "doesn't know anything. He knows he exists"; the mother, who in an "access of madness" was tempted to prostitute her daughter, "the little slut [who] goes to have her body caressed by a filthy Chinese millionaire."

———

Across the city. Two or three landmarks, right off the list: the Charner Theatre, the Cathedral, the Eden Cinema . . . The Continental, the most beautiful hotel in the world.

Saigon. The French Quarter. Midmorning. The tree-lined avenues of the *colons.* Nguyen Hue, the former Boulevard Charner, the "Champs-Elysées of the East." At its top soars the grandiose butter-and-cream Hôtel de Ville, built in 1908 as the city's administrative center, its flamboyant towers, columns, and statuary conspicuous reminders of Europe's doomed efforts to put its stamp on the lands it subjugated. I round a corner onto tamarind-shaded Dong Khoi, the former rue Catinat, heart of French colonial life. Lam Son Square, once the Place Garnier, opens a hundred yards down the rue Catinat. On its western boundary stands the dove gray elegance of the Hotel Continental, onetime center of French society, its terrace the spot to see and be seen. Somerset Maugham wrote: "At the hour of the aperitif, [the hotel terraces] are crowded with bearded, gesticulating Frenchmen drinking the sweet and sickly beverages . . . which they drink in France and they talk nineteen to the dozen in the rolling accent of the Midi." On the square's east is the great domed entrance of the turn-of-the-century Municipal Theater, the Charner Theatre, and beyond it the rue Catinat arrows under tamarinds to the river.

> . . . [The chauffeur] drives down the rue Catinat.
> He sees the child with a young white man who must be her
> brother and a very handsome, similarly dressed young native
> man. The three of them are coming out of the Eden Cin-
> ema.

Along this stretch the *colons* promenaded, shopping in chic boutiques and *parfumeries,* stopping at the Eden Cinema to see the latest films, dropping into the Rotonde and the Taverne Alsacienne for a Chartreuse or Dubonnet. Today souvenir shops and smart new cafés replace the boutiques and bistros of the past, though the ocher facade of the old Hotel Catinat survives in mid-block. At the bottom, overlooking the river, stands the classic Hotel Majestic, a peach and beige confection that has, like most French structures from Vietnam's past, undergone a recent, painstaking restoration—an impressive phenomenon considering the country's history of ruinous colonialism and two tragic wars of liberation.

> The lycée—the halls are full of students. The child is wait-
> ing against a column in the hall.

Noon. The temperature hovers just above one hundred. Duòng Nguyên Thi Minh Khai is a river of motorbikes thundering from curb to curb. Vespas and Honda Dreams, loud, penetrating, unmuffled. The clamor of Saigon, "the noise of old wars, old worn-out armies." The air is thick with exhaust. Heat pulses from the street, the softening tar, the flow of howling vehicles, heat that allows no sweat, that broils your insides.

On the northwest corner of Nam Ky Khoi Nghia, opposite Reunification Palace, stands a graceful two-story structure with green shutters: the Chasseloup-Laubat Secondary School. Tamarind trees shadow its iron gate, which is surmounted by a gold-lettered sign that renames the school for the eighteenth-century Vietnamese poet: "Lê Quy Dôn."

Suddenly it's quiet, motorbikes fled to another part of the city. Students pedal past on bicycles, slender adolescent girls floating in their snowy *ao dias,* broad-brimmed straw hats balanced on blue-black hair.

The concierge is short, barrel-chested, middle-aged, in white shirt and dark trousers. His thick hands clutch a newspaper. I explain my desire to visit Chasseloup-Laubat. He eyes the camera slung over my shoulder, the notebook in my pocket.

I tell him of the child who was a student here, of the French novelist she became, of the importance of this setting to her novels. I want only a few photos of the school, its manicured gardens.

"One hour," he says, tapping the watch on my wrist. "Come then. Take photo."

As I cross the street I notice a pair of stone bollards planted on the sidewalk outside the gate. It's here, parked at the curb in front of the Chasseloup-Laubat Secondary School, that day after day the child found the chauffeur-driven Léon Bollée, "a car as big as a bedroom," the North China lover waiting in the depths of its long black hull, waiting to speed the child across the city to his bachelor quarters in Cholon.

> There is the Léon Bollée, stopped at the entrance of the
> school. You can see the chauffeur of the Léon Bollée. White
> curtains conceal the rear seats, as though the car was carry-
> ing a condemned man one mustn't look at.

I walk as far as the post office, another handsomely restored turn-of-the-century sugar-and-egg confection, its cavernous hall spotless, buffed, gleaming. Two huge map-murals, one plotting the Saigon of 1892, the other the telegraph lines of southern Indochina in 1936, look down on polished hardwood writing desks where people pen letters. On each desk a delicate porcelain bowl bears water and chop sticks for sealing envelopes and gluing stamps.

In exactly an hour a *cyclo,* one of Saigon's ubiquitous pedicabs, takes me back to Chasseloup-Laubat. The concierge nods and steps aside to let me pass. I'm struck by the serenity of the place, as if it were a convent rather than a school. It's meticulously kept, the pristine walls a pale saffron, the shutters a gleaming forest green. The gardens are lush; bonsaied plants line the walk through the columned entry into the inner courtyard. A sign hangs above the opening: "TAT CA VI HOC SINH THN YEU"—

"All for the Student." Girls pass while others appear at upstairs windows, books held carefully to catch the light. These lithe young women, so heartbreakingly beautiful in bridal white, hover in this tranquil space like doves in a well-tended cage.

In the days when this was Chasseloup-Laubat, the *lycée* was strictly for white girls—Europeans, mainly French. Among such well-bred young women the child's presence was a disruption, her affair with the Chinese a scandal. She was "poor, the daughter of poor people, poor ancestors, farmers, cobblers, always first in French at all her schools, yet disgusted by France, and mourning the country of her birth and youth . . . with a taste for weak men, and sexy like you've never seen before."

No, the child did not fit at the *lycée* where she studied nor at the Lyautey Boarding School, where she slept in the dormitory beside the beautiful Hélène Lagonelle, "the child's other, never-to-be-forgotten, love." She slept at Lyautey, that is, when she wasn't sleeping with her North China lover in Cholon.

At last she was caught "in the dragnet of the mothers of the students of Saigon. They want their daughters to keep to their own kind," she is told by the principal of Chasseloup-Laubat. "They say—listen to this— Why does she need a baccalaureate, that little tart." Her mother is called in from Sadec to speak with Lyautey's director about her daughter's sen-sational love affair. Old friends, the mother and the director both came from France in 1905, when the education program for native children began. The mother's reputation as an exemplary teacher, the child's bril-liant schoolwork kept her at Lyautey and at the *lycée*. "She's a child who's always been free, otherwise she'd run away . . . if I want to keep her I have to let her be free."

> In the evening, after school, the same black limousine, the same hat at once impudent and childlike, the same lamé shoes, and away she goes, goes to have her body laid bare by the Chinese millionaire.

I wander into the arcade that runs between the two courtyards, the arcade where the child waited alone: "She is being shunned. She wants it that way, to be in that place." A tap at my shoulder. The concierge takes my arm, leads me to the gate. "Enough. You go."

"I'd like to stay."

"You finish," he says.

Back to the heat and noise of Thi Minh Khai. The Vespas and Honda Dreams, the street awash with their hot, unmuffled roar. My cyclo driver hails me out of the clamor, "the noise of old wars, old worn-out armies." "Where to? Where we go now?"

———

If Saigon is crowded, noisy, intense, the Chinese ghetto of Cholon is chaos, a cacophony of vehicles and people so powerful as to render hearing an affliction, so visually overwhelming as to make one dizzy. The bus from central Saigon drops me outside seething Binh Tay Market, a labyrinth of overflowing stalls surrounded by a block of dilapidated shophouses, the corners surmounted by crumbling Moorish domes. In the dimness under an iron roof I find pickled vegetables and dried fish, blue-and-white pottery stacked to the ceiling, the flowered bonnets favored by urban women and the conical straw "limpet" hats of country people, dozens of varieties of mushrooms and dried roots, eels, snails, frogs, turtles, geese, ducks, chickens, birds' nests and shark fins for soup, hundred-year-old eggs, mountains of plastic frippery, alps of tin gew-gaws, fifty kinds of rice, and fiery vats of crimson chili paste pounded before my streaming eyes.

The Chinese came from enclaves in My Tho and Bien Hoa to set-tle in Cholon at the turn of the nineteenth century. Cholon, "Big Mar-ket," was soon the largest Chinese community in Indochina. By the early twentieth century the great wealth generated by merchants and bankers saw the establishment of lavish restaurants and casinos, brothels, and *fumeries* where opium smokers idled away the hours. With the "scent of a European cologne about him, and the fainter one of opium and silk, tussore silk," the North China lover was one of those rich Chinese haunting Cholon's opulent underworld. "Doing nothing is like a profes-sion for you, having women, smoking opium. Going to clubs, the pool, Paris, New York, Florida."

> It's in Cholon. Opposite the boulevards linking the Chinese part of the city to the center of Saigon, the great American-style streets full of streetcars, rickshaws, and buses . . . It's a native housing estate to the south of the city. His place is modern, hastily furnished . . .

140

This is the sole clue to the whereabouts of "the bachelor quarters."
South of the sweep of "American-style" Tran Hung Dao and behind
Binh Tay Market, Cholon lurches through muddy alleyways to the
waterfront, the embankments of the Bén Nghé Canal. I wander a maze
of steamy lanes, stop at a stall to drink Tiger beer poured over chunks of
ice into a pint mug. Children approach, smiling, curious, good-humored.
I snap pictures. Laughter. They want more. Friends come. More pictures—a whole roll. A cyclo piled with scrap metal pedals past. A boy
beats two pieces of pipe in a monotonous tattoo, advertising a soup stall.
Up and down the lane the windows of two-story dwellings are shuttered, the cramped doorways thronged with grandmothers, cats, crates of
chickens, naked babies in straw bonnets. "This is a street with cubicles
like there are all over Indochina. It has the outdoor taps they call fountains. A covered arcade runs the length of it . . . This is where it is . . .
under this open arcade."

> The lovers' bed.
> They may be sleeping. We don't know.
> The noise of the city has returned. It is continuous, all of
> a piece. It is the noise of vast spaces.
> Through the shutters, sunlight falls in patterns on the bed.

Hai Lon Ong veers south to Tran Van Kieu and the waterfront. I
walk as far as the dried fish market. Its reek sucks up the air, replacing it
with ammonia so pungently dry it's like no air at all. There are a dozen
kinds of fish, each meticulously arranged as if ancient tradition orches-
trated the desiccated wheels, spires, pyramids, and domes. Perch, smelt,
flounder, squid line the aisles like crisp bills stacked at a mint. What do
they do with them? Are they edible? Shoppers ignore the fetor, fondle
the goods like epicures, pop brittle anchovies into their baskets and make
for home.

Through the back door is a wharf where workers weigh fish, spread
them on rattan trays to dry in the sun. The canal flows past.

> She asks him what he does at night. He says he goes and
> drinks choum [rice brandy] with the chauffeur along the
> waterways.

The waterways. Cholon. Upstream from the dried fish market the

Cán Gíuøc Bridge crosses the canal. At midspan old men hawk bric-a-brac and worn shoes, a striking young Humong woman offers videos for sale: Sylvestor Stallone, Chuck Norris, Bruce Lee. The waterway is lined with lopsided old warehouses, houseboats, and stilthouses that look as if they'll topple into their own reflections. A luminescent crust films the canal, where grotesque objects of deformed plastic bubble and fume in an inky cocktail. Sipping *choum* with your chauffeur along its banks may have been pleasant sixty years ago, but today the Bén Nghé Canal is not enticing. I leave it and walk the lanes toward Hai Lon Ong.

> "Tell me again: to be rich, to do nothing and bear it, you need money and what else . . ."
> "To be Chinese"—he smiles—"and play cards. I play a lot . . . often with the scum along the channels at night. Without gambling, you can't go on."

A night at the Cholon Hotel, tossing fitfully beneath a photomural of witless brown cows cropping edelweiss in an alpine meadow. Below, the motor roar quits at two and at four begins again, tuning up for the morning's performance. The breakfast rush is on at the foodstalls below my window. There's nothing for it but to join the crush. By five I'm one of dozens squatting on toy-sized stools of frightening pink, spooning in bowls of *pho* and sipping cups of bitter green tea.

The bus for My Tho and the delta leaves at eight. With two hours to kill I go by cyclo across Cholon to the Quan Am Pagoda. Incense spirals as big around as sumo wrestlers smolder endlessly under an ancient tiled roof crusted with ceramic "glove puppet" figurines. Dedicated by Cholon's Fukien congregation to the goddess of mercy, it's nonetheless A Pho, the Queen of Heaven, who dominates the central hall where worshipers come in a steady flow, smoke floating from their joss-stick bouquets. A familial, easygoing atmosphere permeates Vietnamese pagodas. At Quan Am people gossip, sleep, nibble snacks, read newspapers, and pray.

We jolt out of Cholon Station at 8:15, last-minute food vendors tumbling from the bus into the road as we turn south on Trang Tu. I've found a seat toward the back, with room for my bag in the overhead rack. It's a sturdily built old vehicle with springless seats and windows without glass—a blessing in the heat.

I'm the only European among a busful of Vietnamese country people who've sold their produce, eggs, ducks, geese, and are heading back to their villages with city swag. We backtrack along the road the child and the Chinese lover drove after their meeting on the Vinh Long ferry. Before, when going home for holidays, the child rode the "native" bus between Sadec and Saigon. Then things changed: "She gets into the black car. The door shuts. . . . Never again shall I travel by native bus . . . I've lost, good and bad, the bus, the bus driver I used to laugh with, the old women chewing betel in the back seats, the children on the luggage racks." This morning bicycles are piled on the luggage racks, baskets, boxes bound with twine, bulging burlap sacks slung above like slaughtered stock. In the back, yes, old women punctuate their gossip with splats of betel leveled at the aisle.

The city falls behind, the delta stretches ahead. Water buffalo. Duck ponds. Small houses among banana trees. Flamboyants in full crimson bloom. "The sea of rice paddies of Cochin China. The watery plain crisscrossed by little, straight white roads for the children's carts. The unmoving, monumental hell of the heat. As far as the eye can see, the fabulous, silken flatness of the delta."

Cochin China—the whole of Vietnam to the sixteenth-century Portuguese who tried but failed to found a colony here. To the French, whose missionaries arrived in 1680, it was the south, the region below Phan Thiét. It's Cochin China where the Mekong, after flowing 2,500 miles from its source on the Tibetan Plateau, fans into nine great streams—Cuu Long, "Nine Dragons." They sweep "quietly, without a sound, like blood in the body" over the alluvial flatlands of the delta to the sea.

———

Midmorning. My first glimpse of the Mekong at My Tho on the banks of the Tien Giang River, the northernmost of the Nine Dragons. It was to My Tho that Chinese immigrants fled from Taiwan when the Ming dynasty collapsed in 1644. Chinese still live on the eastern shore of the Bao Dinh Canal, where stilthouse shops are stacked with sugarcane, melons, fish awaiting transport to Saigon. Turning west along a road paralleling the river, we head into the "great plain of rice in southern Cochin China. The Plain of Birds." Another forty miles of rough road between paddyland and riverside villages to My Thuan and the ferry to Vinh Long. The ferry of the child and the North China lover.

> This is the river.
> This is the ferry across the Mekong. The ferry in the books.
> On the river.
> There on the ferry is the native bus, the long black Léon Bollée cars, the North China lovers, looking.

The swiftly flowing Co Chien, a mile wide and swarming with sampans, fragile little rowing boats, ponderous junks, lines of barges drawn by powerful tugs, oceangoing freighters ghosting upriver on the tide. We join a column of vehicles waiting to cross. Makeshift food stalls border the road: the piquant aroma of grilled pork; soft drinks; cool green coconuts. "They gather around the roadside stands. The child looks at the cakes, made of corn soaked in coconut milk, sweetened with molasses and wrapped in a banana leaf. The Chinese treats her to one. She takes it. She devours it. She doesn't say thank you."

The buses idle, creep forward. Motorbikes, trucks on their way south to load cargoes of rice. The bus conductor tracks me down outside a coconut stall, hands me my bag, a ticket for the ferry. There's no need to wait. I can go aboard, travel on my own to Vinh Long.

Two ferries are loading. I choose the smallest, a silver-skinned vessel, open-decked at either end, the upper level for passengers, a pilothouse topside. A truck, groaning under its load, rumbles up the ramp. People pushing bicycles, farm women in black pajamas and limpet hats, children, soldiers. A bus follows. We all come next, scrambling aboard.

> The elegant man has got out of the limousine and is smoking an English cigarette. He looks at the girl in the man's fedora and the gold shoes. He slowly comes over to her.

Today there are no limousines. No elegant men smoking English cigarettes. The days of the *colons* are finished, the days of the millionaire Chinese. From the foredeck the river stretches to the far shore, where trees shield the embankment. We move off, sweeping downstream in a long arc. "The engine of the ferry is the only sound, a rickety old engine with burned-out rods. From time to time, in faint bursts, the sound of voices." We pass an approaching ferry at midstream, then work upriver toward the landing, only twenty minutes until we bump ashore.

———

I don't have any photographs of Vinh Long, not one, of the garden, the river, the straight-tamarind-lined avenues of the French conquest . . .

The Cuu Long Hotel. A ground-floor room facing the river. I drag a chair onto the balcony to watch evening settle over the water. It's sweltering, the ponderous sky a tarnished pewter. "We have just one season, hot, monotonous, we're in the long hot girdle of the earth." The significance of Vinh Long is uncertain to the child. The emphasis shifts between books. *The Lover* delves further into the child's past than does *The North China Lover.* In *The Lover* she speaks of the untaken photographs, writes of the dousing-down of the house as if it were in Vinh Long, not Sadec, where pailfuls of water were splashed through the rooms. "I remember . . . our elder brother wasn't in Vinh Long when we sluiced the house out." She maintains he was in France. Yet in the opening passage of *The North China Lover* she writes, "A house in the middle of a schoolyard. Everything is wide open . . . They're washing down the house." Later that day she observes, "The older brother is watching the mother . . ." Pierre, who was clearly present, wasn't expatriated until after the Chinese lover came into the child's life—a time when she was clearly in Sadec.

What is consistent is the nightmarish recollection of "the local lunatic, the madwoman of Vinh Long." Each novel contains descriptions of the child's fear of this terrifying bogey-person who, shrieking, tracks her through the streets. In *The Lover* she writes, "It's one of the long avenues in Vinh Long that lead down to the Mekong. It's always deserted in the evening . . . She's barefoot, and she's running after me to catch me. . . . I must be eight years old. I can hear her shrieks." When, in *The North China Lover,* she tells this story to the Chinese, he says the person is "one of those beggarwomen between Vinh-Long and Sadec who shrieks while she's laughing."

An unwieldy junk without lights creeps out of a nearby canal and begins a perilous journey across the black night of the Mekong to An Binh Island. Twenty yards off the hotel, sampans lie at anchor. On board, mothers bathe their children while men gossip and fuss with their boats. When the rain starts, a slashing torrent that's the first of the monsoons, everyone scrambles belowdeck in a hopeless effort to stay dry. The Mekong vanishes behind a watery curtain, the laden junk a forgotten comma in the everlasting history of the river.

After the downpour I walk under dripping trees to the riverside market, then west along the embankment through the old French Quarter, "the long avenues in Vinh Long that lead down to the Mekong." Ban Kinh Te, on the banks of the Rach Cai Ca Canal, is the most striking of Vinh Long's colonial buildings. Here lived Anne-Marie Stretter, wife of the general administrator. "In Vinh-Long they call her A.M.S." The child tells the Chinese stories of the woman's lovers, of the young man in Savanna Khet who killed himself for love of her. The child identifies with A.M.S.: they're both outcasts, their disgrace a "matter of course." Her own isolation at Chasseloup-Laubat "brings back a clear memory of the lady in Vinh Long. At that time she'd just turned thirty-eight. And the child is ten. And now, when she remembers, she's sixteen. The lady's on the terrace outside her room, looking at the avenues bordering the Mekong."

The promiscuous Anne-Marie Stretter may have been swept away with French colonialism, but Ban Kinh Te isn't abandoned. The saffron mansion stands freshly painted, its plaster garlands profuse with creamy flowers, the newly tiled roof iridescent after rain. The streets are deserted this evening. The child was right. But as I cross a bridge over the canal and wander roads scattered with forgotten villas, there's no sign of the "the local lunatic, the madwoman of Vinh Long."

———

This is an outpost in southern French Indochina.
The year is 1930.
This is the French Quarter.

Khách San Sadéc—The Hotel Sadec. A heavy, three-story modernistic cube in the Soviet style, something the East Germans in the fifties would have designed, or the Bulgarians. The elevator doesn't work, so I shoulder my bag up a staircase fashioned for the ceremonious entrances of upper-echelon party functionaries. My third-floor room's a no-nonsense chamber with a complicated collapsible mosquito net and cumbersome furniture crafted for maximum discomfort.

I arrived from Vinh Long on the back of a Honda Dream. Fourteen miles of bad road, booming across creaking bridges crossing boat-filled canals. A string of brick kilns along the riverbank, great mosquelike domes with brick minarets spewing smoke into the monsoon sky. Sadec is larger than I expected, dirtier, noisier, poorer. A muddy market sprawls for a mile along the banks of the Sadec River. Among the stalls, *com* shops serve rice with pork, chicken, beef. After a midmorning meal, I drink iced beer and watch shopkeepers play a multidimensional game of Chinese checkers. A hefty twelve-year-old in snowy terrycloth robe kibitzes. Several moves ahead of the opponents, he offers postmortems after every move. The game promises to go on all morning. I leave the threesome in a state of cerebral tension and walk back to the hotel.

Vu T Phuong Trang, in an *ao dai* of Prussian blue, seems no bigger than a puppet behind the hotel's reception desk, a brown monstrosity the size of a newspaper kiosk. She has a Botticelli smile and her English is soft, mellifluous, approximate. Between her rhetorical adventures and my ignorance of Vietnamese, our conversation takes bewildering directions. Still, when I mention Marguerite Duras, Vu brightens, nodding in vigorous affirmation.

With quick strokes of a ballpoint pen she sketches arrows on a map printed across the back of a hotel brochure. It's simple enough—out the entrance and four blocks along Húng Voung Street. "On corner." She draws a dainty X as if annotating a treasure map. "Just here . . . you see."

I stumble into the heat. A block down Húng Voung an accumulation of derelict thrill rides, primitively made as if by some amateur carnival enthusiast, colonize a weedy lot. I pass a *pho* stall, a corner market, a few modest houses. Then, on the corner of Hö Xuän Huong appears "a house in the middle of a school yard . . . This is the gate. This is the schoolyard."

The gaunt old concierge, a thin and pallid opium smoker, peers down from the porch like a starving owl. I ask if this is the school where Marguerite Duras lived as a child, where her mother was headmistress.

"Yes," he says, brushing fanciful crumbs from his stripped pajamas. "Is place of . . . cinema."

Here director Jean-Jacques Annaud shot scenes for *The Lover,* his film based on the Duras novel, starring Jane March as the child and Tony Leung as the Chinese lover. This explains Vu T Phuong Trang's knowledge of the French author, the concierge's familiarity with things cine-matic. With a smile and the sweep of a bony hand, he invites me in.

Three small buildings cluster around the schoolyard, pale ocher walls scarred by the scuffling roughhouse of generations of school kids. Tile roofs, long covered porches, blue louvered shutters opening into class-rooms. One building has a wing, an arcade with several doorways. "The child is in the entryway of the house, over by the dining room that looks into the large schoolyard. Everything is open. . . . And then we see her looking at something she sees but we cannot yet: Paulo . . . He is sleep-ing in the arcade that runs the length of the classrooms, behind a low wall, shaded from the moonlight."

In this school, this small structure where the concierge now lives, the destiny of the child's deeply wounded family played itself out. Here the pathologic Pierre torments Paulo, the younger brother; the mother, egged on by Pierre, beats the child, attacks her, "falls on me, locks me up in my room, punches me, undresses me, comes up to me and smells my body, my underwear, says she can smell the Chinese's scent"—the same despairing, unbalanced mother who "lets the girl go out dressed like a child prostitute."

One morning the Chinese lover arrives at the school. He announces to the mother that he's having an affair with her daughter and sets in motion the denouement. The Chinese owners of La Fumerie du Mékong have spent months trying to collect the money the mother owes for Pierre's opium habit. When they discover the child's Chinese lover is the son of the millionaire "from the blue house" on the river, they quickly depart. The "chettys," Indian moneylenders who sit endlessly under the arcade waiting to be paid, are no longer a threat. The Chinese will pay the debts, pay for Pierre's repatriation to France, then passage for Paulo, the mother, the child. "My father doesn't want a marriage between his son and your daughter, Madame. But he is prepared to give you the money you need to settle your debts and leave Indochina."

On the child's last visit to this school in Sadec, the chettys have laid claim to the furniture, Dö's old sewing machine is gone, the "beds are still in the bedrooms, they've got tags on them with writing in Chinese." She talks with her mother, makes love to her brother Paulo on the cool tiles of the bathroom floor, the "only time in their lives they made love together." Thanh is there, Thanh whom the mother found in the forests of the frontier between Siam and Cambodia and brought into her "family." It is to Thanh that *The North China Lover* is dedicated, Thanh and the mother's servant Dö who provide a center, a sense of coherence in this desolate family, this "family of stone, petrified so deeply it's impenetrable." Only Thanh knows that the father of the Chinese lover has paid off all their debts and laid down just one condition, "that they clear out of the colony."

The life at the school in Sadec is left behind as Thanh drives the child back to Saigon in the mother's battered old car, the B-12. Now there is only the farewell, the ache of love between the child and the Chinese from "the light blue, China blue house" on the banks of the Sadec River.

> ...she tells him that he must talk to his wife about everything that happened—between you and me, she says—between her husband and the girl from the school in Sadec...
>
> The Chinese had asked: Why his wife? Why tell her rather than others?
>
> She said: because for her it's the pain that will make her understand the story.
>
> He asked again:
>
> "And if there is no pain."
>
> "Then it will all be forgotten."

———

The old metal bridge connects the market with the distant bank. Wooden planks clatter on their sleepers under the impact of passing traffic. A sampan floats downstream toward the sea.

When I reach the far side, I discover motorbikes clustered beneath tamarind trees. Burly, grinning Trung detaches himself from his cronies lounging in the shade. "Where to, boss?"

"The Chinese . . . the house of blue tiles on the riverbank."

I brandish Vu's map—only a couple of arrows pointing downstream.

"No problem, boss."

A rutted road leads through ranks of empty police barracks and into the countryside. Trung pilots his blaring Honda with exuberant nonchalance as I cling behind. Soon we rush over an earth-filled dam crossing two sweeping branches of the Mekong, then plunge into a village bordering the track. Emaciated grandmothers and naked, snot-nosed babies share the muddy verges and foul ground between ramshackle shanties, while snarling orange curs snap at my ankles. "They pass through villages of rice, children, and dogs." Of all the hamlets I've encountered in my travels through Vietnam, this shoddy settlement en route to the house of the millionaire Chinese is the most wretched.

Suddenly the road turns between a pair of huts and angles along the riverbank. We slam to a stop before an elaborate, padlocked wrought-iron gate mounted on carved columns. The child said, "The blue house is the most beautiful one in Vinh-Long and Sadec put together, he must be a millionaire, his father." It is large and ungraceful, impressive rather than beautiful. The house is a tile-roofed mansion, oddly Victorian, a central tower flanked by a pair of awkward wings. A dozen lofty shuttered windows face the river, each surmounted by an arc of blue tiles—the only blue tiles to be seen. I'm left with the feeling that writing of Sadec fifty years after departing Indochina, Marguerite Duras let memory beguile her into endowing the house of the Chinese millionaire with qualities reality betrays.

The flag of Vietnam, a yellow star on a red field, flies from the balcony over the entrance. A sign swings above the gate:

Truổng Tiéu Hoc

Tãn Hung

Ironically, the house of the Chinese has become the New Prosperity Primary School, as if in death the child and the North China lover have united in this pair of schools on opposite banks of the Sadec River.

My arrival creates a stir. People from the village gather, peering over my shoulder as I scribble in my small green notebook. They're suspicious, unhappy at my intrusion. A crowd assembles among the reeds along the riverbank to launch a sampan. When I snap a picture, they surge across the road to join the villagers. The smiles, the honeyed politeness usual with Vietnamese, are missing. Instead a sudden threatening truculence makes me pocket my notebook and bury the camera in my bag. Trung grasps my arm.

"Come on, boss . . . time we go."

We turn speedily round, the Honda popping violently as the crowd edges nearer. Trung guns the bike and we bound away. As we smack into the first pothole, I glance back. The knot of people hasn't budged. The villa soars behind them, a slender arc of blue tiles above each shuttered window. The shadow of the house Marguerite Duras described in her books is an ungainly phantom beside the bronze flow of the Mekong.

———

They are by the channel for the Messageries Maritimes, where they've been going every evening during the big heat.

The chauffeur stops in front of a kind of stand covered with branches. They drink choum.

After the delta, Saigon is a blow—raucous, packed. Evening. I drink beer on the banks of the Saigon River. A counter, a dozen stools, a rack of foreign journals: *Cosmopolitan, Stern, Paris-Match.* The owner and his pretty wife sit deep among the magazines, devouring *com tay cam,* rice with chicken and mushrooms, their chopsticks deftly snatching food from Styrofoam boxes. Well-dressed strollers crowd the park where touts hawk boat rides along the Ben Nghe Channel. A fish-snouted ferry sets off for distant An Giang, deep in the delta. Across Ton Duc Thang the Hotel Majestic is a pink bonbon in the fading light.

A hundred yards downstream, at the mouth of the channel, a flagstaff like a ship's mast, tall and heavily-sparred, marks the Pointe des Blagueurs—Jokers' Point—where *colons* ended their promenade after strolling from the cathedral down the rue Catinat. Downstream, moored along the bank, oceangoing freighters, black-hulled vessels from Bangkok, Singapore, Seattle load cargo. Across the waters of the channel stands an oriental mansion, Nha Rong, "Dragon House," now the Ho Chi Minh Museum. From the nearby wharf Ho sailed for Europe in 1911 to begin the long battle for the freedom and independence of his country. Built in the 1860s, Nha Rong was once headquarters of the French shipping firm Messageries Maritimes.

The liners used to go up the Saigon River, engines off, drawn by tugs to the port installations in the bend in the Mekong . . . The boats stopped there for a week. As soon as they berthed, you were in France. You could dine in France and dance there . . .It was the handsome ships of the Mes-

151

sageries Maritimes, the musketeers of the shipping lines, the Porthos, D'Artagnan, and Aramis, that linked Indochina to France.

From here they sailed. Before his meeting with the child the North China lover went to and from the United States and Europe. Later, the child's repatriated addict brother Pierre sailed. "The older brother is on the lower deck of the ship. . . . He is leaving for the first time. He is nineteen years old." He went to France, to Lot-et-Garonne, where he lived with a relative, a village priest. Finally, the mother, the little brother, the child. The propellers churned the river, the great liner pulled from the pier. "And it is done. The ship has left land."

As the vessel slipped downstream, the limousine, the Léon Bollée, came into view: "He was in the back of the big black car that is parked along the wall of a warehouse in the port. In his usual dress. The raw tussore silk suit. As though he were sleeping."

This is it. The end. Though years later, when the woman who was the child lived in Paris, the Chinese telephoned. They talked—reaffirmed their love. Their story, he said, "had remained what it was before." He loved her, would love her always, love her until death.

The stall owner and his wife serve drinks to couples at the bar. The ferry has left for An Giang. A storm approaches, a curtain of rain sweeping over the river. Almost seventy years have passed since the child sailed for France. Not long after, planes replaced the great oceangoing liners. By the spring of 1954 the French themselves were gone, defeated by the Viet Minh at Dien Bien Phu. Then the American war, fifteen years of bloodletting that took three million lives. The rain comes and goes. A cooling breeze blows up from the South China Sea. A freighter, the *Opatija,* flying the Croatian flag, edges from the quay and swings into the current. Everything has changed: the name of the country, the city, everything. Yet nothing. The story, said the North China lover, has remained what it was before.

10

Room over the Rue Catinat

Graham Greene in Vietnam

THE WEDDING GUESTS appeared on the Place Garnier, stepped through gleaming doors into the Continental's lobby. Striding Aussies in sharp suits, escorting chic blondes, followed by clusters of Vietnamese, the women in stunning *ao dais,* the classic dress of Vietnam, exquisitely colored silk tunics over flowing trousers. In his autobiography, *Ways of Escape,* Graham Greene described falling in love with Indochina. "The spell was first cast, I think, by the tall elegant girls in white silk trousers."

Saigon's Hotel Continental stands along Dong Khoi, the former rue Catinat, only a few hundred yards from Notre Dame Cathedral's redbrick spires and four blocks from the Saigon River. From my table in the Continental Bar, where a tuxedoed Vietnamese at a baby grand played melodies I couldn't quite identify, I watched a willowy young woman in an *ao dai* of daffodil yellow meet the wedding guests at the door and lead them beneath a coffered ceiling profuse with chandeliers. Blue-black hair swept to her waist ,and when she turned to gaze through the arched passageway into the bar, I saw a face of such astonishing loveliness that she might have been Phuong, Fowler's lover in Graham Greene's *The Quiet American,* "the most beautiful girl in Saigon."

It was at the Continental that Fowler first met Alden Pyle, the quiet American. "I had seen him last September coming across the square towards the bar of the Continental: an unmistakably young and unused face flung at us like a dart." An innocent American confronting an older, subtler civilization, Pyle seemed to have sprung from the imagination of Henry James. A high-minded CIA operative, he had a naïve faith in democracy and a mission to find a "third force," a way between the colonial French and the Communist Viet Minh, as if he knew what was best for these diverse and ancient peoples. Fowler said of him, "I never knew a man who had better motives for all the trouble he caused."

It was at the Continental two months later that Pyle first met Phuong. She and Fowler sat together on the terrace. "The dice rattled on the tables where the French were playing *Quatre cent Vingt-et-un* and the girls in the white silk trousers bicycled home down the rue Catinat." Later that evening the three dined at the Chalet, a restaurant along the road to Cholon. Pyle instantly fell in love with Phuong and, after months of high-minded moralizing, usurped her from Fowler by promising her marriage and a respectable life in Boston.

The family of the bride arrived: mother, father, aunts, uncles, graceful and austere with exquisite bones and the elegant plumage of rare birds. Again I was reminded of that dinner at the Chalet: "Two Vietnamese couples were dancing, small, neat, aloof, with an air of civilization we couldn't match. . . . They never, one felt, dressed carelessly, said the wrong word, were a prey to untidy passion. If the war seemed medieval, they were like the eighteenth-century future."

A waiter brought another gin and tonic, tall, iced, delicious. The piano player took a break. Beyond the arch the lobby emptied, a half acre of marble and gleaming hardwood where the young woman in yellow suddenly appeared alone. For a heartbeat . . . no, it wasn't for me she waited. The wedding couple was here: the bride in silk of scarlet and gold, a matching hat crowning clipped raven hair, while her groom, a flushed Australian of pudgy middle age, sagged beside her in shapeless gabardine. Cameras flashed, videos whirred as they were drawn triumphantly across the lobby. The party, daffodil girl and all, vanished into a banquet hall. Tall mahogany doors swayed shut.

Born in England in 1904, Graham Greene published his first novel, *The Man Within,* in 1929. *The Quiet American,* his fourteenth, came in 1955, followed by ten more before his death in France in 1991. He also wrote plays, autobiography, essays, children's books, film criticism, and screenplays—most notably *The Third Man.*

In 1951 Greene went to Malaya to cover the Emergency for *Life.* A conflict between anti-Communist parties, inspired and backed by

Britain, and Malayan Communists, the Emergency was another of those ambiguous military actions of the period: "like the French in Indochina," Greene wrote in *Ways of Escape,* "the Government did not officially call it a war."

On his way back to Britain Greene stopped off to visit friends in Vietnam and began his love affair with Indochina. *Life* liked his Malaya article and asked him to cover the French–Viet Minh war. What he wrote appeared in *Paris-Match,* but only after *Life* turned it down. Greene suspected that his "ambivalent attitude to the war was already perceptible— my admiration for the French Army, my admiration for their enemies, and my doubt of any final value in the war."

The prescience of this observation, his "doubt of any final value in the war," informs *The Quiet American,* sets it apart and justifies the claim by the reviewer for *Harper's:* "There has been no novel of any political scope about Vietnam since . . . *The Quiet American.*" The style and form of Greene's novel are relatively simple, its complexities of plot derived from flashbacks and time shifts. It begins with the political assassination of the idealistic Pyle by the forces of Mr. Heng and a mysterious Viet Minh "Committee" and follows with Fowler's recounting of the incidents leading up to the killing.

Much of the story is set "in my room over the rue Catinat" and along the shady street running from the Cathedral to the river. This was Fowler's beat. An English reporter in Vietnam covering the French–Viet Minh war for a London paper, Fowler was uncommitted: "The human condition being what it was, let them fight, let them love, let them murder. I would not be involved."

A true believer in democracy and the responsibilities of the West, Pyle was Fowler's opposite. Their conflicting values generated a colloquy between doctrine and doubt, innocence and experience, idealism and realism. The debate began the morning Pyle arrived on the terrace of the Continental and Fowler gave him a rundown on the political and military situation in the country. "The French control the main roads until seven in the evening; they control the watch towers after that, and the towns—part of them. That doesn't mean you are safe, or there wouldn't be iron grilles in front of the restaurants." Fowler informed Pyle of General Thé, the Caodaist chief of staff who led his forces into the hills to fight both the Communists and the French.

At mention of Thé, Pyle told Fowler of his hero and mentor York Harding, the American author of *The Advance of Red China:* "'York,' Pyle said, 'wrote that what the East needed was a Third Force.' Perhaps I should have seen that fanatic gleam, the quick response to a phrase, the magic sound of figures: Fifth Column, Third Force, Seventh Day. I might have saved all of us a lot of trouble, even Pyle, if I had realized the direction of that indefatigable young brain." Their meeting over, Fowler left Pyle "with arid bones of background" and took his "daily walk up and down the rue Catinat."

With the wedding party launched into a nightlong banquet, I left the Continental and strolled across Lam Son Square, the Place Garnier of Greene's day. I passed the belle époque Municipal Theater, its domed entrance jacketed in the scaffolding of reconstruction, then walked down rue Catinat.

A hot June night, the street a river of cyclos (Greene called them *trishaws*), motorbikes and taxis, the cafés and coffee bars packed. In dedicating *The Quiet American* to "Réné and Phuong," Greene thanked the couple for allowing him to have "quite shamelessly borrowed the location of your flat to house one of my characters." The character was Fowler, the flat somewhere above the treetops in this block midway between the Continental and the Hotel Majestic on the riverfront. Outside, in the hallway, old women gossiped as always, and Fowler opened his book to a poem, then turned and looked out the window to the cyclo parked across the street. Which flat exactly? Which building? I had no way of knowing, although a cyclo was parked across from where I stood outside the saffron facade of the old Hotel Catinat.

"I had a drink at the Continental at six," Fowler recounted when Inspector Vigot of the French Sûreté questioned him the night of Pyle's murder. "At six forty-five I walked down to the quay to watch the American planes unloaded. I saw Wilkins of the Associated News by the door of the Majestic. Then I went into the cinema next door."

I had coffee in the crowded Paloma Café, across the street from the Hotel Catinat, then continued along rue Catinat to the Hotel Majestic. Traffic accelerated down Ton Duc Thang, while across the way couples crowded the riverfront park and a floating restaurant disgorged its passengers. From here Fowler watched the unloading of the American bombers. Tonight, red, blue, and green neon shone on the dark sweep of water from the Canon and Carlsberg signs across the river and down-stream, moored along the quay, black-hulled freighters from Shanghai, Singapore, and San Francisco loaded cargo under arc lamps in the steamy Saigon night.

———

In the morning, under the clock tower at the Ben Thanh Market, I caught a cyclo and was pedaled through the clamor of traffic down Le Loi, once the Boulevard Bonnard. We passed the Rex Hotel at Nguyen Hue, the former Boulevard Charner. On our left soared the belle époque Hôtel de Ville, and a moment later we burst into Lam Son Square, the old Place Garnier.

At precisely 11:30 on a hot monsoon morning while Fowler drank iced beer at the Pavilion, a coffee bar favored by expatriate women, "two of the mirrors on the wall flew at me and collapsed half-way." For a moment Fowler thought it another joke, like General Thé's bicycle bombs, for which, according to Fowler's informant Mr. Heng, Pyle sup-plied the ingredients. The bicycle bombs, however, were more or less harmless. When he stepped onto the Place Garnier, Fowler "realized by the heavy clouds of smoke that this was no joke. The smoke came from cars burning in the car-park in front of the national theatre . . . a man without his legs lay twitching at the edge of the ornamental gardens."

Fowler's first thought was personal: at this hour, Phuong, now Pyle's mistress, would be in the milk bar across the square. He tried to reach her but was stopped by the police. Then Pyle suddenly appeared: "Pyle . . . for Christ's sake, where's your Legation pass? We've got to get across. Phuong's in the milk bar." She wasn't there, Pyle informed Fowler. He'd warned her not to come. Fowler remembered two young American women in the Pavilion who said they'd been warned to leave before 11:30 and realized that Pyle and the Americans were responsible for the blast. From the moment he saw a peasant woman "on the ground with what was left of her baby in her lap," Fowler's avowed noninvolvement evaporated and he was suddenly committed. Not to an idea, but to indi-viduals horribly damaged by the quiet American's intrusive "innocence." When Pyle observed that he must have the blood cleaned from his shoe before appearing at the legation, Fowler's course was clear.

———

We swung past the scaffolded facade of the Municipal Theater, turned beneath the huge revolving globe on the corner of the Hotel Continental, and continued up the rue Catinat until "the hideous pink Cathedral blocked the way." We circled the cathedral and turned right onto Le Duan. After two blocks we came to a derelict windowless honeycomb of reinforced concrete surrounded by wire-topped walls and spiked gates—the former American embassy, the "Legation," where Fowler, furious at the loss of Phuong, looked for Pyle and instead found Joe, the economic attaché: "He sleeps with my girl, Fowler shouted—your typist's sister."

From the embassy we continued up Le Doun as far as the Botanical Gardens, where Pyle and Phuong "had been photographed beside a large stone dragon. She held Pyle's dog on a leash—a black chow with a black tongue." Fowler found the photo among Pyle's things after his death, along with a copy of York Harding's *The Rôle of the West,* and took both as mementos. At the Botanical Gardens we turned left along Nguyén Binh Khiêm and crossed the Boulevard Dien Bien Phu. We were now in Dakow, the neighborhood of the Jade Emperor Pagoda, a heavily ornamented turn-of-the-century Buddhist-Taoist temple. In its shadow a narrow span crossed the Thi Nghe Channel: Pyle's body was found "in the river by the bridge to Dakow—Vietminh territory when your police withdraw at night." On the night of the murder, Fowler identified Pyle's body. "He wasn't dead from this, Vigot said, pointing at a [bayonet] wound in the chest. He was drowned in the mud. We found the mud in his lungs."

—•—

After the bomb blast in the Place Garnier, Fowler took a motor trishaw to the Quay Mytho in Cholon to see Mr. Heng.

> "Bombs aren't for boys from Boston. Who is Pyle's chief, Heng?"
>
> "I have the impression that Mr. Pyle is very much his own master."
>
> "What is he? O.S.S.?"
>
> "The initial letters are not very important. I think now they are different."
>
> "What can I do, Heng? He's got to be stopped."

Heng advised Fowler to write the truth of what happened, but Fowler reminded him that his paper was not interested in General Thé, only in the Viet Minh. Then he might go to the police, Heng suggested. The police wouldn't touch an American—besides, Pyle had diplomatic privileges, he was a graduate of Harvard, and the minister was fond of him. Heng took a more pragmatic turn: would Fowler invite Pyle to dinner at the Vieux Moulin?

> "Why the Vieux Moulin?"
> "It is by the bridge to Dakow—I think we shall be able
> to find a spot and talk undisturbed."

Fowler knew quite well that the Viet Minh would not talk with Pyle. They would simply kill him. Yet Fowler agreed to invite Pyle to dinner and set the quiet American up for assassination. Though he'd hoped to remain "not *engagé*," he was now wholly involved. At the outset his motives appeared sound. He thought of the woman in the Place Garnier with the dead baby in her lap, the legless man twitching by the flower beds, the bomb victims who Pyle said "had died for democracy." And he thought of the quiet American with his bloodied shoe among the dead.

But his motives were clouded by his passion: his jealousy, his desire to have Phuong back. Phoung, "the most beautiful girl in Saigon," embodied Greene's Indochina and, by extension, Fowler's. In *Ways of Escape,* Greene wrote that in Vietnam he'd "drained a magic potion, a loving cup." Phuong was not someone Fowler could give up.

I left my driver with his cyclo parked outside the Jade Emperor Pagoda, crossed Mai Thi Luum and walked onto the Dakow Bridge. The canal was pestilential, a foul gravy frothing between its embankments. No sign of the Vieux Moulin that had been "wired against grenades," with "two armed policemen . . . on duty at the end of the bridge." Traffic sped past, the omnipresent motorbikes assaulting the nerve ends with their smoke and incessant blare. I stopped at midspan and peered down. It was there they had found Pyle: "He was in the water under the bridge to Dakow." A few days later Pyle's missing dog turned up with its throat cut. "It was in the mud fifty yards away. Perhaps it dragged itself that far."

I went into the pagoda, the air heavy with the smoke of smoldering incense. Among a carved panoply of gods and goddesses, Ngoc Hoang, the Jade Emperor of the Taoists, dominated the main sanctuary. Ornately robed and heavily mustached, Ngoc Hoang is an Asian Saint Peter who oversees entry into Heaven. I stood among a crowd before the central altar, where supplicants arrived in a steady flow, smoke floating from their bundled joss sticks. And what was the Jade Emperor's judgment the night Pyle died? Who was bound for heaven? Who for hell? Fowler? Pyle? Mr. Heng and the Viet Minh? Or had Ngoc Hoang settled it like Inspector Vigot: "I'm just making a report, that's all. So long as it's an act of war—well, there are thousands killed every year."

———

Northwest of Saigon, across fifty miles of paddy land, Tay Ninh lies at the foot of Nui Ba Den, Black Lady Mountain. In a part of the world where every faith has its sacred mountain, Nui Ba Den, the only hillock in flat countryside not far from the Cambodian frontier, is the setting of the Holy See of the Caodai. Dreamed up by Ngo Minh Chieu, a civil servant turned mystic, and officially sanctioned by the French in 1926, Caodaism is a mélange of oriental faiths—Confucian, Taoist, Buddhist—organized along the lines of Roman Catholicism with "a Pope and female cardinals. Prophecy by planchette [Ouija board]. Saint Victor Hugo. Christ and Buddha looking down from the roof of the Cathedral on a Walt Disney fantasia of the East, dragons and snakes in technicolour."

In *A Dragon Apparent,* Norman Lewis' account of his travels in Indochina, the English writer also drew on Disney to describe the Caodaists: "There was a cathedral . . . that looked like a fantasy from the brain of Disney, and all the faiths of the Orient had been ransacked to create the pompous ritual."

In the early 1950s, when Greene and Lewis traveled to Indochina on quite separate journeys, each discovered that the Caodaists maintained a large army. Lewis wrote, "Cao-Daïsts had a formidable private army with which they controlled a portion of Cochin-China. The French tolerated them because they were anti-Viet-Minh." In *The Quiet American* Greene wrote that the Caodaists had "twenty-five thousand men, armed with mortars made out of the exhaust pipes of old cars, allies of the French who turned neutral at the moment of danger." Both travelers described the watchtowers that lined Route 22 from Saigon to the heart of the Holy See. "Every kilometer," Greene wrote, "a small mud watch tower stood up above the flat fields." Lewis found: "These pigmy forts lent a rather pleasant accent, a faintly Tuscan flavour, to the flat monotony of the landscape."

Lewis' allusion to Tuscany seemed a bit farfetched on a stifling

morning in griddle-flat paddy land where small boys rode water buf-
faloes up to their bellies in mud. My driver, Trinhn, and I left at dawn to
beat Saigon's rush hour and stopped for tea at Cu Chi. Cu Chi is famous
for its network of tunnels used by the Viet Cong to infiltrate Saigon—
deep passageways possessing living quarters, weapons factories, field hos-
pitals. A cloud passed over Trinhn's pinched face when I told him not to
stop for it.

"But, boss," Trinhn said, "everybody want to see Cu Chi tunnel."

"Not everyone, Trinhn."

We set off toward Cambodia across the alluvial monotony of soil
deposited over centuries by the Saigon River a dozen miles to the north.
Rice appeared in various guises, from seedlings planted by rows of
women stooped in their straw limpet hats to golden stands ready for harvest. Houses appeared here and there, tile-roofed bungalows, some of
whose front gardens sported topiary dragons. Tombs rose in the fields,
concrete bunkers in shocking pastels bearing the names of the honored
dead.

At Go Dau we turned away from Moc Bai and the Cambodian
frontier, continuing up Route 22 toward Tay Ninh. In the distance Nui
Ba Den rose three thousand feet above the plain like a vegetable cro-
quette. "That was where General Thé held out, the dissident Chief of
Staff who had recently declared his intention of fighting both the French
and the Vietminh."

A half dozen miles from Tay Ninh, Trinhn turned up a branch road
to Long Hoa. We traveled between roadside joss stick factories, sheaves
of incense stacked along the shoulders to dry. After a couple of miles we
reached the Caodai cathedral—the Great Temple of the Holy See.

Disney did immediately come to mind. Impossible to describe what
Norman Lewis called "the most outrageously vulgar building ever to
have been erected with serious intent," without invoking the cartoonist.
And why wasn't the creator of Mickey Mouse among the host of saints
conjured up by Caodaists? Saints like Winston Churchill, Louis Pasteur,
William Shakespeare, René Descartes, Victor Hugo, and V. I. Lenin, all of
whom prophesize through Caodiast mediums who employ a planchette,
the celebrated *corbeille à bec*.

With its omnipresent "divine eye" surrounded by a triangle and
reminiscent of the eye on the reverse of an American dollar, its flam-

boyant dragon-entwined columns, its great mural depicting the "Third Alliance Between God and Man," a vibrant painting that includes Sun Yat-sen holding an inkwell while Victor Hugo and the Vietnamese poet Nguyen Binh Khiem write "God and Humanity" and "Love and Justice" in Chinese and French, the Great Temple of the Holy See is remarkably kitsch. Beneath the star-spangled dome, eight dragons guard an eight-sided dais supporting a bird's egg blue sphere from which, through fluffy clouds, the divine eye peers.

At noon, accompanied by a string-and-gong band, several hundred worshipers gathered for one of four daily services. Most were garbed in white, while notables wore hats stitched with the divine eye and robes of red, blue, or gold. The orchestra scratched and clanged; prayers, hymns, and chants floated heavenward. As I watched sacrificial flowers, incense, tea, and alcohol being offered to the Supreme Being, I had a hunch that, with fervent young missionaries and sharp marketing, Caodaisim might yet capture the imagination of the West to become the creed of the millennium, spiritual fodder for the New Age.

———

After the service and a scratch lunch at a market stall in Long Hoa, Trinhn and I left the Holy See for Saigon. At a latitude where night falls without the luxury of an extended dusk, Black Lady Mountain was fading when we reached Go Dau. On such an evening Fowler and Pyle found themselves on this road. They'd been to an annual celebration given by the Coadais that foreign dignitaries felt was politically expedient to attend. About to leave so he would arrive before curfew, Fowler discovered Pyle in the parking lot. The American's Buick wouldn't start. Reluctantly, Fowler offered him a lift. They were the last to begin the long trip home. "The procession of cars was well ahead . . . I put on speed to try to overtake it, but we had passed out of the Caodaist zone into the zone of the Hoa-Haos with not even a dust cloud ahead of us. The world was flat and empty in the evening."

As we began the long run to Tráng Báng, I asked Trinhn if we had enough gas.

"No problem, boss," he said without glancing at the gauge. "Plenty gas."

I leaned across to see for myself. The gauge rested on half. "Okay, Trinhn, no problem."

Somewhere in the darkening paddy land ahead, Fowler's car had sputtered, then limped to a halt thirty yards from a watchtower—out of fuel. "Those bastards at Tanyin [Tay Ninh] have siphoned it out . . . It's like them to leave us enough to get out of their zone."

With no alternative, the two men climbed into the watchtower, where they found a pair of young conscripts from the Vietnamese army—minions of the French. One held a rifle, the other a Sten gun that Pyle quickly commandeered.

"We've got a long night ahead," Fowler told Pyle.

"What if the Viets [Viet Minh] attack them? Pyle asked." He meant the conscripts.

The conscripts would "fire a shot and run," Fowler said. "You read it every morning in the *Extrème Orient.* 'A post south-west of Saigon was temporarily occupied last night by the Vietminh.'"

When Trinhn and I got to Tráng Báng, darkness engulfed us. No moon, only the muted lights of motorbikes ahead and astern. "How long, Trinhn?"

"Not long, boss, you'll be drinking *bia hoa* on Bui Vien Street."

"I think the Continental, Trinhn, for a vermouth cassis."

"Vermouth . . .?"

"It's what Fowler would have."

"Who's Fowler, boss?"

Pyle and Fowler talked in the darkness, first of politics, then women. They heard a distant watchtower under attack, the crump of a Vietnamese army tank striking a mine. Then Viet Minh guerrillas discovered Fowler's car. A moment later a "megaphone voice" ordered the sentries to turn over the Europeans. Pyle and Fowler made a run for it. Leaping from the tower, Fowler broke his leg. He lay in the darkness, "breathless" with pain, unable to move and easy prey. Then a bazooka shell exploded on the tower.

When we reached Tan Son Nhat Airport it began to rain, hard drops like coins flung against the windshield, then a thrashing tropical downpour. In the distance, where runway lights were awash, stood weathered rows of parking bays for U.S. Phantom fighters and blackened concrete bunkers that once stored bombs, rockets, napalm.

Pyle dragged Fowler into a flooded paddy, held him down while the Viet Minh raked the rice with a Sten. Proving himself decisive and courageous, he rescued Fowler—an act for which Fowler was not altogether grateful: "Who the hell asked you to save my life?" Pyle claimed he did it so as not to feel guilty about pursuing Fowler's girlfriend: "I couldn't have faced Phuong." Fowler and Pyle, the realist and the idealist, utterly incomprehensible to each other: "We had spent what seemed to have been a week of nights together, but he could no more understand me than he could understand French."

From Tan Son Nhat we arrowed straight to the city's heart. The Rex, the Caravelle, the Majestic drenched by the storm, streets gleaming under streaming motorbikes. Trinhn dropped me in Lam Son Square, and I ducked into the Continental. I looked around for the daffodil girl, but except for the desk clerk, the place was deserted. In the bar the pianist played "Stardust," but the key wasn't right and the melody wandered vaguely in the direction of "My Reverie." Settling into an oversized bamboo chair, I ordered a gin and tonic. A dripping American couple in jogging shoes and basketball shorts strode across the lobby as if it were a gymnasium and called for their key. My drink arrived. Outside, rain slashed down on the rue Catinat. The vermouth cassis could wait for Fowler to arrive. On a night like this you might expect him at any moment.

———

Graham Greene last visited Vietnam in 1955. "After the defeat of the French in the North," he wrote in *Ways of Escape*, "and with some difficulty I reached Hanoi—a sad city abandoned by the French." I, too, headed north to Nha Trang, Hoi An, Da Nang. It was the hot season of a hot year, and by the time I reached Hué it was a stifling hundred degrees. A hundred and five in Hanoi.

I took a room at the Hanh My Hotel, on the edge of the old city, a short walk from Hoan Kiem Lake. Each evening I found Doan on the corner of Hang Gai and Hang Tróng, and he piloted me around the lake in his cyclo. He had a broad Tartar face and perpetual smile thatched by a dark mustache. I rode through the tree-lined boulevards of the French Quarter, along streets of Parisian villas. We passed the Opera House at the eastern end of Trang Tien—a replica of the neo-baroque Paris Opéra, with columns and slate brought from France. Then the State Bank, an Art Deco gem once the Bank of France, and the restored residence of the governor of Tonkin, now the State Guest House. At last we came to the Hotel Metropole, where Doan chatted with fellow cyclo drivers and I had a drink in the bar—the bar Fowler shunned the night he came back from the press camp after an excursion to Phat Diem: "It was cold after dark in Hanoi and the lights were lower than those in Saigon, more suited to the darker clothes of the women and the fact of war . . . I didn't want to drink at the Metropole with the senior French officers, their wives and their girls."

Later, Doan pedaled me through crowds leaving the water puppet theater after the evening's performance, then around Hoan Kiem to catch the meager coolness panting off the lake. People milled in the streets of the old city, sat on corners drinking *bia hoi,* sought air by the lakefront in the stifling city.

On a morning thick with heat and cloud, I walked through the ancient grounds of the Temple of Literature, then joined a long, swiftly moving line, monitored by soldiers in immaculate white, to visit the somber columned mass of the Ho Chi Minh Mausoleum. Engraved in stone at the entrance was Ho's maxim: "Nothing is more important than independence and freedom." We streamed up a wide staircase into a cool room, circled the solemn chamber where Ho lay under glass, a frail figure aglow in soft light. Below the white wisps of his beard birdlike hands nested on a shrunken chest.

From the mausoleum I continued through the gardens to the stilt-house Ho had built after independence in 1954. It's a simple structure of bamboo screens, modeled on the houses of ethnic minorities. Downstairs is an open-sided meeting area; upstairs, two spare, highly polished rooms—Ho's study and bedroom, left as they were when he died here in 1969. At this modest dwelling beside a lake teeming with carp, Graham Greene had tea with the president of the Democratic Republic of Vietnam on the author's final visit to Indochina.

———

Across the Frisian flatness of the Red River delta the church at Phu Ly rose in a Gothic dream—the cathedral at Ely, in the Cambridgeshire fens, came to mind, soaring perpendiculars above the River Ouse. We were on the road to Ninh Bính. Njuyên Ngoc Thanh picked me up at 6 A.M., his sensitive face as pale and finely boned as his hands on the wheel of his aging Toyota. He drove fast, though with care, through thinning traffic. It was my chance to see the cathedral at Phat Diem. In *Ways of Escape* Greene wrote, "I was anxious on this first visit in 1951 to pay a visit to Phat Diem, one of the two Prince Bishoprics of the North . . . The two bishops, like the Caodaist Pope, were allies rather than subjects of the French, and maintained small private armies." In December 1951 Greene and *The Quiet American's* protagonist, Fowler, climbed the cathedral's bell tower to witness a Viet Minh assault on French forces in Phat Diem.

Phu Ly was a squat village cut up by a maze of canals. As we drew near, its church of damp-blackened concrete rose steeply among scattered village houses. It seemed enormous, like Chartres Cathedral in the thirteenth century, when the town comprised a few thousand souls.

As Phu Ly fell behind, another church came into view, this one vaguely Austrian baroque, dwarfing another village. Portuguese missionaries, particularly the brilliant Jesuit Alexandre de Rhodes, who developed the Latin-based *guoc ngu* script currently in use, preached in this region in the sixteenth century, converting people to Catholicism in droves. It's estimated that 95 percent of the locals attend mass regularly. The villages grew smaller the further we went, the churches larger. How large, I wondered, was the cathedral at Phat Diem?—picturing a vast Nôtre Dame among the lotus ponds and paddy lands of northern Vietnam.

By eight o'clock a steep range of sawtooth peaks marched across our path. They were peculiarly Asian, like mountains in a Li Ch'êng scroll, angular and eroded, with surreal gullies brushed against precipitous forest greens. In the foreground were fruit trees, lakes brimming with lotus flowers like flocks of flamingos, and in every direction churches, a jumble of European architectural styles, their spires soaring.

We swung east of the mountains, left them shimmering behind as we reached Ninh Bính, a market town on the main road. Dusty, sprawling, thronged. The railroad came through Ninh Bính, and while we waited for a bright blue passenger train to clatter past, a cart creaked up beside us, drawn by a shaggy red ox. The driver, thin as a sheet of cardboard, slept on the seat behind the great russet beast while the ox watched the train rush by, then plodded on as it vanished and the barrier swept upward.

Beyond Ninh Bính the road dwindled to a track that ran along a dike between canals and flooded fields. Bicycles replaced motorbikes. A few small houses clustered in tiny hamlets. Lotus ponds. Ducks. A woman, pedaling precariously, hauled hundred-pound sacks of rice, four of them, on her sagging bicycle. Boys riding water buffalo stared as we passed. Five miles from Phat Diem a capacious church dwarfed the feudal landscape and, a quarter mile farther, another—a matched pair of Gothic edifices, as if medieval masons from Amiens and the Île de France had loosed themselves on an unsuspecting Indochina.

The road intersected a canal, and we turned west. Following the canal a few hundred yards, we bridged the wider, deeper waterway Fowler had navigated from Nam Dinh in a landing craft. Sampans drifted on the quiet surface; a covered footbridge crossed to the other side. We paralleled the canal until we came to the village. When Fowler arrived he found Phat Diem surrounded by Viet Minh forces, the market burning. "We were an easy target in the light of the flames, but for some reason no one fired."

A roadside market faced both canal and scattered farms beyond. To the south rose a rib of the *calcaire*, "those strange weather-eroded mountains on the Annam border that look like piles of pumice." In town a surf of winnowed rice broke against the curbing. We turned at the main crossroads and drove a hundred yards up a street lined with shops. At the top Thanh killed the engine. So this was Phat Diem.

All the Gothic churches in Christendom couldn't have prepared me: first "the white statue of the Sacred Heart . . . stood on an island in the little lake before the Cathedral," then, lifting beyond it, the remarkable Sino-Vietnamese Cathedral itself, with its monumental bell pavilion whose upswept roofs and triple gateway might have marked the entrance to a great Buddhist shrine except for its crosses and carved angels. The facade of the church, set a few yards behind the bell pavilion, was its mirror image. If the Caodai cathedral at Tay Ninh reminded me of Disney, Phat Diem was reminiscent of Grumman's Chinese Theater. But as we circled the lake and parked outside the gate to the grounds, my notion of Hollywood swiftly vanished. Conceived and designed by Bishop Tran Luc, this massive edifice of timber and dressed stone, completed in 1899, was constructed on a foundation of bamboo poles driven into the swampy ground. It was anything but kitsch. Instead, an aesthetic and cultural aptness pervaded, a balanced simplicity and integrity of workmanship that made the baroque and Gothic churches along the roadside seem shoddy intruders in an alien world.

Thanh drank tea at a shady stall while I walked under massive tamarind trees to the perfectly proportioned bell pavilion, its central tower three dragon-roofed tiers capped by a stone cross. In the top tier, accompanied by a priest—"European, but not French, for the Bishop would not have tolerated a French priest in his diocese"—Fowler witnessed the Viet Minh attack, then the counterattack by French paratroopers. "From the bell tower of the Cathedral the battle was only picturesque, fixed like a panorama of the Boer War in an old *Illustrated London News*."

Beneath an arch in the bell pavilion a barefoot man in tattered shorts slept on the stone slab of Bishop Tran Luc's tomb. I left him undisturbed and walked around the cathedral, past four auxiliary churches, to the back, where I found the piled stones of the Grotto of Our Lady of Fatima. On a trip to Europe the bishop of Phat Diem became devoted to the cult of the virgin that Catholics believe appeared to a group of Portuguese children. He had the grotto built and held a procession each year on the feast day of Our Lady of Fatima. In December 1951 the participants were a broad mix that included Catholics, Buddhists, and pagans, as well as French officers and infiltrators from the Viet Minh. Then, while "the main Communist battalion moved through the passes in the *calcaire,* into the Tonkin plain, watched helplessly by the French outpost in the mountains above, the advance agents struck in Phat Diem."

It was a Saturday and there weren't many visitors. A young man wrestling an armload of chrysanthemums shouldered open a low door at the back of the cathedral and disappeared. I followed him into a shadowy room where he and another young man arranged flowers. We conversed in impromptu sign language, and they showed me through a door.

I passed through the vestry and emerged beside the high altar like a cardinal sent to offer his blessing. Nearby, a priest slouched in a ladder-back chair tilted against the chancel rail. Glancing over his newspaper, he adjusted his glasses, then went on reading. There was no one else—I had the run of the place. And what a place. Through the cool dimness the nave extended the length of a football field. Overhead, carved beams and rafters bore a tiled double roof supported by fifty-two immense ironwood pillars three feet in diameter and thirty-five high.

I walked the length of the church, admiring wood and stone carvings in the lateral naves, the thick overhead beams sculpted in motifs of flowers and flames, the simple teakwood pulpit with its portrait of Karol Wojtyla painted when he became Pope John Paul II. I paced the central aisle to the high altar hewn from a single block of marble. Above it the tall altarpiece gleamed in reds and golds. As Greene described it, "the bell tower with spreading oriental wings and . . . the carved wooden Cathedral with its gigantic pillars formed out of single trees and the scarlet lacquer work of the altar, more Buddhist than Christian." The young men appeared, bearing sprays of flowers in their arms, the carmine of the chrysanthemums intensifying the deep reds of the shrine. The priest shifted in his chair, humming softly to himself, but never stopped reading.

———

Fowler made his way down the tower and through the cathedral grounds. The citizens of Phat Diem, "Catholics, Buddhists, pagans, they had all packed their most valued possessions . . . and moved into the Cathedral precincts. . . . I said, It's like an enormous fair, isn't it, but without one smiling face." He crossed the grounds and went down the main street. There, he turned along the canal Thanh and I paralleled on our way into town. "When I had crossed two canals, I took a turning that led to a church."

Thanh drove at a walking pace, negotiated the short shopping street, turned. Counting bridges, we found the church just as Fowler had, a squat, vaguely European structure, an anticlimax after the cathedral. We sat for a while in its shade. Fowler met a platoon of French paratroops here—at least the lieutenant was French, though his men were German mercenaries. Three hundred Viet Minh, possibly preparing for a night attack, were reported in the village ahead. The platoon moved out to make contact. The English journalist went along.

Thanh dozed while I walked the road behind the church and crossed a canal over a flimsy wooden bridge. Here the platoon met its first obstacle: the bridge was out, the water filled with the bodies of villagers caught in a crossfire. The men found a punt: "Six of us got in and he began to pole towards the other bank, but we ran on a shoal of bodies and stuck . . . one body was released and floated up all its length beside the boat like a bather lying in the sun."

169

I stood at the edge of a paddy, the flooded land stretching away at my feet. The *calcaire* scribbled the horizon like sapphire chalk, and a few farm buildings stood among the trees across a field. People labored nearby: stooped women in conical hats planting rice, men at some task requiring unnamable tools, children leading a buffalo, a thick gray creature like some improbable prehistoric beast stitched hastily together in the back room of a provincial museum.

Fowler accompanied the paratroopers to the farm. "The lieutenant went in first, hugging the wall, and we followed at six-foot intervals in single file." Inside the farmhouse the reporter found "two hideous oleographs of the Sacred Heart and the Mother and Child." They gave the place a strangely European feel. At least Fowler knew what the occupants believed. They were human, "not just grey drained cadavers." This is the first evidence of the compassion Fowler later displayed in the Place Garnier, the concern for individual victims of the war that sent him to Mr. Heng and eventually led Pyle to the Dakow Bridge. While Fowler and the lieutenant waited, sentries pushed beyond the farm. They fired two shots. "*Deux civils.*" A mother and her small son. "They were clearly dead: a small neat clot of blood on the woman's forehead, and the child might have been sleeping. . . . I thought, I hate war."

I found Thanh behind the wheel of the Toyota, the engine running. "Getting late . . . time we go."

Turning at the main road, we drove along the canal and through the village. Fowler had made his way back and spent the night at the officer's quarters. "With one wall destroyed by a bazooka and the doors buckled, canvas curtains couldn't shut out the draughts." He slept on the floor clutching a borrowed pistol. Sometime in the night, to Fowler's complete surprise, Pyle arrived. He was let through as far as Nam Dinh, he claimed, where he bought a boat and rowed himself to Phat Diem. "It wasn't really difficult, you know. The current was with me." Fowler told Pyle he was mad, he could have been killed by a naval patrol or a French plane, or had his throat cut by the Viet Minh. "He laughed shyly. Well, I'm here anyway, he said." And why had he come? To tell Fowler he'd fallen in love with Phuong, planned to take her from him, to marry her and carry her off to respectability in Boston. What seems a kind of joke, one of Greene's comic turns, is deadly serious. With Phuong at stake, Phuong who represents Indochina and the future, the clash of values, of world views is personalized. The outcome was inevitable—the death of the "innocent" Pyle. "They killed him because he was too innocent to live. He was young and ignorant and silly and he got involved . . . you gave him money and York Harding's books on the East and said, Go ahead. Win the East for Democracy."

It was late when we got to Ninh Bính, where we stopped at a road-side stall to eat bowls of *com tay cam,* the clicking of our chopsticks barely audible above the blare of passing trucks. Darkness came as we got back on the road, blinded by approaching headlights flaring against the wind-shield. Rounding the steep karst mountains, we were on the long flat run to Hanoi.

It is nearly fifty years since Graham Greene "fell in love with Indochina." He quickly learned that the days of the French were num-bered, the numbers running out. He knew the French commander, Gen-eral De Lattre, saw him pass from confidence to despair. Greene spent a "doom laden twenty-four hours" in the valley at Dien Bien Phu, know-ing instinctively it was a trap the French had laid for themselves. He wrote of Dien Bien Phu in *Ways of Escape:* "The battle marked virtually the end of any hope the Western Powers might have entertained that they could dominate the East. The French, with Cartesian clarity, accepted the verdict. So too, to a lesser extent, did the British . . . That young Americans were still to die in Vietnam only shows that it takes time for the echoes even of a total defeat to encircle the globe." After the French withdrawal from the north, he came back to have tea with Ho Chi Minh. When Greene died in 1991 Vietnam had been united and independent for a quarter century. What would he make of it now? What would he think of this fast drive across the Red River delta, the lights of Hanoi ablaze against a towering sky? This weathered land with its helter-skelter dash into the twenty-first century?

11

The Only Mzungu Afoot
Maria Thomas' Dar es Salaam

> Like an African, the white doctor came to work on foot,
> along the road that lined the port of Dar es Salaam . . . But
> the aberration, since no one white ever walked in Africa . .
> . pleased her in ways, even if the walk did not.
>
> Maria Thomas, *Antonia Saw the Oryx First*

DAWN COMES TO Dar es Salaam like pale smoke from across the Indian Ocean, bringing with it smells of smoldering garbage and the first racketing calls of crows. Even before the light takes shape, women appear, saronged in vivid lengths of *kanga* cloth, streaming along the waterfront, whole shops full of freight balanced on their heads: cooking pots, baskets of mangoes, hardware in wooden crates, loaves of sugared bread, dried fish like stacks of new money. One sports an ax atop her head like a deadly hat. Another glides by beneath a silvery fish, a barracuda, as if they're partners in a carnival act.

Midmorning the procession slows. Young men settle under palms, gossiping as they listen to soccer on hand-held transistors, hawking peanuts, fresh fried cassava chips, oranges, and gum. A boy, sharpening knives, pedals an upside-down bicycle, its rear wheel a grindstone flashing sparks as he works. At dusk a cooling wind ruffles the harbor. The crows swarm back, searching out roosts high in the casuarina trees. And the women return, a continuous river. Like travelers in a mythic caravan they slide south through spreading darkness.

———

I came to Dar es Salaam from England aboard an Italian cargo ship.

It was summer, some years after Roberta Warrick's death. On August 7, 1989, she died in an airplane crash on her way to the Fugnido refugee camp on Ethiopia's border with Sudan. Also killed were her husband, Tom, deputy director of the U.S. Agency for International Development in Ethiopia, and U.S. Congressman Mickey Leland of Texas, one of the most vigorous and informed champions of Africa in America's legislature.

Under the name of Maria Thomas (Thomas was Roberta Warrick's maiden name) she wrote two short-story collections and the novel *Antonia Saw the Oryx First.* As a Peace Corps volunteer she, with her husband and four-year-old son, first traveled to Ethiopia in 1971. With time out for a Wallace E. Stegner Fellowship at Stanford University, she remained in Africa for seventeen years, subsequently living in Tanzania, Liberia, Nigeria, and Kenya. But it was Ethiopia that held her, inspiring several stories in her collection *African Visas.* Her early work was published in periodicals such as *Redbook, North American Review,* and the *Antioch Review.* She received the *StoryQuarterly* Fiction Prize, the *Chicago Review* Annual Fiction Award, and a National Magazine Award for several stories later collected in *Come to Africa and Save Your Marriage.* After an absence of many years, she returned to Addis Ababa and was moved to write an essay for *Harper's* (January 1987), "A State of Permanent Revolution: Ethiopia Bleeds Red," which won the Overseas Press Club's Commendation.

If it was Ethiopia, scene of her Peace Corps work, to which Maria Thomas was drawn, it was Tanzania, particularly its principal city, Dar es Salaam, that provided the setting for her novel *Antonia Saw the Oryx First.*

A wise and sensitively written double portrait, the novel tells the story of the growth of a complex friendship between the African-born American doctor Antonia Redmond and an African patient, the "traditional healer" Esther Moro. "They were both attracted to something in the raveling themes of sickness and healing, of destiny and the nature of men . . . this black village girl and the white doctor." Like any white, or *mzungu,* Antonia faces exile from the newly independent nation, while Esther confronts her awakening "desire to touch, to help, to clear away contamination." Esther is the future, Antonia the past. Yet in a moment of equilibrium each reflects the other, like mirrors, one black, one white. Dar es Salaam provides the frame for the mirrors. With economy and a penetrating eye, Maria Thomas captures the soul of this poignant, plundered city poised at the end of a ruinous colonialism.

———

Rose Mbwambo spreads a map on the counter and examines it with dark, intelligent eyes. Across Azikiwe Road from the New Africa Hotel, the Tourist Information Center is in a large brownish space that has the look and feel of a 1940s American Legion hall. There's a buttoned couch and a threadbare Makonde drum. Shabby posters trumpeting the joys of "Big Game Hunting" picture fiendish lions, reprehensible elephants, rhinos big and dumb as dump trucks. The city map is badly printed in four colors that bleed into one another. It's impossible to read street names, though the city's essential outline is legible, if smeared.

Rose is about to answer questions I've asked since first planning this trip: How much of Maria Thomas' Dar es Salaam was spun from her imagination, and how much will I find? I've made a list of neighborhoods, districts, and landmarks from the pages of *Antonia*. Will I get a geography lesson, or will geography prove a phantom?

———

"You're sure this is Ocean Road Hospital, Juma?"

A rangy, open-faced teenager, Juma peddles homemade cane chairs to passing Sunday drivers. It's a busy corner where Land Rovers wheel northward toward Sealands Bridge and the posh enclave at Oyster Bay. He points a bare arm across a great lawn being mowed by a party of goats. On its far edge is what I take to be a grand ruin. Juma nods wisely. "Yes, *bwana*. It is very old indeed."

It's Ocean Road Hospital that continually attracts Maria Thomas, for it's here her protagonist Antonia Redmond spends her days treating patients, her evenings meeting with Esther Moro. "Sometimes Esther and Antonia would sit together across a desktop and their tea that was never boiled long enough to give a taste, with no words between them. Sometimes, they explored: 'Water is dangerous,' Esther said . . . Then [Antonia] let Esther look at everything through a special glass . . . that penetrated to reveal what eyes couldn't see. Even a drop of water opened to a world of shapes."

In frustration, Antonia witnesses the hospital's ruinous decline. "They don't even clean up, she said, aware that she was overheard. Nurses disappeared as if by magic. At least you ought to get them to clean up."

A goatherd, no older than five, accompanies me on my trek across the grass.

> Heavy walls cut from stone and a red tile roof, set in a
> widening spread of trampled grass . . . wide corridors and
> porches where patients waited, it was not so much falling
> apart as it was calcifying like tartar on neglected teeth.

A three-tiered gallery broken by rows of shuttered windows is surmounted by twin spires of carved stone capped by bristling globes of iron. On the corners stand whimsical towers with Moorish openings and a crenelated keep straight from a Scottish castle.

A nanny goat mounts the steps at my side. Together we peer along the dimness of the lower porch, where walls rubbed smooth by generations of waiting backsides part with their ancient layers of plaster and paint. Not a sound. A thin layer of sand. All is empty, barren, woebegone. It seems Antonia's fear of disintegration has been realized. Through a warped shutter, I make out a shadowy floor drifted in fallen plaster, remnants of upturned furniture in a lonely pile.

A hundred yards from the crumbling hospital, beside a seldom-used road that follows the beach back to town, a fictional image unexpectedly takes shape. So perfectly does it mirror the pages of *Antonia,* I'm caught between hallucination and déjà vu. Between the road and the sea, women squat among mounds of discarded shells. Florid *kanga* cloth is the only color in a gray sierra to which generations of clam cookers have contributed. Over smoldering fires of driftwood, oil drums bubble and, through a layer of steam and a thick cover of weeds and barnacles, clams with bright orange gills and long blue-black necks slowly open.

> [Antonia] walked instead along a lane behind the hospital
> toward the sea. The sky and tide were swept back. . . . There
> were no people around save two old women steaming
> something in an oil drum using driftwood sticks for fuel.
> The doctor watched them. They had clams, very large and
> thick shelled.

Stunned by this literary vision turned real, I watch the women work.

They hardly notice me. No one offers a taste or tries to make a sale. When I turn to leave, a crone with scars arabesqued over her leathered face says a soft *kwa heri,* good-bye.

Farther on, at the tip of a grassy promontory, I watch fishing dhows running for port, their patched sails ballooning. The wind is steady, the sea a choppy aquamarine. Behind me—where it *must* be—beyond acres of lawn, big and imposing as a turn-of-the-century luxury hotel, the Presidential Palace rises with its creamy walls and Mediterranean arches.

> As she . . . saw fishermen like a migration of white butter-flies returning on the tide in dhows, as the green lawns of the presidential palace cut into the brown swing of the hospital path . . .

The tropical dusk falls with urgency. In the fading light I turn into Magogoni Street and start back to town. Mine is the solitary white face in a flow of Africans. I'm the only *mzungu* afoot.

———

Dominic Kizua is slight and quiet, with the soft yellow eyes of a malaria sufferer. With care, as if he expects the thing to come apart like wet paper in his hands, he nurses the fragile old Peugeot into the enclave at Oyster Bay. It was to Oyster Bay that Antonia Redmond's parents retired from a coffee farm at the foot of Mount Kilimanjaro when Tanganyika became independent. "The Redmonds' house on the coast was a wandering pink stucco affair in the diplomatic enclave . . . The garden was pink to match, bougainvillaea, hibiscus, frangipani."

After her father died and her mother returned to Philadelphia, "Antonia still went to the pink stucco house on Oyster Bay, but now as the guest of strangers. The last time it was Italians." Among a dwindling number of whites, in a country increasingly chaotic, where luxury is smuggled butter and bottled gherkins from China, Antonia attends diplomatic dinners.

> Dinner parties were blurred together. Candles in paper bags around a circular drive . . . voices pitched to some standard, an aggregate laughter accompanied by the clinking of glasses . . . It was part of her blasphemy to walk those sweeping drive-ways on foot through the heavy incense of wet *frangipani.*

176

While the sputtering tape deck offers Nat and Natalie Cole croon-ing "Unforgettable," embassy flags flash past: Swiss, French, Japanese, Russian, Canadian, and the Union Jack. The houses face white water and a wide sweep of bay. They're large, with deep verandas, tile roofs, cool, shadowy gardens. One senses that easy living has returned. But it isn't all soft lights and diplomatic privilege. Even here Africa intrudes.

Dominic steers into a side road jagged with potholes and awash with sand. Ragged vendors squat along its margins, peddling woven grass mats and one-at-a-time cigarettes. Nearby, on a lane behind the seafront, an American flag trails from a squat pole erected for endurance. Built in the "Fortress America" style that followed the Beirut bombing, the embassy is a sugar-white blockhouse, grim, sturdy, and pugnacious, bristling antennae. In the fortified gatehouse behind bombproof glass, a marine corporal raises a telephone to his sunburned face and reports our passage.

> Sprawling gardens and billowing porches, once dreams now delusions; all the houses on Oyster Bay were touched by the sadness of fantasy.

> Now Antonia lived in "housing," different, she told people, from a house. The development was called Kinondoni and was planned and built by foreigners . . . It might have been East Germans who designed the place. Or Bulgarians.

The tarmac ends abruptly where Kinondoni begins; deep ruts swal-low the car, camouflage it in scarves of dust. "The asphalt . . . had never arrived. In the rains, red mud washed over everything. What she enjoyed about the place was the feel . . . of village energies breaking into what the planners had tried to organize away." Village energies *are* in abundance, erasing European "efficiency," rewriting it in Africa's vibrant scrawl.

On the verges of impossible roads men parade in tattered shorts and fragmentary T-shirts. Women wear *kangas* and bits of satin party dresses, while armies of children go naked. We're greeted with good-humored banter, the rich laughter and expressions of welcome that come from people unburdened by competitive egos and self-consciousness. A man in tartan pedal-pushers ambles past, followed by a boy wheeling a toy truck woven entirely from twigs.

The houses are the sort built across America after World War II, what we called "ticky-tacky boxes," though smaller, shabbier. By now they've sloughed their European facades. Doors and windows have been hacked or walled up at random. Lean-tos of tin and thatch offer space for ever-extending families. Above a sagging porch the bloody carcass of a goat hangs from a hook. A man plucks a chicken in a trashy yard. Soda pop. Cigarettes. Fruit. Houses double as shops and cafés. A constant coming and going—a unity of family life and commerce.

The farther into the interior, the worse the roads. Suddenly, heaving between a collapsed shed and a broken pump, we swerve from urban Africa, that tragic shadow of Europe, and enter a grassy clearing. In the shade of a gigantic baobab, bare-chested men play *bao,* a board game as ancient as the tree they sit beneath. Women's eyes follow us as we motor past.

———

Mikorosheni, "among the cashew trees."

"You won't find cashews these days," Rose Mbwambo told me. Spilling across the great brown counter, she scanned *Antonia.* "She must mean Esther *Moru,"* she said, fingering a page, "not *Moro.* The one they say touches sick people and makes them well. A healer. But I don't believe it. Not many do anymore. It's not scientific. There were barren women she made pregnant. Their bellies blew up and stayed like that for years. False pregnancies. Now we call them "Esther pregnancies." All over the country. She's famous. If she's still alive, she's in Mikorosheni. Who knows? You might find her."

If Kinondoni is Africa overlaid on a blueprint of Europe, Mikorosheni is the opposite, a bush village of mud-and-wattle turning tenuously European. How tenuous is reflected by roadside business: a derelict taxi from the Kamikaze Cab Co. parked outside the Just Take A Chance Beauty Salon.

In this squatter village Antonia Redmond's patient Esther Moro shared a tin-roofed shack with her girlfriend Hadija and their landlady, Zobetta. Permanently injured by a Greek sailor wielding a broken bottle, Esther could no longer work as a prostitute. She had no way to live. "No one did . . . They were all gathered in Mikorosheni, she thought, around catastrophe, living in danger, against the law, with broken, foreign things." She described a recent disaster: an oil lamp had spilled, igniting a neighbor's cardboard house; five babies perished. "Because we have no electricity, Esther told Zobetta. Because our houses aren't made of stones and cement. I wish there were no lamps."

Nothing has changed. The houses are still of mud and tin, their walls fashioned of cardboard picked from the trash. The potholed tracks wind around pit latrines and garbage dumps and the place smells "of cookfires, of charcoal and kerosene and the rancid coconut oil in which everything was fried."

Despite its poverty, its permanent dereliction, Mikorosheni is thronged, spirited, gaudy, alive with hawkers, crowded with scores of *vitumbua,* traditional African "bun" shops selling everything from smuggled sanitary napkins to kerosene and *chapatis.* Dominic steers tentatively along roads mobbed with shoppers. He's jumpy. Although a native of Dar es Salaam, he considers this distant suburb alien territory, as outlandish as Switzerland, say, or, God help us, the U.S.A.

When I ask him about Esther Moru, his face clouds. He insists he's never heard of her. Maybe so. Or maybe he thinks Esther is a *mganga,* a witch doctor, and a white man shouldn't become involved. At my urging he reluctantly agrees to look for her. On a corner, vendors offer mosquito nets, holding them aloft on tall poles like ghostly brides. Dominic puts his head out the window and calls in Swahili: "Esta Moru? *Unaweza kunipeleka,* Esta Moru?" Blank looks and headshakes.

At the Cold Drinks Hilton, a mud room with a deep tin-roofed porch, we sip warm Cokes and question the waitress. At a corner table two prostitutes eye us, then lose interest. The waitress swipes at the table with a rat-colored rag. No, no. *Hapana.* She doesn't know any Esta. No one called Esta ever came in here. Before my Coke is quite finished, she snatches the bottle away and vanishes with it into the papaya patch out back.

We stop at the cassava market, visit barber shops, open-air clothing stores, thatch-walled beauty salons, and flyblown "butcheries." Wherever we go we ask about "Esta." Even at the Ice Cube Fruits Parlour the headshakes and shrugs, the blank looks and vague "hapanas" are the same. Dominic is too shy and out of place to be forceful, my Swahili too weak to press. Esther Moro goes unfound. But from among the young women swarming on corners, stepping from doorways, she and Hadija seem to loom "arm in arm, in their tight pants and high shoes, laughing and . . . jiggling beads and bangles, the girls came forth . . . noses in the air, tripping in the pits and ruts of the village paths."

———

The Peugeot swings into the parking lot and stops before steps rising to a broad entrance. Hand lettering follows a curve of archway:

TANZANIA TUMOR CENTER

OCEAN ROAD HOSPITAL

It had seemed a ruin on Sunday; today nurses in starched blue and white stride along dim corridors through flurries of plaster sleeting from twenty-foot ceilings. In even dimmer rooms women wait stoically along scarred walls, black faces swept clear of emotion, eyes blank. At the end of the corridor, through a low doorway, sagging shelves are stacked with yellowing medical records; on a table sits a telephone, cord ripped from the wall.

On my way upstairs I stop a nurse on the landing. She's small and quick, but hesitant to speak. Does she remember a *mzungu* doctor? A woman, young, pretty, blonde? Yes. Maybe. Sometimes there are *mzungu* doctors. But a woman . . .? She doesn't know. She's new here. She has to attend to a patient. Hurrying downstairs she glances over her shoulder, then vanishes into the gloom.

From a ward smelling of nothing you'd want to remember, a nurse steps, blocking my way. Black arms fold across a white apron; shrewd eyes appraise me. I ask about Antonia. The eyes remain fixed. It's a long time before she answers. Again, as if not wanting to disappoint, it's yes, followed by a shrug, a vague, noncommittal maybe—but who can remember? In talking with Africans, Antonia at some point "had forgotten how to build a conversation of parable and innuendo, how to find answers in allusions and indirections." I've never known. The nurses simply confound me.

———

Dominic waits on the steps outside. Together we cross the parking lot to the car. No one will speak of the *mzungu* doctor. These two extraordinary women, Antonia and Esther, must remain fictional, as probably they should, creations of deep insight, sympathy, and spirit, wise and complex portraits from Maria Thomas' imagination.

We turn south along Ocean Road. Soon we pass the women simmering clams, then the green lawns enclosing the Presidential Palace. Fishermen heave a pirogue onto the sand near the Kigamboni ferry, while a ship flying the azure and white of Greece threads the narrows of Mzinga Creek. The smoke of trash fires drifts over the sea. Unclouded by romanticism, Maria Thomas' Dar es Salaam, down-at-heels, exotic, "primitive," dazzles along the curl of its wind-ruffled bay.

Dominic shifts gears and encourages the old Peugeot around a sweeping curve. "Where to now?"

The city lies ahead. Nowhere, Dominic. We've found it. This is it.

Honourable Lioness
In Karen Blixen's Africa

During my first years in Africa I had a Somali gunbearer
named Ismail . . . he spoke an English of the hunting world,
so that he would talk of my big and my young rifle. After
Ismail had gone back to Somaliland, I had a letter from him
which was addressed to *Lioness Blixen*, and opened: *Honourable Lioness*.

Karen Blixen, *Out of Africa*

The Coast

THE BUS FROM LAMU takes a paralyzing eight hours, most of it over
hopeless roads chaperoned by an infantry platoon intended to frighten
off *shifta*, Somali gunmen who won't suffer Kenyan sovereignty over the
old Northern Frontier District. Waylaying buses is a tactic in their
makeshift civil war. This time the *shifta* leave us in peace, and on a rainy
afternoon in late November I reach Mombasa and check into the New
Palm Tree Hotel. After trading gossip with the Baluyia desk clerk Francis Makokha, I receive a message left by friends: "Come for sundowners
at the Mombasa Club."

———

On the thirteenth of January, 1914, after a nineteen-day voyage from
Europe, Karen Dinesen (1885–1962), who was later to write under her
married name, Karen Blixen, and her pseudonym, Isak Dinesen, arrived
in East Africa aboard the S.S. *Admiral*. When her ship anchored in Mombasa, she was met by her fiancé, a Swedish cousin, Baron Bror Blixen-

Finecke. She lived in Africa for seventeen years on her farm "at the foot of the Ngong Hills." Six years after her return to Denmark in 1931, she published *Out of Africa*, the classic account of her stay—not so much a traditional autobiography of event and character as a distillation of her passion for a landscape and its people, and for her lover, the professional hunter Denys Finch Hatton.

———

On Easter Sunday 1498, Vasco da Gama sailed through Mombasa's reef and conquered the seven-hundred-year-old Swahili town. Random pillaging soon became organized, and the Portuguese quickly crushed coastal strongholds, plundered trade routes, decimated an ancient and vital culture. In 1593, to consolidate their control over this corner of the Indian Ocean, the Portuguese built Fort Jesus. The fort still holds the high ground above Mombasa Harbor; tonight it is radiant in the wash of a tropical moon, its weathered walls shimmering in patterns of mauve and pink like the abstract canvases of Helen Frankenthaler or Mark Rothko. Its long and savage history, though not forgotten, seems remote in the moonlight, distant as dhows ghosting before an easterly monsoon.

Below the ramparts sprawls an antiquated accumulation of tin roofs and broad verandas—the Mombasa Club. My friends wait under shadowy neem trees at its entrance, and together we mount the stairs and cross rambling terraces. Moonlight burnishes the water below, silhouettes the headlands opposite. Out beyond the harbor's mouth, a white curl of surf slips across the reef.

———

On that January day in 1914, when the *Admiral* steamed into port, there was no wharf at Mombasa, and Bror Blixen brought his bride-to-be ashore in a rowboat. She was twenty-seven, the daughter of an intensely bourgeois mother and a troubled, romantic father who had killed himself when Karen was nine. Now, with Denmark behind her, and in the company of the exuberant and singularly irresponsible Bror, she began a new life: coffee farming in Africa.

———

We gather around a table on a second-floor veranda and the waiter, an austere Somali in impeccable white, looks askance at my khaki shorts.

I can only shrug: "Sorry, shorts are all I brought." I've scoured away layers of bundu dust, but by the club's old-fashioned code, I'm too informally dressed. Happily, at a word from my hosts, club members for years, the Somali refrains from tossing me out and brings gin and tonics—tall, icy and welcome. We toast the soft African night as a dhow, outward bound for Zanzibar, slips silently past, making for deep water through the reef.

———

Karen Blixen acquired an enduring affection for the East African coast, though in her day it was considered "the white man's grave." With her close friend Berkeley Cole, who owned a farm on the slopes of Mt. Kenya, she fantasized the life they might lead: "Berkeley had a great, ever unsatisfied, love of the sea. It was a favourite dream of his that he and I should . . . buy a dhow and go trading to Lamu, Mombasa, and Zanzibar." Berkeley and Denys Finch Hatton, good friends, were often together at Karen Blixen's Ngong Farm, where from the early 1920s, Finch Hatton lived, at least between safaris. Karen and Denys sometimes flew in his Gypsy Moth to Takaungu—a few whitewashed Swahili houses along a cobalt blue creek, just thirty miles up the coast, off the Lamu-Mombasa Road, along a track through a sisal plantation Finch Hatton once owned. He built a house at Takaungu, two rooms and a veranda made of coral blocks carved from the reef. On a bluff above the Indian Ocean, it stands near a ruined mosque.

> It was a full moon while I was down at Takaunga, and the beauty of the radiant, still nights was so perfect that the heart bent under it. You slept with the door open to the silver sea; the playing warm breeze in a low whisper swept in a little loose sand, on to the stone floor. One night a row of Arab dhows came along, close to the coast, running noiselessly before the monsoon, a file of brown shadow-sails under the moon.

That was years after the *Admiral* put into Mombasa and Bror Blixen rowed Karen ashore. It was after she found her ideal in Denys Finch Hatton. It was very near the end. The beginning was here at the Mombasa Club, where Bror brought her that first night.

On the voyage out Karen met and befriended Colonel Paul von Lettow, on his way to Dar es Salaam to take command of forces in German East Africa. By August that year England and Germany were at war, and the legendary von Lettow led devastating attacks against British irregulars in Kenya. But on this steamy January night the possibility of war seemed far away, and the urbane colonel joined Bror and his bride-to-be for supper at the club. After coffee and cognac, Bror led Karen across a shadowy garden that tonight is drenched in frangipani and bougainvillaea. They slept together in a cottage under the palms. Judith Thurman, Karen Blixen's biographer, writes that "Tanne [Karen] had told her family, for propriety's sake, that they were married the morning of her arrival, but, in fact, the ceremony took place the next day."

———

The moon is midnight high when I leave the club for my hotel. On the morning of January 14, 1914, the wedding party walked this way— Karen and Bror, and Bror's witness, Prince Wilhelm of Sweden. They passed the walls of Fort Jesus, then the Court House and Legal Chambers. Tonight, the fort is in darkness, the streets cooled by a spattering rain. At the top of the hill Treasury Square and the colonial relic of the District Commissioner's Office, with its tin roofs and dim verandas, are shadowed by mango and banyan trees.

Here, with the D.C. officiating, Karen Dinesen became the Baroness Blixen in a ceremony that, as she wrote her mother, was "easy and simple and only took ten minutes." By four that afternoon, accompanied by Prince Wilhelm and his entourage and using the governor of the protectorate's private dining car for their wedding supper, the newlyweds set off upcountry by rail—for Nairobi, and the Ngong Farm.

The Ngong Farm

. . . at one time I drove through the streets and thought:
There is no world without Nairobi's streets.

A stocky Kikuyu with a stubble beard, Wilson Keemani pilots his sky-blue Toyota through downtown traffic. Tom Mboya Street. Moi Avenue. Parliament Road. Wilson's Toyota, like most Nairobi cabs, has a case of the hacks and shudders, lurching out of control now and then. But reassuring stickers embellish the dash:

> With God all things are possible.
> VICTORY
> When satan reminds you of your past,
> remind him of his future.

Across Uhuru Highway we turn west out Ngong Road, struggling among a conflagration of smoking minibuses, smoldering trucks, and a roadful of shabby secondhand cars. Finally, after passing the Nairobi Show Grounds, then the Ngong Race Course, traffic thins. Eucalyptus, flame trees, and jacarandas shade the narrow road.

A dozen miles out of town, beyond Ngong Forest and the threadbare collection of shops clustered at Karen, named for Karen Blixen, we pull into a sweeping drive and up to a fieldstone bungalow. Wide and low, it's fronted by a broad, tree-shaded lawn—Mbogani, Karen's "house in the woods," subdued, classic, altogether lovely. The pain of her departure from the farm becomes doubly poignant the instant you see it.

> When I had sold all the contents of my house, my panelled rooms became sounding boards. If I sat down on one of the packing cases containing things to be sent off . . . voices and tunes of old rang through the nobly bare room intensified, clear.

By 1931, when she left Africa, Karen was broke. Her husband Bror, ever the charming spendthrift, had gone through large amounts of money their families had provided for their farming venture. When Karen and Bror separated and divorced, and Karen took over management of the farm, it was too late. "My farm was a little too high up for growing coffee. It happened in the cold months that we would get frost on the lower land and in the morning the shoots of the coffee-trees, and the young coffee-berries on them, would all be brown and withered." The Ngong country was short of rain as well, and for three years there were ruinous droughts: "Those years were disastrous to the farm . . . At the same time coffee-prices fell: where we had got a hundred pounds a ton we now got sixty or seventy. Times grew hard on the farm. We could not pay our debts."

When she arrived in 1914, however, she was filled with hope and high expectations. Twelve hundred Kikuyu gathered to roar their welcome. The moment established an abiding affinity with Africans, an affinity she described in *Shadows on the Grass:* "The introduction into my life of another race, essentially different from mine, in Africa became to me a mysterious expansion of my world. My own voice and song in life there had a second set to it and grew fuller and richer in the duet."

Africa's appeal is its emotional resonance—a resonance, as Karen found, not only in landscape and wildlife but in its people. And, though her alliance with her "Natives" would, in the light of today's racial sensitivities, be seen as paternal, her view of Africans was always lucid, never superficial, superior, or sentimental.

Today I'm met by Peter Kandie, a young Kikuyu turned out nattily in white shirt and snowy jacket. He leads me under the mugumu trees and into the house, now the Karen Blixen Museum. At the entrance, near the old kitchen, are photos of Meryl Streep and Robert Redford, who portrayed Karen and her lover Finch Hatton in the film version of *Out of Africa*. To the left of the kitchen is the "guest bedroom," now furnished as a study. The floors are of burnished parquet, the walls paneled in dark wood, the beams hand-hewn timbers set against creamy plaster. Beside a gun rack stands an antique bookcase holding first editions of Karen's books and behind an oak desk are blowups of old photos. One of Karen taken at the farm with her beloved deerhound Dusk, another of her in old age, her limpid eyes gazing from an almost transparent face—photographic parentheses around Karen's writing life.

Storytelling was always central to Karen. Her father's book, *Letters from the Hunt,* about his adventures among the Chippewa in the wilds of Wisconsin, was a minor Danish classic. As a girl, Karen wrote family theatricals, and as a young woman using the nom de plume of Osceola, wrote several tales, publishing three in Danish literary reviews between 1907 and 1909.

In Africa she turned to letters, evocative narratives of her new world, written primarily to her mother, her Aunt Bess, and her brother Thomas. These detailed chronicles tell the story she later distilled in *Out of Africa*. From its opening phrase, "I had a farm in Africa . . . ," poignant with loss, the prose as spare and inviolate as if she were describing her life in Africa from a great and clarifying height. Her description of the terrain at the book's outset perfectly defines her writing style: "The geographical position and the height of the land combined to create a landscape that had not its like in all the world. There was no fat on it and no luxuriance anywhere; it was Africa distilled up through six thousand feet, like the strong and refined essence of a continent."

From the study a hallway opens into the dining room. An antique table stands on a Persian carpet, six chairs arranged around it. A massive set of buffalo horns is mounted on the wall. Buffalo were talismans for Karen and Denys. They often flew to watch the herd in the Ngong Hills: "We flew in the sun, but the hillside lay in a transparent brown shade . . . It did not take us long to spy the buffalo from the air." Though little of Karen's furniture remains at Mbogani House—most was sold, although some can be seen at the Macmillan Library in Nairobi—the buffalo horns seem especially appropriate.

Copies of two skillfully done portraits by Karen, the originals of which are in Copenhagen, hang on the walls. One is of Kalyim Njais, a young Kikuyu woman whom Karen painted because she was so beautiful. The other is of Abdullai, younger brother of Farah Aden, Karen's all-important majordomo. As a boy Abdullai learned chess watching Berkeley Cole and Denys play in the evenings before the fire. When Abdullai challenged and beat Denys, Denys recommended that Karen pay for the boy's education. After finishing school, Abdullai went to Somalia, where he became an attorney and later a judge.

In 1913, Abdullai's brother, Farah Aden, had been sent ahead by Bror to join Karen's ship in Aden and escort her to Mombasa. He remained with her throughout her years in Africa, managing the house, the stables, and her safaris. He was adviser, friend, and confidant. "I talked to him about my worries as about my successes, and he knew all that I did or thought. Farah, by the time I had had to give up the farm and was leaving Africa, saw me off at Mombasa. And as I watched his dark immovable figure on the quay growing smaller and at last disappear, I felt as if I were losing a part of myself, as if I were having my right hand set off."

———

To the right of the doorway leading from the hall into the dining room, illuminated by an open window, is a painting by René Bouché— a striking portrait of the seventy-four-year-old Karen Blixen, by then known as the writer Isak Dinesen, painted during her American sojourn.

Her 1959 American journey was a triumphal tour, the climax of her writing life. She had published *Seven Gothic Tales* (1935), *Out of Africa* (1937), *Winter's Tales* (1942), *Last Tales* (1957), and *Anecdotes of Destiny* (1958). *Shadows on the Grass* would appear in 1961. Her books, generally Book-of-the-Month Club selections, sold well in America. She was twice nominated for a Nobel Prize. When Ernest Hemingway won the Nobel in 1954, he suggested it should have gone to her. In America during the winter of 1959, as a guest of the Ford Foundation, she made a film for their "greatest living writers" series, and another for the *Encyclopaedia Britannica.* She gave readings at Radcliffe, Brandeis, and the Y.M.H.A. Poetry Center, where the crowds were large and enthusiastic. She was lionized by the literary establishment. The Institute of Contemporary Arts arranged appearances in Boston, New York, and Washington. She spoke on Shakespeare at the Folger Library and, as an honorary member of the American Academy of Arts and Letters, was the honored guest at its annual dinner and gave the keynote speech, "On Mottoes of My Life." Social events were as intense as official affairs. Possibly no occasion meant more than a lunch given her by Carson McCullers, at which Arthur Miller and Marilyn Monroe were the only other guests.

———

It was in this room, with views across the terrace and west lawn to the Ngong Hills, that Karen Blixen, coffee farmer, began her metamorphosis into Isak Dinesen, storyteller and literary lioness. So often, after dinner, she and Denys talked until dawn, discussing literature, music, life. Long before Karen's divorce from Bror, in 1921, Denys moved to the farm, where he stayed between his hunting safaris. "When Denys Finch-Hatton came back after one of his long expeditions, he was starved for talk, and found me on the farm starved for talk, so that we sat over the dinner-table . . . talking of all the things we could think of, and mastering them all, and laughing at them."

From the dining room a portal leads to the living room, where French windows open onto a broad veranda. The room is furnished with a lion skin rug, a Turkish carpet, an antique Victor phonograph. Denys' bookcase, on which Karen mounted brass plaques engraved "D.H.F.," is filled not with his books, but books placed there for the film. Denys' books and the folding screen that once graced the room were among the few possessions Karen took back to Denmark. Painted with exotic figures of "Chinamen, Sultans and Negroes, with dogs on leads," the screen was the source for many of the stories Karen told Denys when they settled before the fire, stories that reappeared, transformed, in Isak Dinesen's tales.

———

But it's *Out of Africa* I've come for, and *Out of Africa* I find at every turn. The house sings with it. Peter Kandie leads me along a breezeway to the kitchen where Karen's eminent cook, the brilliant and eccentric Kamante, prepared a triumphant repast for the Prince of Wales in November 1928. In a letter to her mother, Karen wrote: "All honour is due to Kamante. I gave them clear soup with marrow, fish from Mombasa, a kind of turbot, with sauce hollandaise, ham, that Denys had given me, with Cumberland sauce . . . partridges with peas, croustades with mushrooms, a kind of savarin and fruit—strawberries and grenadillas." After the meal an *ngoma,* a native dance, was held for the prince under the Cape chestnut trees on the great east lawn. It was not the season for *ngomas,* and in *Shadows on the Grass* Isak Dinesen wrote of Farah Aden's skill in convincing the old chiefs to send their people to perform the dance: "Memsahib . . . they are coming. They are coming all of them, and they are bringing with them their young men and their virgins."

On the terrace beyond the dining room, at a pair of millstone tables, Karen carried on farm business and doctored her workers' families: "My consultation hour was vaguely from nine to ten, my consultation room the stone-paved terrace east of my house." Here, when dinner was finished and the stories told, she and Denys sat up late, enjoying a last cigarette and watching the stars. In the distance: "The Mountain of Ngong stretches in a long ridge from north to south, and is crowned with four noble peaks like immovable darker blue waves against the sky."

The Grave

There was a place in the hills . . . when I thought that I was to live and die in Africa, [I] had pointed out to Denys as my future burial-place. In the evening, while we sat and looked at the hills from my house, he remarked that then he would like to be buried there himself as well. Since then, sometimes

when we drove out in the hills, Denys had said: 'Let us go as
far as our graves.'

Early morning in the dry season, February 10, *Id al Fitr,* the end of
Ramadan and a national holiday. As we leave Nairobi, the roads are
empty, Ngong itself nearly deserted. Wrapped in scarlet *shukas,* a dozen
Maasai *morani,* warriors with ochered hair, loiter outside closed shops. In
front of the Diamond Cafe a Maasai woman, deep in beaded necklaces,
gazes absently as my driver, Steven Maina, and I roll up in a pearl-gray
Peugeot.

Ngong has the look of a frontier town, its shabby businesses strung
along bad roads: butcheries, Indian shops, native *hotelis* offering single cigarettes and warm Cokes. The Diamond Cafe is painted in great blue dia-
monds like a Mardi Gras costume, and when the waiter deposits a can of
Nescafé Classic on our blue table, he fills our cups with water from a
bright blue thermos. The water is tepid but the coffee welcome—the
morning's first cup. With it we wolf big doughy *mandazi,* three-cornered
doughnuts—Africa's basic breakfast.

Over our second coffee, I ask Steven if, to go on, we need a police
escort. Holdup men, I'm told, work the back roads of the game reserve.
Steven Maina's a wizened Kikuyu *mzee* like the old chiefs who sent "their
young men and their virgins" to Karen's *ngoma* for the Prince of Wales.
Formal, earnest, reserved, he's from Muranga, beyond Thika, on the road
to Mount Kenya. "Yes," he says, after great thought. "We shall ask."

At police headquarters, a bungalow set in an acacia grove at the edge
of town, we're joined by Lucas Auma. A burly Luo from the great
Nilotic fisher-farmer tribe of Lake Victoria, he's turned out smartly in
police blues. He sits beside Steven, a well-oiled assault rifle wedged
between thick knees. I ride in back and ask discreetly if it's far.

Officer Auma adjusts his sunglasses, peers ahead, then offers a classic
African equivocation: "A bit far."

———

On May 8, 1931, Denys Finch Hatton flew to the coast to look after
the small house he owned at Takaungu. With Karen forced to sell the
Ngong Farm and soon to leave Africa for Denmark, he might have to
make Takaungu his home. On the return flight he would stop over at Voi
to try his hand at scouting elephant from the air. In *Out of Africa* Karen

wrote, "I asked him to let me come with him, for I thought what a lovely thing it would be to see the sea." Denys told her yes, then no. It would be a rough trip; he might have to land and sleep in the bush. "I reminded him that he had said that he had taken out the aeroplane to fly me over Africa. Yes, he said, so he had; and if there were elephants at Voi, he would fly me down there to have a look."

Karen's despair at losing her farm and leaving Africa, and her increasing possessiveness toward Denys, caused a serious rift between the lovers. When Denys refused to take her on the flight and left for Takaungu with only his servant, Kamau, Karen was shaken. On his way back, Denys scouted elephant from the air over Tsavo, then stayed the night with friends at Voi. On the morning of May 14, 1931, Denys and Kamau took off from the nearby airstrip, circling the field once to wave goodbye to friends gathered below. Then, as the Gypsy Moth headed low over the Mwakangale Hills for Nairobi, the engine sputtered and misfired. The plane plunged out of sight into thick bush, clouds of smoke blackening the sky. When Denys' friends reached the crash they found the Gypsy Moth in flames, Denys and Kamau trapped in the inferno.

———

Around the corner from police headquarters the road winds uphill past *shambas,* small farms where corn struggles in skimpy plots and cows browse weedy fields. At the first bend Lucas Auma shifts his weapon and looks back at Ngong, pointing out a hillside of tin-roofed shanties. "You have slums like that in America?"

The bedrock road is sharp and bone-shattering; dust flies in ocher scarves. Eucalyptus line the road as we mount the high, hilly country. Despite a national holiday, people work in their fields. A four-year-old tends sheep in a scruffy meadow while teenagers plow with ponderous hoes, breaking the ground and their backs in the bargain.

Hilltops rise above the *shambas,* golden with dry-season grass, branded here and there with clumps of wild olives. An old Maasai herder trails behind a dozen humped cows, and a flock of goats, hellbent on crossing the road, collides with our Peugeot. They bounce away and bolt into a thicket of thorn scrub.

———

... they informed me that they would bring Denys's body
up by train next morning, so that the funeral could take
place in the hills at noon. I must have his grave ready by
then.

May is the season of the long rains, and on the morning of the fif-
teenth a drizzle falls over the Ngong Hills. Karen, with her friend Gustav Mohr, drove up early to find the site for Denys' grave. It was hard
going in the wet, and a long time before they found it. Karen stopped to
smoke a cigarette and had just thrown it away when, briefly, the weather
cleared: "In ten minutes we could see where we were." They were close
to where Denys and Karen had planned their graves. To the south lay the
foothills of Kilimanjaro; to the north, "a shining silver drew up the shoulder of Mount Kenya. Suddenly, much closer, to the East below us, was a
little red spot in the grey and green, the only red there was, the tiled roof
of my house on its cleared place in the forest."

Mourners arrived from Naivasha, Gilgil, and Elmentetita, "their cars
all covered with mud from the long fast drive." The Somalis of Nairobi
came in mule carts. Early in the afternoon they brought out Denys' body,
"following his old safari-track to Tanganyika, and driving slowly on the
wet road." Karen learned that the bishop of Nairobi would not come, as
the ground wasn't consecrated. But a cleric was present, and he read the
service. "The priest read out a Psalm: 'I will lift up mine eyes unto the
hills.'"

———

After half an hour we turn into a track mounting toward the game
reserve. Fishtailing over loose stones, we climb steeply through curtains
of dust. A quarter mile up, we come upon a hand-lettered sign:

STOP—FINCH HATTON

There is a gate of sorts, a single strand of barbed wire taut between
weathered posts, corn in weedy fields and banana trees crowding around
a low, board house. Lucas speaks with a woman chopping weeds. Yes, this
is the grave. An entrance fee of two hundred shillings is required, about
four dollars, which the *mzee,* the woman's father, will eventually collect.

Across the field a slender column of lion-colored stone rises above
the corn. Clusters of bougainvillaea and great clumps of rosemary blos-

193

som nearby. Pale stones stand at the grave's corners: "We marked out the place for the grave, by the compass, laying it east to west." Gustav Mohr wrote to Karen in Denmark: The Masai have reported to the District Commissioner at Ngong, that many times, at sunrise and sunset, they have seen lions on Finch-Hatton's grave. A lion and a lioness have come there, and stood, or lain, on the grave for a long time." The lions come no more. Still, in the dry season, late in the afternoon, the buffalo Denys and Karen visited so often graze the golden hillside above the grave. Though there's a haze, Lucas points far down the slope and assures me that during the season of the long rains Karen's house is visible in the forest below.

The column was raised by Denys' brother Toby, after Karen left Kenya. A brass plaque is fixed to its south face. Toby chose the epithet from "The Rime of the Ancient Mariner," one of Denys' favorite poems.

DENYS GEORGE FINCH HATTON

1887—1931

"HE PRAYETH WELL WHO LOVETH WELL,

BOTH MAN AND BIRD AND BEAST"

Lucas and Steven stand solemnly in the presence of this white man's grave, gazing a long time at the inscription a long time. Then Lucas turns to ask, "What was this man to the woman . . . to Karen?"

"They were lovers."

"Ah, I see."

"Denys was killed when his plane crashed at Voi. A long time ago—1931. The same year Karen left Africa. Her coffee farm failed. It was too high, not enough rain, her money gone. She went back to Denmark and wrote a book about her life here, about Africa and her love of it and for this man. It is called *Out of Africa,* and it begins, 'I had a farm in Africa, at the foot of the Ngong Hills . . .'"

Lucas nods. This big, dark-skinned policeman in a smart blue uniform—a Luo from Kisumu on the distant shores of Lake Victoria. He turns thoughtfully to look away, down the cool hillside, toward the Ngong Farm. "Yes," he says. "Yes."

> If I know a song of Africa . . . of the giraffe, and the African
> new moon . . . of the ploughs in the fields, and the sweaty

faces of the coffee-pickers, does Africa know a song of me? Would the air over the plain quiver with a colour that I had had on, or the children invent a game in which my name was, or the full moon throw a shadow over the gravel of the drive that was like me, or would the eagles of Ngong look out for me?

Shella—Epilogue

It's a hot hour's walk out the waterfront to the village of Shella on Lamu Island's southeast corner. The reward is a cooling swim from a beach of fine silvery sand, an icy beer on the terrace at Peponi Hotel and a visit with Bunny Allen at his Arab-Swahili house on the seafront.

At ninety-three, Bunny is a handsome fellow with keen eyes and a high, intelligent forehead. A golden hoop dangles from his left ear. His nose is a classic appendage, first broken during his days as a boxer at Sir William Borlase School, at Marlow, in Buckinghamshire, and again in Kenya by a pouncing leopard. Born, he says, of Gypsy stock and raised in the Thames Valley, Bunny earned his name as a boy skilled at snaring rabbits. He took the hunting lore learned in Windsor Forest to Africa and applied it to stalking game.

Assistant to Denys Finch Hatton on the 1928 Prince of Wales' safari, Bunny also hunted with Bror Blixen, J. A. Hunter, and Philip Percival, the doyen of African safari guides immortalized as Pop in Ernest Hemingway's *The Green Hills of Africa*. But it's Finch Hatton Bunny remembers with affection. "Bror was known for his cool courage, his knowledge of the bush and uncanny skill with a gun. But if Bror had a drink of gin, his safari clients could go thirsty for all he cared. A month in the bush can bring friction between people. A good safari guide has to spread oil on the waters if he wants everyone happy and content around the evening fire. Denys was the opposite of Bror. He not only kept his clients happy, he offered them chilled champagne."

As a young apprentice hunter just out from England, Bunny was often the guest of Denys and Karen at the Ngong Farm and saw them together frequently at Nairobi's legendary Muthaiga Club. By this time it was rumored that Finch Hatton was having an affair with the young aviatrix Beryl Markham, later to publish *West with the Night,* her own fine memoir of Africa. Maybe Denys and Beryl were having an affair, maybe not. "But," says Bunny, with the confidence of a man who knows the nature of romance, "I never saw two people more in love than Denys and Karen."

Late in the afternoon, monsoon clouds pile up over Manda Island and a honed *kusi* blows in across the reef. Bunny throws a shawl across his shoulders, and together we cross beneath the flat-topped thorn trees in his garden and through a creaking gate to the beach. A dhow sails past, its crew waving. *"Jambo, fundi!"*—"Hello, builder!" Bunny is more famous in Shella for building houses than for being a survivor of the era of great white hunters.

"This Somali shawl," he says, adjusting the threadbare garment, "was given me by Denys Finch Hatton. It's a bit worn, but it will see me through."

"It's lasted quite well."

"Sixty-five years is it?"

"A bit more—he crashed in the spring of thirty-one."

Bunny gazes at Manda's swollen old baobabs across the water. "It was two weeks before the accident . . ." For the first time this afternoon he leaves me, sliding into a deep, mysterious recess of his memory. He speaks to himself, to someone far inside. "Denys and Karen asked me down to Takaungu for a weekend. It was a lovely place, a small house on a bluff above the sea. There was a ruined mosque nearby and a creek of transparent blue water where we swam when the tide was out. When the tide turned and washed across the coral flats we sat on the veranda listening to the waves rush into the caves below the house.

"Whenever one of them stepped inside for drinks or a bit of food, they touched the other, a hand trailing across a shoulder or a brush of a kiss. When they returned, it was the same. They never took their eyes off each other. Later, walking on the beach, arm in arm or holding hands, they kept their heads close together, talking softly, always talking. No two people had more to say to one another, no two people were ever more in love."

"And the shawl?"

"Denys asked if I'd like it as a present. A memento of a fine weekend. That was late in April. By the fourteenth of May he was dead."

"And Karen?"

"Sailed at the end of July."

"Out of Africa."

"Out of Africa."

We recross the garden and go out through an iron gate into Bunny's *shamba*. A hundred yards behind the sprawling house we make our way through the bush and up an incline. Here, in the shade of umbrella thorns, stands the headstone Bunny erected to honor Tabei, his gun bearer and companion of many hunts.

"I depended on him entirely," Bunny says, moving into reverie once again. "He was wonderful company, tracked game, read the bush, was there to put in the killing shot when it was needed. He saved my life a half dozen times by steering me around wounded buffalo. When we were separated out there, I tell you, I was extremely lonely.

"He came to me one night complaining of stomach cramp. I massaged him with lion fat—always keep lion fat for the purpose—and he felt a bit better. In the morning Mwenji came to say he was improved. A quarter hour later, when I finished breakfast and was going to see him, Mwenji was back. 'Tabei died.'" Tears fill Bunny's eyes as he looks back on that morning. "I can tell you, we were pretty broken up around here." He gazes down at Tabei's tombstone.

Tabei A. Tilmet

1920–1983

A Fine Man

Someday, one imagines, Bunny will join Tabei under Shella's umbrella thorns for their last safari. And an era will end—the era of Denys Finch Hatton, Takaungu, the Ngong Farm, the last link with Karen Blixen in Africa.

Will such an era return? Without Denys and Karen, without Kamante and Berkeley Cole and Farah Aden, without Bunny Allen, will the lions roar? This is a question, since there is no measuring a lion's roar, to which no answer can be given.

Selected Bibliography

Allen, Bunny. *First Wheel*. African Hunting Heritage Collection. Clinton, N.J.: Amwell Press, 1983.

————. *Second Wheel*. African Hunting Heritage Collection. Clinton, N.J.: Amwell Press, 1983.

Aschan, Ulf. *The Man Whom Women Loved: The Life of Bror Blixen*. New York: St. Martin's, 1987.

Asher, Michael. *Thesiger: A Biography*. New York: Viking, 1994.

Bassani, Giorgio. *The Garden of the Finzi-Continis*. Translated by William Weaver. A Helen and Kurt Wolff Book. New York: Harcourt, Brace, 1977.

Brinnin, John Malcolm. *Dylan Thomas in America: An Intimate Journal*. Boston: Atlantic Monthly Press, 1955.

Cavafy, Constantine. *Collected Poems*. Translated by Edmund Keeley and Philip Sherrard, edited by George Savidis. Revised edition. Princeton, N.J.: Princeton University Press, 1992.

Clark, Kenneth. *Civilization: A Personal View*. New York: Harper & Row, 1969.

Dinesen, Isak [Karen Blixen]. *Letters from Africa, 1914–1931*. Translated by Anne Born, edited by Frans Lasson. Chicago: University of Chicago Press, 1981.

————. *Out of Africa and Shadows on the Grass*. New York: Vintage, 1989.

Duras, Marguerite. *The Lover*. Translated by Barbara Bray. New York: Harper-Collins, 1985.

————. *The North China Lover*. Translated by Leigh Hafrey. New York: New Press, 1992.

Durrell, Lawrence. *The Alexandria Quartet*. London: Faber and Faber, 1962.

————. *Bitter Lemons*. London: Faber and Faber, 1957.

————. *The Greek Islands*. New York: Viking, 1978.

————. *Prospero's Cell*. London: Faber and Faber, 1945.

————. *Reflections on a Marine Venus*. New York: Dutton, 1960.

Forster, E. M. *A Room with a View*. London: Penguin, 1990.

————. *Where Angels Fear to Tread*. London: Penguin, 1975.

Greene, Graham. *A Sort of Life*. New York: Simon and Schuster, 1971.

————. *The Quiet American*. New York: Viking, 1956.

————. *Ways of Escape*. New York: Simon and Schuster, 1980.

Lawrence, T. E. *The Selected Letters of T. E. Lawrence*. Edited by Malcolm Brown. New York: Norton, 1989.

————. *Seven Pillars of Wisdom*. New York: Doubleday, 1936.

Lewis, Norman. *A Dragon Apparent*. London: Picador, 1982.

Liddell, Robert. *Cavafy: A Critical Biography*. London: Duckworth, 1974.

Lovell, Mary S. *Straight On till Morning: The Life of Beryl Markham*. London: Hutchinson, 1987.

Mahfouz, Naguib. *Autumn Quail*. Translated by Roger Allen and John Rodenbeck. Cairo: American University in Cairo Press, 1985.

————. *Midaq Alley*. Translated by Trevor Le Gassick. Cairo: American University in Cairo Press, 1985.

————. *Palace of Desire*. Translated by William Maynard Hutchins, Lorne M. Kenny, and Olive E. Kenny. New York: Doubleday, 1991.

————. *Palace Walk*. Translated by William Maynard Hutchins and Olive E. Kenny. New York: Doubleday, 1990.

————. *Sugar Street*. Translated by William Maynard Hutchins and Angele Botros Samaan. New York: Doubleday, 1992.

Mann, Thomas. *Death in Venice and Other Stories*. Translated and with an introduction by David Luke. New York: Bantam, 1988.

————. *A Sketch of My Life*. New York: Knopf, 1960.

Manzalini, Heidmarie Stücher, and Albarosa Catelan, with the collaboration of Eberrhard Schmidt. *Un romanzo per Ferrara*. Ferrara: Spazio Libri Editori, 1992.

O'Prey, Paul. *A Reader's Guide to Graham Greene*. London: Thames and Hudson, 1988.

Read, Bill. *The Days of Dylan Thomas*. New York: McGraw-Hill, 1964.

Severy, Merle, ed. *The Renaissance: Maker of Modern Man*. Washington, D.C.: National Geographic Society, 1970.

Stark, Freya. *Dust in the Lion's Paw, Autobiography 1939–1946*. London: John Murray, 1985.

Thesiger, Wilfred. *Arabian Sands*. New York: Dutton, 1959.

————. *The Life of My Choice*. New York: Norton, 1988.

Thomas, Dylan. *The Collected Poems*. New York: New Directions, 1957.

————. *Portrait of the Artist as a Young Dog*. New York: New Directions, 1940.

————. *Under Milk Wood*. New York: New Directions, 1954.

Thomas, Maria. *African Visas*. New York: Soho Press, 1991.

————. *Antonia Saw the Oryx First*. New York: Soho Press, 1987.

————. *Come to Africa and Save Your Marriage*. New York: Soho Press, 1987.

Thurman, Judith. *Isak Dinesen: The Life of a Storyteller.* New York: St. Martin's, 1982.

Tremlett, George. *Dylan Thomas: In the Mercy of His Means.* New York: St. Martin's, 1992.

Trzebinski, Errol. *Silence Will Speak: The Life of Denys Finch Hatton and His Relationship with Karen Blixen.* London: Heinemann, 1977.

———. *The Lives of Beryl Markham.* London: Heinemann, 1993.

Young, Gavin. *Slow Boats to China.* London: Penguin, 1983.